ABOVE US,
THE STARS

ABOVE US, THE STARS

10 Squadron Bomber Command:
The Wireless Operator's Story

JANE GULLIFORD LOWES

Matador
9 Priory Business Park,
Wistow Road, Kibworth Beauchamp,
Leicestershire. LE8 0RX
Tel: 0116 279 2299
Email: books@troubador.co.uk
Web: www.troubador.co.uk/matador
Twitter: @matadorbooks

ISBN 978 1838595 555

British Library Cataloguing in Publication Data.
A catalogue record for this book is available from the British Library.

Printed and bound in the UK by TJ Books Limited, Padstow, Cornwall
Typeset in 12pt Adobe Jenson Pro by Troubador Publishing Ltd, Leicester, UK

Matador is an imprint of Troubador Publishing Ltd

In memory of Lydia, Jim, Jack and George
&
"Penny's Prangers" and the men of "Shiny Ten"

Acknowledgements

I owe an enormous debt of gratitude to so many people who have assisted me with my research for this book. I am especially indebted to those professional historians whose published works became my "bibles" whilst I was attempting to piece together Jack's story – Martin Middlebrook, Chris Everitt, Max Hastings, James Holland, Alan Cooper, Jonathan Falconer and Kevin Wilson. Particular thanks go to Jonathan Falconer and Stephen Bungay who assisted me at the outset, and to Alan Cooper, for permission to quote from his work.

There would have been no book at all if it weren't for the wonderful people at 10 Squadron Association, especially Ian McMillan, whose history of the squadron, *From Brooklands to Brize*, provided so much material. Ian, Phil Marter and Dick King at the association (of which I am now a proud member) have been so helpful and have patiently dealt with my never-ending questions.

I knew at the outset that I needed to interview veterans, and I am most grateful to Graham Cowie and the organisers of Project Propeller for inviting me along to their annual aircrew reunion, where I was able to speak to so many men who were contemporaries of Jack and the Pennicott crew. The gentlemen who so kindly shared their precious time with me, some of whom have now passed away, are listed at the back of this book. Special thanks also go to my friend Jill Rose for the introduction to Tom Davidson, and to Tom himself who provided so much information.

There's only one way to visualise the inside of a Halifax bomber, and that's to actually climb aboard one. I'm very grateful to Ian Richardson and Barry Fisher at the Yorkshire Air Museum who allowed me to scramble around their Halifax, *Friday 13th*, and particularly to Barry for answering all my technical questions. It's a wonderful museum, and I heartily recommend it to anyone who has any interest in the Second World War or in aviation generally. The staff at the International Bomber Command Centre in Lincoln were so helpful, especially Dr Dan Ellin.

For their assistance with information on the members of the Pennicott crew, I would like to thank Anthony Pennicott and Maureen Cowles-Curtis. An extra special mention goes to Angela Gill, whose contribution will become evident. Tobin Roberts kindly gave permission to reproduce the words of his late father's poem, *To the Men of My Squadron*. Paul Mitchell helped with information on "lack of moral fibre."

For the Seaham part of this book, I am indebted to my family, especially my mother, Moira Gulliford, for all her memories, family stories and her description of 7 Caroline Street. George Clyde, who passed away in 2016, had also provided a lot of details about his family home. Special thanks also go to all those who kindly provided me with their wartime reminiscences of Seaham, in particular Con Vickers, Cecily Guy, Ron Toft, Harry Sayer, Alan Lowes, Greta Meek (who also provided a copy of the Reverend Duncan's pamphlet) and George Meek. Sadly, George passed away in 2019, before the book was completed. Kathleen Anderson provided lots of help on Seaham casualties, and Brian Slee helped with photographs. Louize Cross provided information regarding her later father, Jimmy Thornton. I am also grateful to the many others who provided information which could not be included due to lack of space.

In Germany, Ian McNee and Heilgard Hacker have been very generous with assistance regarding the Wuppertal raid, and I am especially grateful to Heilgard for allowing me to use her family's story.

Paul Hewitt at Battlefield Design created the stunning book cover and drew up the map of the Pennicott crew's raids. Colourisation of the crew photo and Jack's portrait is by the very talented Marina Amaral. I thoroughly recommend her books *The Colour of Time* and *World on Fire*.

There are more photographs on the Gallery page of my website, www.justcuriousjane.com. You will also find articles on Seaham's history there. You can read more about Edith Threadkell, Jack's neighbour, in my first book, *The Horsekeeper's Daughter* (Matador, 2017).

I'd like to thank my family (and Merry the Spaniel) and close friends (you all know who you are) for their input, suggestions and never-ending support. Finally, I want to mention four very special people who were the inspiration for this book but who are no longer with us: Lydia and Jim Groark (my grandparents), Jack and George Clyde (my great-uncles).

Forever grateful. Never forgotten.

Contents

Acknowledgements   vii

Map   xii

Introduction   xiii

1	Roses in December	1
2	A Breed To Be Proud Of	6
3	A Call To Arms	14
4	The Means Of Victory	24
5	Silver Wings	31
6	American Friends	41
7	Unnecessary Railings	52
8	Airborne	67
9	Penny's Prangers	79
10	Home Fires Burning	93
11	The Gathering Storm	101
12	The Shape of Fear	109
13	Wings Over Wuppertal	120
14	Innocence Lost	134

15	The Gates of Hell	145
16	Wizard Prang	157
17	Purgatory	171
18	A Ticklish Business	183
19	Finest of Mortal Friends	197
20	Paper Daddy	204
21	Mephistopheles	214
22	The Navigator	225
23	The Big One	236
24	Lady Luck	248
25	Permission to Land	261
26	Absent Friends	270
27	"For Gallantry"	279
28	Return to Happy Valley	291
29	At Ease	306
Postscript		320
Bibliography		327

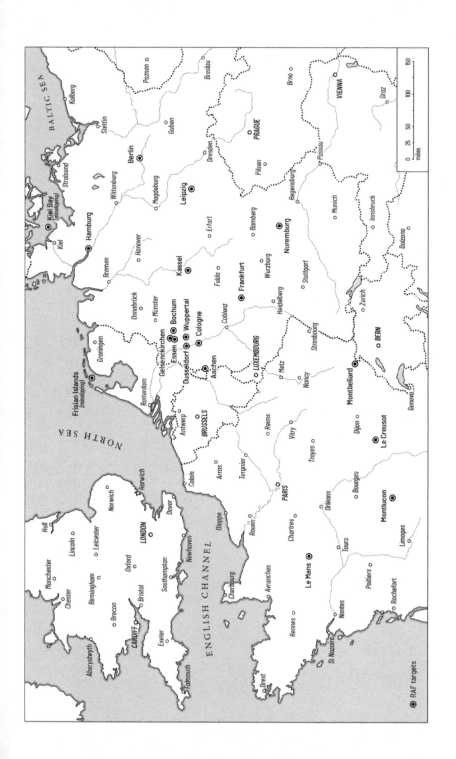

Introduction

The Second World War ended twenty-five years before I was born, and yet it shaped me. The emotions experienced by those who endured those six long years – the hardships, the fear, the pain of separation, the emptiness of uncertainty, grief, love, disappointment and ultimately joy and relief – lived on, diminished but never entirely extinguished. Some dealt with those emotions by burying them, never revealing their stories and memories to their loved ones; others, like my grandparents, talked about their experiences constantly.

As I grew older, I began to understand concepts of catharsis and of "collective family memory." They talked because it helped them process the things they had seen, the things they had lived through, and in some cases the things they had had to do.

Their history became my history.

We cannot comprehend the enormity of the threat that generation faced, the social chaos and upheaval which ensued, nor the bravery of the millions of men and women who served. It is very easy to lapse into the clichés of "keeping a stiff upper lip" and "doing your bit." In reality in every city, town and village, ordinary life went on, just in a different way, and in extraordinary circumstances. It had to. People still went out to work and to the cinema, children went to school and played in the streets, babies were born, lovers were married and the dead were buried.

What follows is a narrative I've wanted to know, understand, and ultimately tell, since childhood. This book tells the stories of Jack Clyde, a young RAF Bomber Command wireless operator, of his crewmates in 10 Squadron, and of the family he left behind in the small Durham mining town of Seaham Harbour. Jack was my great-uncle, and one of the many of thousands of men who never spoke about his experiences after the war. Working from Jack's personal papers, from contemporaneous sources and original squadron records, from family recollections and, most importantly, from conducting interviews with surviving veterans, I have pieced together his story.

I am not a professional historian, nor do I claim to possess any special expertise on the subject matter. This book is not meant to be a full account of the Second World War, nor a technical reference work on the operations of Bomber Command or 10 Squadron. It is not a detailed description of every event which befell my hometown in wartime. It is simply the story of one man among millions, and the role he played; it is part social history, part military history and part family memoir. I have done my utmost to ensure that the historical details are correct, but I bow to those with greater knowledge than I on these matters in the event of any errors. All the events, places, dates and people in this account are historically documented. Some of the conversations recounted here (particularly between the members of the crew) were relayed to me second or even third hand, and, by necessity, I have had to "imagine" the exact words used.

This book is for all the silent heroes.

1

Roses in December

The dust had already begun to settle when seventeen-year-old Jack Clyde arrived at what was left of Ilchester Street. Amid the sound of broken glass being removed from the shattered window frames of the terraced houses that still stood, the gurgle of water streaming from broken pipes and the sobbing of women stood crowded around, there was the constant clang-scrape of metal shovels hitting brick and roof slates.

Every now and then the air wardens and the men assisting would pause, listening intently, to make sure they could still hear the baby crying. They came upon his young mother first, her body crushed and broken in her shroud of plaster dust. Moving wooden beams, negotiating the remnants of the family's furniture and possessions, and lifting brick after fractured brick, eventually the rescuers found little Michael Johnson, still in the arms of his dead grandmother. She was still sat in her chair; unable to reach the air raid shelter before the first bomb hit, she had used her body to shield the infant from the blast. She had been killed outright by a piece of shrapnel which had pierced her lungs. Dusty and still bawling, Michael had barely a scratch.

Baby Michael's mother, Mary, and his grandmother, Sarah Shaw, were not the only ones to perish that day. The small mining community of Dawdon, on the southern fringes of the County Durham mining town of Seaham Harbour, was hit hard. Houses were destroyed in Ilchester Street, Stavordale Street and Fenwick Row. Twelve dead, forty-one injured, 230 houses damaged and 119 poor souls made homeless. Among those killed were whole families, including the Rochesters. Thomas Rochester was a deputy at the local colliery. He died with his wife, Eleanor, and teenage daughters, Eileen and Joyce, when their house took a direct hit.

The entire bombing raid had been witnessed by the passengers on a stationary train, just a few hundred yards away. The force of the explosions had blown out the train windows and showered it with splinters. One of those on board, a chap by the name of Harrison, described in an interview with a local newspaper how he had seen an enemy aircraft, believed to be one of those responsible for the raid, come from the north, pursued by British fighter aircraft. It seemed to be crippled and was flying very low. It unloaded its bombs in the sea and they exploded with a deafening crash. Three RAF Hurricanes then came up from the south and gave the German two or three bursts of fire and he plunged into the sea. The plane rested on the water for about five minutes and then sank. The lifeboat was sent out but no survivors were found.

A Mrs Dyson, who lived opposite one of the houses which had suffered a direct hit, described the terrible noise of the explosions. She, her husband and two children had managed to get to an air raid shelter in their neighbours' backyard. She explained breathlessly to waiting reporters:

"Two of our windows and part of the front door were blown in. The knocker, doorknob, key and nameplate from the house opposite came flying through our front window, while the curtains from the same house were blown into our passage." [1]

The feeling of shock hung heavy in the air, palpable. War had finally reached Seaham Harbour, on a sunny August afternoon. For young Jack and his friends, this was their first experience of the realities of a conflict which was to have an unimaginable impact on them, their families and the town they called home.

15 August 1940. Black Thursday. The significance of that date is all but forgotten, but it marked some of the heaviest fighting and most intense bombing of the entire Battle of Britain. When we think of the Battle of Britain today, our understanding perhaps influenced by the black and white films of the 1950s, or the glossy Hollywood epics of the 1960s, we tend to imagine Spitfires and Messerschmitts locked in aerial combat and dogfights above the green fields of Kent; in fact, the Battle of Britain was fought down the entire length of the English coast.

Mid-morning, a force of 122 Heinkel and Junkers bombers, escorted by the fighter aircraft (mainly Messerschmitts), left their bases in German-occupied Norway and Denmark, and headed for the northeast coast of England. Their target? The shipyards, coal mines and steel furnaces so essential to the British war effort. The raiders were intercepted by RAF Hurricanes from RAF Usworth (now the site of the aircraft museum, in the shadow of the huge Nissan car factory), RAF Middleton St George (now Teesside Airport) and the various RAF stations that peppered the North Yorkshire countryside. The German force was decimated by the RAF, losing some twenty-eight

---

1   The *Sunderland Echo* Archives, 16.8.1940.

aircraft, most shot down over the North Sea. Although the RAF lost no aircraft that day, there were numerous civilian casualties scattered around this little corner of County Durham, with twelve dead in Seaham, another nine in the neighbouring village of Easington Colliery, two in Hawthorn, four in Sunderland and single deaths in several other villages.

Newspaper reporting restrictions prevented individual towns and streets from being identified, so as not to pass vital information to the enemy as to the success or otherwise of the raids. Due to government propaganda rules, the casualty lists never made headlines, but were usually mentioned further down in the body of the newspaper article. Instead, emphasis was placed on Luftwaffe losses; the *Sunderland Echo* headline the day after the raid was simply:

> "*MORE RAIDERS SHOT DOWN DURING THE NIGHT*
>
> *Enemy raiders… attacked areas on the North East Coast, where one was seen in a beam of searchlights to fall to destruction… GERMANS LOST 169 PLANES… OUT OF ALL PROPORTION TO DAMAGE.*"[2]

The funerals for the Dawdon victims were held the following Monday, their remains being interred in the nearby Princess Road Cemetery. The officiating vicar, the Reverend James Duncan, had himself narrowly escaped injury when his parish church of St Hild and St Helen was hit in the raid. At the behest of his housemaid, he had sought refuge at the very last moment in the understairs cupboard.[3] In his inimitable fashion, he later described to a journalist that as the bombs

---

2   *Ibid.*
3   Rev. James Duncan, Vicar of Dawdon, *Story of an Air Raid*, Seaham, 1940.

exploded all around him, his life had not in fact flashed before him, and that he had experienced greater thrills and deeper depressions watching his beloved Sunderland football club play at Roker Park. At the memorial service held in his church on Sunday 25 August, some ten days after the raid, Reverend Duncan paid tribute to the victims and those they had left behind:

"God gave us memory that we might have roses in December. We walk in the garden and we gather fragrant flowers of proud remembrance."

Having viewed the damage, Jack walked back along Princess Road, mulling over the day's events with his best friend, Jimmy Thornton. He paused only once, at the cemetery and his mother Lydia's grave, twisting her rose-gold wedding band around his right ring finger as he always did, subconsciously, whenever anxious or upset, as he struggled to deal with what he had just witnessed. Jack and Jimmy crossed the metal bridge over the railway line, skirted the wagon works and the Londonderry Yard with its row of ambulance drivers' cottages, made their way past St John's Church and headed home, to Caroline Street. Jack hesitated momentarily on the freshly scrubbed front step of Number 7, and called after his friend:

"Jimmy, I've made my mind up. I'm joining the RAF."

2

A Breed To Be Proud Of

Jack Clyde was a quiet, shy sort of lad. Never one for making a fuss, never at the centre of the action, he was always to be found hanging around in the background, not saying much, his large, piercing blue eyes observing everything. He would brush his dark blonde hair back off his face and smile bashfully, his cheeks flushing with colour if anyone spoke to him. Underneath this shy exterior lay a will of iron, a quiet determination to always "do the right thing."

Jack was born in a tiny terraced house in Caroline Street, at the top of the main street, Church Street, Seaham Harbour, on 9 September 1922. He was the second child of miner John Clyde and his young wife, Lydia. The Clydes had moved into the cramped terrace in the summer of 1921, six months after the birth of their daughter, who was named after her mother. Another boy, George, had followed ten years later in March 1932. Jack remained deeply affected by the death of his mother in April 1937, at the age of only forty-three. His sister, Lydia, had had to leave her job as a shop assistant at the Thompsons grocery store to take over the running of the household and care for her father and brothers. Supported by close friends and good neighbours, the Clyde family tried to make the best of things. There was no other option.

Life in this small, grim mining town which clung to the grey Durham coast, with its three collieries (Seaham, Dawdon and Vane Tempest) and busy harbour, had always been tough, even more so in the years after Jack was born. Industrial unrest and political upheaval were the norm, and in their wake followed grinding poverty and quiet desperation. Strike followed strike, as the Durham miners and their representatives fought for better pay, shorter hours and collective bargaining. At the root of the disputes was the mine owners' opposition to the trade unions and their demands for uniform rates of pay and conditions, and nationalisation of the coal industry. Even after war was declared, the town's mines were still on "short hours;" sometimes there would be no work for weeks. The townsfolk came to dread the sound of the caller, ringing a handbell at the bottom of each street, announcing, "Dawdon Colliery's idle the morn!" In the days before the establishment of the Welfare State, no work meant no pay. A collective fear of revolution hung about the ruling classes – the Russian Revolution was not ten years old at the time of the General Strike in 1926 – and many in government and business feared that Britain would fall into some sort of Bolshevik chaos.

Coal had created this town, and a huge proportion of its men were employed in the mines owned by the aristocratic Londonderry family. The 3rd Marquis had built the harbour in 1828, to transport coal from his wife's pits at Rainton near Durham. Gradually the coalfields crept eastwards, and the first of the Seaham collieries began to draw coal in 1852, followed by Dawdon in 1907 and Vane Tempest in 1928. A vast network of railways connected the collieries, transporting the coal to the little port at Seaham whence it was shipped to London and beyond, in dozens of small collier vessels owned by the Londonderry Line.

The Londonderrys were fabulously wealthy; as well as their estate at Mount Stewart in County Down in Northern Ireland, they owned five "stately homes" in England, including Seaham Hall and Wynyard Hall near Stockton, both now luxury hotels. Their London home, Londonderry House in Park Lane, was at the very centre of high society. Here they hosted lavish receptions and parties for the aristocracy, government leaders and foreign dignitaries, a world away from the often desperate lives of their employees in the Durham coalfields. Their wealth was accrued at great cost; hundreds of their employees were killed in their pits over the years, including two of John Clyde's brothers, the youngest at just thirteen. The Londonderrys enjoyed positions in successive governments as cabinet ministers, as befitted their rank and social status.

By the mid-1920s the Londonderry family had sold off Seaham Hall; they retained ownership of the collieries and much of the surrounding land, but their everyday involvement in the lives of their employees and their interest in the town waned. They were but infrequent visitors, although the seventh Marquis, Charles Stewart Henry Vane-Tempest-Stewart, still retained a very close interest and "hands-on" approach to the running of his mines. His pathological fear of the political left, like so many of his class, had resulted in him taking a very hard line against his striking miners during the general strikes of 1921 and 1926. Although Lord Londonderry perhaps viewed his role as that of the benevolent dictator, his family had historically governed the lives of their mineworkers with a rod of iron. Although not as militant as some of the other mine owners, the position adopted by Londonderry during the 1926 strike, ramping up the anti-left rhetoric and the fear of revolution, earned him a reputation as a right-wing reactionary. Londonderry was no friend of the working man. Even his cousin Winston Churchill (who had advocated the installation of machine gun posts at pitheads to counter the potential threat of rioting from striking miners) accused him of turning an industrial dispute into a political battleground. Londonderry had gone so far as to accuse his striking employees (who included Jack's father) of being revolutionaries, in league with Moscow. However, it wasn't Londonderry's treatment of his employees which led to the end of his political career; by the time war broke out, he had become a figure of ridicule and hate to the British people, despised by the men who worked in his collieries, and an outcast among his own class.

After the bombs fell on Ilchester Street, the Reverend Duncan was desperate to raise funds for the repairs to his church, St Hild and St Helen. He alighted upon the idea of a pamphlet which would tell the story of the town's experience of the air raid, and which would be sold for sixpence to all interested parties as a memento. Lord Londonderry was invited to write the foreword, and his words give a hint as to the reason for his downfall:

> "Many of us had hoped that by statesmanship this war could have been avoided and that the nations of the world could have arrived at some international understanding... It is quite obvious that the war could have been avoided if the nations of Europe, all of whom were peaceably inclined with perhaps the exception of those who felt they were labouring under the disabilities imposed upon them by the Peace Treaties, could have been made to realise that the German nation, by being unsatisfied, was the potential aggressor... Statesmanship has

sadly failed during these last 20 years and it is necessary for us to bear the consequences with fortitude and determination."

Mount Stewart, 1 October 1940[4]

In the years before the war, Londonderry had been a very vocal supporter of the policy of appeasement. Many considered him a Nazi sympathiser, and his conduct prior to the outbreak of war on 1 September 1939 had done nothing to extinguish this reputation. He had been a frequent visitor to Nazi Germany throughout the 1930s. Motivated not least by bitterness at his sacking from his government post of Air Minister in 1935, he had found himself drawn to Hitler's regime. Was he genuinely a Nazi supporter? That is very unlikely. Was he naïve and flattered by the attention he received from those at the very top of the Nazi Party? Most definitely. He continued to express horror at the excesses of the regime, particularly with regard to the treatment of Jews and minorities as the full extent of Hitler's policies became clear; by the same token, he had been aware of what was going on since 1933, and that had prevented neither him nor his family from associating with the hierarchy of the Third Reich. Like many of his generation, he thought that these events, whilst deeply regrettable and unpleasant, were "domestic matters," and that once Hitler was in government, he would "settle down."

Londonderry had visited Germany with his wife and daughters on many occasions, and was a regular guest of Hermann Goering, the head of the German Air Force. In early 1936, the Londonderrys had travelled to the Winter Olympics in Garmisch, staying with Goering at Berchtesgaden, and visiting Munich and Berlin en route, where the Führer hosted a small dinner party in their honour.

---

4   Rev. James Duncan, Vicar of Dawdon, *Story of an Air Raid*, Seaham, 1940.

Both the Marquis and Lady Londonderry wrote numerous effusive letters to Goering, Goebbels and Hitler, praising their lavish hospitality. "I feel that we have never spent so full, interesting and delightful a time as the last three weeks," enthused Her Ladyship in a letter to the British Ambassador in Berlin. To the Führer himself she wrote, "... to say that I was deeply impressed is not adequate. I am amazed. You and Germany remind me of the Book of Genesis in the Bible. Nothing else describes the position accurately."[5] Such sentiments did not go down well at home.

Londonderry was dazzled by all he had seen – by Hitler's popularity with the German people, the military parades, the thriving industries, and by the hospitality he and his family had been shown. In a speech in Durham not long after his return, he allegedly referred to Hitler as "a kindly man with a receding chin and an impressive face". He stated that he had left Germany with "the strongest impression that the German nation as a whole, and the German Government, are actuated by a desire for friendliness towards this country."[6] Londonderry genuinely believed that a friendly approach to Germany, coupled with British strength by rearmament, would avoid a future war.

Von Ribbentrop, the German Ambassador, had visited the Londonderrys at their home at Mount Stewart at the end of May 1936, presenting the Marquis with a Meissen porcelain figurine of an SS Stormtrooper. Mount Stewart now belongs to the National Trust, but the figurine is still there, a permanent reminder of the folly of its owner. Von Ribbentrop even came to stay with the Londonderrys at Wynyard Hall. It

---

5   PRONI, D/3099/3/35/2a, Letter to Hitler, 21.2.1936, cited in Kershaw, Ian, *Making Friends With Hitler: Lord Londonderry and Britain's Road to War*, Penguin, London, 2004.
6   *The Times*, 24.2.1936; *Durham Chronicle*, 28.2.1936.

was during this visit, in November 1936, that the infamous "Durham Cathedral" incident occurred. The ambassador was invited to attend a service at the magnificent Norman cathedral to pay tribute to the Marquis who had just been appointed Mayor of Durham; as the service was concluding, the organist began to play the German national anthem, "Deutschland Uber Alles," in honour of the important guest. Von Ribbentrop automatically began to raise his right arm in salute to his Führer, until the offending limb was grabbed by the embarrassed Marquis and shoved politely but firmly back down to his side.

Londonderry was ridiculed by his political opponents for his views, though of course after the annexation of Austria in 1938, appeasement was precisely the policy adopted by the British Government for a time, until Hitler's assurances were proved to be as worthless as Prime Minister Neville Chamberlain's "piece of paper" upon which they were written. The Marquis felt great bitterness and believed his intentions had always been misunderstood. However, his support for Germany began to waver and by the time of the German invasion of Czechoslovakia in March 1939, Londonderry's eyes had been well and truly opened, and he voiced fully and repeatedly his opposition to the regime. By that time of course it was too late. In the eyes of the British public and many in government, his reputation was destroyed forever. He was already despised by much of his Seaham workforce, Jack Clyde's family among them.

Even while the folk of Seaham had been preparing for war, as late as August 1939 Londonderry was planning to visit Germany. Convinced as to the extent of his prestige and influence, and so completely assured of the validity of his views, the Marquis naively believed he could achieve by private diplomacy and persuasion what the governments of

Europe had failed to do: make Hitler "see sense" and curtail his ambitions. As soon as the Government got wind of the plan they stepped in and he was "advised" to cancel the visit.

One can only guess at the reception he received when he and Lady Londonderry arrived in Seaham to attend the memorial service for the Dawdon air raid victims. That said, Her Ladyship had been in London at the time of the raid; as soon as she had learned of the tragic events, she travelled immediately to Seaham to see what could be done. Her account of what she saw is set out in an article in the Reverend Duncan's pamphlet, entitled, *Everyday Life in War Time*:

> "People were standing about in groups in the streets. There was no sign of panic; instead there was fierce determination to carry on and make good the losses. Twelve people only had been killed. I say only as when the various scenes of desolation had been visited, you could not but marvel that there were not many more victims, although a number of people were injured. Here was a street with three or four houses in a row absolutely reduced to rubbish heaps. In one, an entire family had perished; two young daughters, who were in domestic service in the south and who had come home on holiday, were amongst the dead. The next house belonged to a miner, who had left home a few hours earlier on a glorious summer morning... On his return, having been hastily summoned from the pit, he finds his home a heap of debris, piled up in overwhelming heaps and stacks of mortar and bricks. After hours of work, the dead body of his wife is recovered, then that of his little daughter is brought out, and last of all the boy is found. He is alive but badly injured... These people in the pit villages are a breed to be proud of." [7]

---

7   Rev. James Duncan, Vicar of Dawdon, *Story of an Air Raid*, Seaham, 1940.

3

A Call To Arms

For months and months, the war had seemed so far away to Jack and his family. Real, and yet distant, its impact was limited to radio and newspaper reports, and Pathé newsreels in cinemas, rationing and blackouts, and the gradual absence of increasing numbers of husbands, fathers, sons and brothers. The people of Seaham, in their collective preparations, had felt in no physical personal danger from Nazi Germany. Why on earth would the Luftwaffe target this small, rather nondescript, mining town? Surrounded by farmland, and bordered by the ancient villages of Dalton-le-Dale to the south, Old Seaham to the north and agricultural Seaton to the northwest, the town had a population at that time of some 15,000 souls, the vast majority of whom were connected in some way either to the three coal mines, the railways that linked them, or the docks from which the coal was transported. The memories of the First World War were still fresh in the minds of the many who had served, especially Jack's father, John Clyde, and in the hearts of those whose menfolk had not returned. A gathering dread, tempered with no small amount of hope, hung over the town.

Ron Toft, a regular visitor to the Clyde family home (his mother and Lydia were second cousins), was six years old when war was declared. He vividly remembers sitting around the wireless with his mother and two siblings in the two rooms they rented at 8 Frederick Street, listening to Neville Chamberlain's speech on 3 September 1939, in which he announced to the nation, "We are at war with Germany."

"We were expecting bombs straightaway," Ron recalled. In fact, all the town's schools were closed on 4 September 1939 because the air raid shelters weren't ready. "It didn't happen. Nothing happened. All the children at my school were issued with gas masks, and the beaches where we used to play were cordoned off with barbed wire."

Ron has clear memories of air raid shelters being constructed in backyards and gardens across the town. The Tofts didn't have one, and his mother showed the children how to take shelter in the cupboard under the stairs or under the table. After the Ilchester Street raid, Mrs Toft, a single mother, had toyed with the idea of sending her three children to Australia or Canada where she hoped they'd be safe. She submitted her application and the children attended their medical examination, before being approved for the evacuation scheme. The family received notification of their embarkation date but Mrs Toft changed her mind when news broke of the sinking of one of the evacuation ships, the SS City of Benares on 18 September 1940, torpedoed by a German submarine just five days into its journey across the Atlantic to Quebec and Montreal. Of the ninety child evacuees on board, seventy-seven were drowned. The transatlantic evacuation scheme was swiftly cancelled – it was simply too dangerous – and city children were dispersed instead to the countryside.

No bombs had fallen on Seaham (nor indeed anywhere else) during the period known as the "Phoney War," but the town was not immune from the creeping but unrelenting aggression of the Nazis. On 9 November 1939, the merchant vessel *SS Carmarthen* struck a mine and sank just three miles off the coast. Fourteen of the crew were rescued by the Seaham lifeboat, the *Elizabeth Wills Allen*, but two perished. Just ten days later, on 19 November, the *SS Torchbearer*, a collier carrying Londonderry coal from Seaham Harbour, bound for London, was sunk by a German U-boat off Harwich in Suffolk with the loss of four crew.[8] The brave men of the Merchant Marine are so often overlooked but without their contribution, transporting coal and food and raw materials to where they were most needed, the country would have been on its knees and quite possibly starved into submission within a matter of months. Taking to mine-infested waters in their little ships, armed with a single machine gun if they were lucky but many without any defences at all, they were hunted mercilessly by U-boats and E-boats, and attacked from the skies. Many of the colliers departing from Seaham met the same fate as the *Carmarthen* and *Torchbearer*.

The Clyde family, like every other in Britain, was still coming to terms with the concept of food rationing, which had been introduced in January 1940. The maximum rations for each person (depending on supply) was 8 oz of bacon and ham, 16 oz of sugar, one shilling and tuppence worth of meat, 4 oz of cheese, a pound of jam a month, 8 oz of butter, 12 oz of margarine, 3oz of lard and 16 oz of sweets, together with a single egg a week and three pints of milk. By 1945, some of these amounts had been almost halved. Those who worked in certain occupations (including mining) which required hard physical labour were allowed extra protein in the form of a

8   www.bpears.org.uk/Misc/War_NE, accessed 25.2.2016.

double cheese ration. Eventually soap, fuel, clothing and paper began to be rationed too, and even Christmas trees could not be bought, as the precious timber was required for the war effort. As raw materials became increasingly scarce, every possible item that could be recycled, was. Many young women made wedding dresses out of tablecloths, curtains and even parachute silk; the bottom two tiers of their wedding cakes were made from cardboard. Nothing went to waste.

Each family was allocated a particular shop from which to purchase their rations, and to avoid shortages, different shops issued rations on different days of the week. The Clyde family purchased their rations on a Wednesday, their next-door neighbour, Miss Edith Threadkell, on a Thursday, and the Kelly family across the backyard on a Monday. This "staggered" purchasing was designed to avoid shortages, but if a family's allocated shop had run out of a certain item by the time the lady of the house got to the front of the queue, then it was tough luck. Greta Meek, who was five when war was declared, can recall being sent out by her mother to queue up at Tinnion's on The Avenue. Frequently people would join the line without knowing what it was they were actually queuing for, and rumours would spread along the queue like Chinese whispers:

"It's apples!"

"No, it's oranges!"

Greta's stepmother was the housemaid who had saved the Reverend Duncan's life, insisting he take cover under the stairs during the Ilchester Street air raid.

Various schemes were introduced throughout the country to persuade the population to grow as much of their own food as possible, including one which encouraged families with sufficient garden space or an allotment to rear a pig. George Meek, Greta's husband, who grew up in one of the ambulance drivers' cottages on the edge of the Londonderry Yard, recalled how folk kept all sorts of animals to supplement their meagre rations – hens, geese, rabbits, ducks, even goats. His father (who drove one of the Rolls-Royce ambulances allocated to the three local collieries) had an allotment, and the family took on a pig under the government scheme. When the time came for the unfortunate animals to be slaughtered, they had to be taken to government-approved abattoirs or butchers; the family would receive a small proportion of the meat, and the rest would be sent off to be sold and distributed in accordance with rationing entitlements. However, wherever there is a rule there is always a way to bend it, and many a family kept a "secret pig" in addition to their "official" one. George's mother had four children at home and a husband to feed. He had very clear memories of her collecting two stones of flour a week, and baking cakes using liquid paraffin as there was no lard available.

As news of the evacuation of British Forces from Dunkirk gripped the nation, the Clyde (and every other) household had been issued with a leaflet explaining "How to Deal with a Bomb." Jack pored over the contents, memorising the advice, so that he was perfectly prepared should the need arise. Strict instructions were given to clear out attics and lofts and roof spaces of any junk and rubbish that might easily catch fire in the event of an incendiary bomb coming through the roof. Incendiaries weren't explosive; their purpose was simply to start and spread fires, and they did so to huge effect. Weighing only two pounds or so, generally they would pierce a roof but come to rest on the first boarded floor they struck, usually the attic. Citizens were instructed to "have ready at least four large buckets, a shovel or scoop, preferably with a long handle, and a fair quantity of sand or dry earth. Provide also what appliances you can; if possible, a stirrup handpump with the special nozzle giving either a jet of water for playing on a fire, or spray for dealing with the bomb itself. Failing this, a garden syringe would be useful, or even old blankets soaked in water."

Seaham resident Cecily Guy remembers starting St Cuthbert's School in Cornish Street, Seaham Colliery in 1940. The favourite "lesson" was the air raid drill. The children would be ordered to put on their coats, collect their gas masks and stand in a line. "Forward… march!" The children then hurried across the yard and out of the school gate, down the steps and into the air raid shelter. Wooden benches lined both sides of the dimly lit shelter, and when all children were seated, one of the teachers would check all were present by calling out the register. In order to keep up the children's spirits, and to try to prevent them being frightened, the teacher in charge would start them off singing. Cecily remembers they would sing all the most cheerful, loudest songs they knew. Next came the most anticipated part of the drill. The teacher would bring out the emergency rations from large tin boxes stored beneath the seats; each child would be given one or two ginger snaps and two or three Horlicks' tablets. After further songs and perhaps practising putting on their gas masks, the children would troop out of the shelter and back to their classrooms. For them, it was all just a huge game. For their teachers, it must have been utterly horrifying.

After the fall of France in June 1940, German eyes were fixed firmly on British shores and the nation was warned to prepare for invasion. The Germans knew that for an invasion to succeed, they had first to destroy the Royal Air Force. On 30 June, Hermann Goering, head of the Luftwaffe and former hunting companion of Lord Londonderry, gave the order to draw the RAF into battle. From mid-July, shipping convoys were attacked in the English Channel, and there were nightly bombing raids along the south coast, targeting the Channel ports and coastal radar stations. On 16 July, Hitler issued a directive calling for preparations to be made for Operation Sea Lion – the codename for the invasion of Britain. The Führer ordered that "The British Airforce must be eliminated to such an extent that it will be incapable of putting up any sustained opposition to the invading troops."

Even before the bombs fell on Ilchester Street, there had been a foretaste of what was to come, just a few days earlier. On the night of 12 August, sixteen high explosives (HEs) were dropped in the vicinity of Seaton Village railway station.[9] Most fell in the open fields that still surround the village, setting the yet-to-be-harvested crops ablaze. It's possible that they were jettisoned by an enemy bomber before it turned for home, having been unable to locate its target, or that they had simply been dropped in the wrong place. Con Vickers, born in Seaton in 1930, recalls well that very first night of terror. At that time, he was living in Hoy Crescent, about half a mile from Seaton station. He remembers the house being in total darkness, the family, including his sick father, all sitting around the wireless listening to the news. Just as he and his brothers were getting ready for bed, the air raid siren started up and panic set in. His mother herded the family into the "Anderson" shelter in the garden, where they said prayers that they would be kept safe. Soon the distant hum of approaching aircraft could be heard, growing ever louder, accompanied by the rumble and thump from the anti-aircraft batteries positioned all down the coast as they opened fire on the invaders. Mrs Vickers instructed her family to "pray harder" but by this time the fields were alight. A landmine exploded in farmland right next to the houses, causing some damage. Thirty-year-old Andrew Errington, the village gamekeeper and air warden, was struck directly by a falling bomb as he attempted to put out the fires. He died

9   www.bpears.org.uk/Misc/War_NE, accessed 25.2.2016.

the next day in Sunderland Royal Infirmary. The first civilian casualty of enemy action in Seaham, he was buried in the little sloping graveyard at Christ Church on 16 August 1940.

As usual, the local newspapers focused on enemy losses. The *Sunderland Echo*[10] had reported on 15 August:

"NAZI AIR ACTIVITY IN THE NORTH EAST
Hot Reception from RAF and Ground Defences
British Fighters Harass Raiders
Large numbers of Spitfires and Hurricanes were flashing in and out of the clouds engaging unseen enemy raiders."

From 13 August, the Luftwaffe began to target airfields and radar stations; whilst the RAF airfields in South East England suffered the heaviest losses, damage and casualties were widespread. Many aircraft were destroyed on the ground, and airfields rendered unusable due to bomb damage. Fierce air battles raged between the fighters of the RAF – Spitfires and Hurricanes mainly – and the heavy bombers of the German Air Force, none more so than on "The Hardest Day," 18 August. The Luftwaffe continued to bomb towns, cities and airfields all along the south coast and in the Midlands from its bases in France, Germany and the Netherlands, while the squadrons stationed in Stavanger in Norway and Aalborg in Denmark were dispatched to attack the industrial centres of North East England in "nuisance raids."

It wasn't just the people of Seaham who suffered in those attacks. There was widespread loss of life and significant damage to property in Sunderland, Newcastle, Hartlepool, Middlesbrough and especially Hull, which suffered terribly throughout the war, and in the surrounding small towns and villages. On 24 August, the first German bombs fell upon

10   The *Sunderland Echo* Archives, 15.8.1940.

London, when a lost formation of German bomber aircraft erroneously dropped their bombloads; in retaliation, the first RAF raid on Berlin took place the following day. This in effect marked the beginning of the Blitz: the gloves were off, and it seemed that as far as the Luftwaffe was concerned, no target – whether military, industrial or civilian – was off limits. The RAF suffered its heaviest losses of the entire Battle of Britain on 31 August, but still they fought on.

On 15 September, two huge waves of German attacks were fought off by the RAF fighters, by deploying every single aircraft in 11 Group. Sixty German and twenty-six RAF aircraft were shot down. By 16 September the tide had begun to turn: the Luftwaffe simply could not sustain the high losses of men and aircraft, and on 17 September Hitler made the momentous decision to "postpone" Operation Sea Lion. Instead, in an attempt to reduce Luftwaffe casualties, he focused the attention of his forces on night-time bombing raids over London and other British cities, attacking the more easily reached coastal towns during the day. This fatal decision would begin, slowly, to turn the tide of the war. For the first time during the conflict British aircraft production began to outstrip losses, and as those pilots recruited earlier in the year completed their training, the RAF found itself with slightly more pilots than the Luftwaffe. The invasion never came, but an incredibly high cost was paid; by the time the Battle of Britain was over, at the end of October 1940, 1495 RAF aircrew (from Britain, France, Poland and all over the Commonwealth) had lost their lives. It is estimated that 2585 German airmen were killed. Every year, these events are commemorated on 15 September – Battle of Britain Day.

To help the war effort, individual towns and cities were encouraged to fundraise for, and "adopt", individual ships and aircraft. The men of New Seaham Working Men's Club gave the Government an interest-free loan of £1000, and the entire community rallied round to contribute to a Spitfire fund, with local children even contributing their pocket money. The Durham Miners' Federation had even voted to donate the then enormous sum of £10,000 towards the purchase of two Spitfires.

In late September, as the battle still raged, and even as Lord Londonderry sat ensconced in the luxury of his home at Mount Stewart, composing his foreword to the Reverend Duncan's pamphlet about the Ilchester Street raid, Jack Clyde was formulating his own plan. After leaving school, Jack had been working as an apprentice joiner at Tomlin's Yard, overlooking the docks. Keen, quiet and methodical, a perfectionist with an unending attention to detail, he enjoyed his chosen trade, and was well thought of by his elders.

However, on the morning of Monday 23 September 1940, Jack didn't report for work. With a calm sense of purpose, he boarded the train for Sunderland at Seaham station. Jack never did anything without careful consideration, and he had already weighed up his options. Upon arrival, he hopped on a bus to the other side of the river and made his way to the temporary recruiting office housed in the premises of the YMCA at Park Terrace. Without making any fuss about the matter, as was his usual way of doing things, Jack enlisted as "aircrew" in the Royal Air Force. He had celebrated his eighteenth birthday just two weeks earlier.

4

The Means Of Victory

Conscription had been introduced at the very beginning of the war; at first, only young men aged between twenty and twenty-two had been called up, but with losses spiralling and the threat of invasion ever growing, this was quickly extended to other age groups. Jack's sister's husband, Jim Groark, who had celebrated his twenty-second birthday two weeks before war broke out, was one of the first to receive his call-up papers in January 1940. Jim was drafted into the Army and allotted to the Royal Corps of Engineers. He had left Seaham to train with 5th Corps on Salisbury Plain in March 1940; on his first spell of leave a month later, he and Lydia were married. She was just nineteen, Jim twenty-two.

Motivated by a fervent, almost hysterical patriotism, and the need to be seen to be "doing one's bit," many men volunteered before they were called up, particularly for the more "glamorous" services, the Royal Navy and the Royal Air Force. Jack was one of them. Jim's motto, however, was always

"Never volunteer. Don't be a hero; you're no good to anybody if you're dead."

One can only guess at the conversation that took place in the small downstairs room at 7 Caroline Street which served as kitchen, dining room and parlour, as Jack revealed his intentions to his family. What did his father say? Did he encourage him or dissuade him? John Clyde had left behind the coal mines of Seaham, where he had worked from the age of twelve, for the killing fields of France and Belgium in the First World War. He had served as a medical orderly and stretcher bearer, fully exposed to the terror of trench warfare. His name and that of his brother Septimus are recorded on the Roll of Honour of those of Lord Londonderry's employees who had answered the call in 1915. Perhaps John tried to talk his boy out of it, hoping at least to defer the inevitable for another six months or so, until he was conscripted. Maybe he encouraged him to pursue a career in the Royal Air Force, in the misplaced hope that he would be spared the horrors he himself had witnessed in the infantry.

However, not only had Jack enlisted as RAF aircrew, in direct contravention of the sentiments expressed by his older and wiser brother-in-law, Jim, he had volunteered for Bomber Command.

In 1936, as the growing military threat from Germany was capturing the attention of governments from Moscow to Paris, and even as Lord Londonderry was being wined and dined by the leaders of the Third Reich, plans were implemented to restructure the Royal Air Force in readiness for the possibility of war. The RAF was divided up into three "areas of command:" Coastal Command, Fighter Command and Bomber Command.

The aims of each were clear, separate yet complementary. Coastal Command was established to keep open the sea lanes, the crucial lines of supply of food and materials, to ensure

Britain did not starve and could continue to function as an industrial nation; the purpose of Fighter Command was to co-ordinate air defences (in the form of fighter aeroplanes) against attacking enemy aircraft, to repel both would-be invaders and the German heavy bombers; Bomber Command would take the air war to the enemy, with the heavy, long-range bombing of industrial, economic and military targets.

As the Battle of Britain had raged, on 20 August 1940, just five days after the Ilchester Street air raid, the new Prime Minister, Winston Churchill, gave his famous speech about the contribution and sacrifice of the RAF's fighter pilots. Few today realise that he also went on to praise the actions of those airmen who served with Bomber Command:

> "Never in the field of human conflict has so much been owed by so many to so few. All hearts go out to the fighter pilots whose brilliant actions we see with our own eyes day after day, but we must never forget that all the time, night after night, month after month, our bomber squadrons travel far into Germany, find their targets, often under the heaviest fire, often with serious loss, with deliberate, careful discrimination, and inflict shattering blows upon the whole of the technical and war-making structure of the Nazi power. On no part of the Royal Air Force does the weight of the war fall more heavily…"

Much to Lydia's horror, and the consternation of their father John, this was what young Jack had signed up for.

The importance of the role that Bomber Command was to play in the coming years was already self-evident to Churchill, even as early as September 1940: "The fighters are our salvation, but the bombers alone can provide the means of victory."

RAF chiefs had begun to formulate plans for attacking the Ruhr area of Germany back in March 1938. Intelligence reports had been received identifying potential targets in the event of war being declared. The Ruhr was the industrial nerve centre of Nazi Germany – the equivalent of Manchester, Birmingham, Newcastle, the northern coalfields, Leeds and the steel-producing city of Sheffield all combined in one concentrated, densely populated area. Peppered with chemical works, engineering factories, aircraft production plants, steel mills, power stations, ports and railways, the area produced some 75% of Germany's coal and iron.[11]

In order to avoid civilian casualties, and so as not to alienate neutral countries and potential allies (including the United States), the British Government had decided that if war did break out, as seemed inevitable, any aerial bombardment by RAF bombers would have to be restricted to military targets. In August 1939, the American President, Theodore Roosevelt, appealed to the European nations not to bomb civilian populations; this was accepted, as long as the Germans agreed to adopt the same policy. The French had in any event been vehemently opposed to any bombing raids on the Ruhr, in case it provoked attacks on its undefended factories. On 1 September 1939, Hitler had famously announced, "I will not wage war against women and children." On the same day the Luftwaffe bombed over sixty Polish towns and villages.

Despite attempts to increase production of aircraft from 1936, when war was finally declared, Bomber Command had only thirty-three squadrons (each of around eighteen to twenty aircraft) at its disposal. Of its 638 aircraft, just under 400 had only two engines. In practical terms, this meant that just over two thirds of its aircraft were not equipped to carry heavy payloads of bombs, nor could they travel any significant distance. Their twin engines were simply not powerful enough.

---

11   Cooper, Alan, *Air Battle of the Ruhr*, Airlife Publishing, Shrewsbury, 1992, pp. 4-5.

The aircraft available to the RAF in 1939 were mainly old Fairey Battlers, Blenheims, as well as a few Hampdens, Whitleys and Wellingtons. These were probably best described as medium rather than heavy bombers, both in terms of the distances they could fly, and the number of bombs they could carry.[12]

Given that the Germans had 1600 long-range bombers, capable of striking at the heart of the British mainland, 335 dive bombers and around 50,000 aircrew, Britain was in something of a pickle, and facing apparently insurmountable odds. As a result, the Ministry of Aircraft Production was formed on 10 May 1940 – the same day that Churchill had become Prime Minister. Plans were immediately put in place to provide the RAF with new long-range, heavy bombers, which would be able to fly higher, further and carry much heavier payloads than their predecessors. Soon the famous Handley-Page Halifaxes and Avro Lancasters would take to the air, assisted by the double-manned Mosquitoes, and supported by the older bombers.[13]

At that time Bomber Command's squadrons were divided into five groups, spread out down the eastern coast of England, but with No. 1 Group (focusing on aerial photographic reconnaissance) based in Northern France. No. 2 Group, another reconnaissance unit consisting mainly of Blenheims, was based in East Anglia; the Wellingtons of No. 3 Group were scattered around airfields in Norfolk and Cambridgeshire, tasked with bombing operations; No. 4 Group, consisting mainly of Whitleys and based in Yorkshire, were allocated the job of dropping propaganda leaflets over Germany; No. 5 Group, made up largely of Hampdens, were based in South Lincolnshire.

The swift and brutal invasion of Holland and Belgium on the same day that Churchill had become Prime Minister, and the subsequent fall of France on 15 May, resulted in a speedy

12 *Ibid*, pp. 7-8.
13 *Ibid*, p. 10.

decision by Bomber Command chiefs to change tactics, and attention switched to the Ruhr and the bombing of industrial targets, particularly oil plants and railway yards. The plan was to disrupt the German transport system, and to try to restrict the movement of both men and raw materials, thereby slowing down production of aircraft, tanks and armaments.

The very first raid took place on the night of 15 May 1940, when eighty-three aircraft – a combination of Whitleys, Wellingtons and Hampdens – set off to attack some fourteen separate targets in the Ruhr Valley. Nine days later, the first raid of many on the huge industrial complex that was the Krupps factory in Essen took place. These early bombing missions met with only very limited success, not least due to the difficulty in identifying targets in the dark and in cloud. It soon became apparent to the RAF chiefs of staff that if the campaign was to succeed, vast numbers of aircraft would need to be employed in individual operations. The Germans were of course fully prepared, and the attacks were expected. The Ruhr was one of the most heavily defended areas in Germany, as its continued industrial output was absolutely crucial to an eventual Nazi victory; protected by enormous anti-aircraft gun installations, searchlight batteries and flak guns, the skies above the valley were patrolled by the Luftwaffe night fighters.

"Flak" was the curse, and quite often the means of destruction, of every RAF aircraft. The German military leaders had at their disposal the 900,000 men of the Flakartillerie anti-aircraft section. Roughly translated as "defence against aviation," all German men aged between eighteen and sixty (with the exclusion of medical personnel) were liable for service in Home Guard flak units, and they were employed to lethal effect. Thousands of anti-aircraft batteries had been constructed, especially down the western borders and encircling the towns and cities of the Ruhr Valley, from which

30mm shells could be fired at aerial targets many thousands of feet high. Such was the intensity of fire that pilots simply had to fly their aircraft straight through the barrage of exploding shells, and simply hope, or pray, that they weren't struck.[14]

During those first early raids over the Ruhr, the old Hampdens along with the Wellingtons and Blenheims, which had a ceiling (maximum flying height) of only 12,000 to 15,000 feet, proved no match for the sophisticated air defences of the Third Reich. They were sitting ducks. Losses of men and aircraft were massive, and unsustainable.

By this time the British Expeditionary Force was in rapid retreat in Northern France, and between 27 May and 4 June 1940 all efforts were focused on supporting the evacuation of 300,000 Allied troops from the beaches in Dunkirk. In what would later become known as the Battle of France, aircraft from Bomber Command bombarded the positions of the advancing German Army units to provide some protection for the encircled forces. A hundred and forty-five British aircraft from No. 2 Group and their crews were lost in the course of the battle, most of whom fell victim to mobile flak guns, the whereabouts of which were largely unknown to, and undetected by, British Intelligence. Once the miraculous evacuation from Dunkirk had been completed, notwithstanding huge loss of life, attention once again switched back to the Ruhr.

When Jack Clyde enlisted in the RAF on that September morning in 1940 he had no comprehension of just how much he would come to dread the very phrase "Ruhr Valley," or how those two simple words, announced to the assembled aircrews by a superior officer in the briefing hall, would tie his stomach in knots of fear. "Happy Valley," the early bomber aircrews had nicknamed it, with the typical gallows humour of the RAF. It would soon become known as "The Land of No Future."

---

14 *Ibid*, p. 22.

5

Silver Wings

The very first entry on Jack's official service record is dated 22 October 1940. Earlier that morning, he had set off to travel to Padgate, near Warrington, to attend his RAF aircrew assessment. Upon arrival at Seaham station, he spotted another boy from the recruitment office in Sunderland. The boys acknowledged each other with the standard greeting in these parts, a raised eyebrow and a slight nod of recognition.

"Alreet?"

"Aye. Alreet. You?"

"Aye. Canny."

Jack reported for duty at the No. 2 Reception Centre, Padgate late that afternoon. After being issued with basic kit, including two bedsheets, cutlery, a mug and several blankets he was required to attend a number of medical examinations. Over the course of the next two days, he underwent a series of tests to assess his suitability for aircrew. Those young men with an aptitude for mathematics or science, particularly those with a grammar school education, were selected for "PNB" training – as pilots, navigators and bomb aimers. The remainder, perhaps those with more practical skills like Jack, would be sent to be trained as wireless operators, flight engineers and gunners. Each individual role was essential to the safe operation of a bomber aircraft and the survival of its crew.

Social status was no guarantee of ability, and the RAF was probably the first of the services to recognise this. It was all down to the aptitude and to the skill set of the individual. Not all pilots were officers; a pilot could be a sergeant (a non-commissioned officer) for example, and he would have command of the aircraft, regardless of whether there were officers or non-commissioned officers on board. Consequently, a particular middle-class lieutenant fresh out of officers' training school may have been more intellectually suited to be an air gunner, while a bright young chap straight off the factory floor may have been considered to have the required attributes to train as a pilot. Many who applied were deemed unsuitable and were assigned to general duties or allocated for groundcrew training. From May 1940, all aircrew held the rank of sergeant or above.

With his methodical nature, attention to detail and fascination with all things electronic, after attending an aircrew selection board, Jack was recommended for training as a wireless operator. He would be responsible for all communications on board an aircraft, for relaying orders received from base, notifying base of the success or otherwise of the mission, and sending distress signals and last known position in the event of an emergency. Of all the roles, apart from that of pilot, wireless operator training was the most intensive and took the longest. As he travelled back home to Seaham, Jack was flushed with pride, bursting to tell his family of his success.

As 1940 drew to a close, Britain was in the grip of war, and subject to incessant bombing from the Luftwaffe, day and night. Large areas of towns and cities throughout the country lay in smouldering ruins; on 14 November, Coventry had been bombed by 449 enemy aircraft, and the subsequent firestorm had caused the lead roof of the fourteenth-century cathedral to melt and flow down the adjacent streets like a river. The city was virtually destroyed, and 568 civilians had been killed on that night alone, with over 2500 homes destroyed and another 41,500 rendered uninhabitable. More attacks followed on successive nights. What remained of the city's streets were strewn with debris and charred human remains, the air thick with dust and ash, and the smell of burning flesh.

In the very early days of the Nazi air campaign against Britain, it could be argued that the "Blitz Spirit" was a myth. Chaos, panic, hysteria and fear reigned among the survivors. Public disorder and looting soon followed, as traumatised civilians struggled to deal with the horrors they had encountered and wandered around the smoking shell of their city, dislocated, confused, with nowhere to go, many of them injured and left with only the clothes on their backs. This hellish scene was replicated throughout the country, in London, Glasgow, Hull, Bristol, Southampton, the Midlands and Sheffield, where over 600 people lost their lives in air raids on the nights of 12 and 15 December alone. The authorities were completely unprepared, and at first there was simply no provision made for the huge numbers of homeless families.

In the wider theatre of war, the Italian Fascist leader, Mussolini, keen to extend his power and to demonstrate his strength to his Axis ally Germany, had invaded Egypt in September and Greece in October 1940; this aggression had inevitably spread the conflict to the Mediterranean, the Aegean, North Africa and the Balkans. In response, the first

Allied offensive in the Western Desert, Operation Compass, had got underway on 9 December. Although they were blissfully unaware of it at the time, these events thousands of miles away would have a lifelong impact on the lives of Jack's family, and especially upon Lydia and Jim.

Christmas 1940 was a somewhat subdued (and very overcrowded) affair in the Clyde household. Midnight Mass and Christmas Eve church services had been cancelled throughout the town because of the blackout. Jim was home on a few days' leave from the Army, so he and Lydia, her father, John, and brothers, Jack and George, were all crammed into the tiny terraced house. Jim and Lydia slept upstairs in the big bedroom, George in the box room, John and Jack in the parlour. It was fortunate that they were rarely all together simultaneously. In the coming months Jim would joke that he and Jack could share a suit, as they were never home at the same time. There was no Christmas tree that year (the wood could not be spared), but Lydia and little George had made some paper cut-out decorations which were pinned around the room, and Jack had fashioned a "tree" of sorts from scraps from the joiners' yard, from which they hung pine cones, painted bobbins, trinkets and the few of their late mother's painted glass baubles which had not been broken.

After attending Christmas morning Mass at St Mary Magdalene's Church, where she had married Jim eight months earlier, Lydia set about putting the family's rations to creative use and managed to conjure up something resembling a Christmas lunch; Edie Threadkell next door had contributed her rations too. Edie's mother, Fanny, had passed away the preceding January, and she was now on her own, her seafaring father having died many years before. John was eternally grateful to Edie for the help and support she had given the family following his wife's death just three years before, and

Edie joined the Clydes for dinner on Christmas Day. Edie had always been very fond of "Jackie" as she called him, and the sole topic of conversation as the family tucked into their festive fare was Jack's imminent departure to the RAF. After dinner, the family gathered around the old upright piano and John banged out a few old tunes and Christmas carols while Jim made sure the blackout curtains were all shut.

Like every other family in the country that Christmas, the Clydes (and Edie, who was considered part of the family) faced a very uncertain future. The whole of continental Europe was now under the control of Hitler and his allies, and the odds against a British victory were lengthening daily. Air raids, rationing, "make do and mend," the absence of loved ones, in some cases forever, had quickly become part of everyday life. There was, quite simply, no light at the end of the tunnel. There was no alternative but to press on and make the best of things, each man, woman and child "doing their bit" to help the war effort, with the ultimate goal of staving off invasion, and simply surviving.

Once the temporary distraction of the festive period had subsided, the gnawing and nagging fear of what lay ahead consumed the family. Of all of them, only John had real experience of war and its horrors. His stomach was in knots as he, Lydia and George said goodbye to Jack on the chilly platform of Seaham station just two days after Christmas, not knowing when, or if, he would see his lad again. He prayed that Jack would never have to witness what he himself had endured in Flanders.

For Jack, like so many raw recruits of his age, it was all a huge adventure. He was eighteen, and like every other eighteen-year-old before and since, he considered himself to be immortal. He had never really been away from Seaham Harbour, nor from his family, apart from when he had attended his RAF assessment at Padgate, and the occasional day trip to Blackpool or Scarborough. Emboldened by his sense of patriotism, his excitement tempered with nerves, Jack kissed his sister, shook his father's hand, ruffled his little brother's hair and pushed his way onto the train, crammed with other servicemen leaving their loved ones behind. Some of the women and girls on the platform were crying, others stood stony-faced. If Jack felt the sting of tears, he didn't show it. Grabbing a seat next to two young men in naval uniform, he closed his eyes momentarily and twisted his mother's wedding ring around his right ring finger. The train shuddered slowly away from the platform, and in a moment, he was gone. He did not see Lydia sobbing into her handkerchief as she grabbed George by the hand and began the short walk back to Caroline Street. She would have to do it all again two days later when her husband, Jim, returned to his Royal Engineers Unit in Dorset.

For Lydia, George and John, as for all the other residents of the small mining community, life went on. John walked the mile or so to Seaham Colliery every day, where he worked as a coal hewer, hundreds of feet underground, often in coal seams only a couple of feet high; it was filthy, hot, backbreaking and hugely dangerous work, with the ever-present threat of rock falls and roof collapses. Lydia kept the household running, queuing for the family's rations at the various shops in Church Street, doing the laundry in the washhouse in the backyard they shared with five other families, and helping George with his schoolwork. When she had a spare moment, she would pop next door to see Edie or Mrs Thornton and her son Jimmy, Jack's best friend, or write letters to Jim.

A programme of slum clearances had begun in the mid-1930s, and new housing estates were being built all over the town. Despite the war – or perhaps maybe because of it, due to the anticipated need for new accommodation as the result of air raids – construction continued. In January 1941, Ron Toft and his mother, brother and sister were one of the first families to benefit and were moved from their rooms at 8 Frederick Street, a few hundred yards from where the Clydes lived in Caroline Street, to a brand new house on the Parkside Estate. For the first time in their lives, they and many families like them had an inside bathroom and toilet, a kitchen with hot and cold running water, and a small garden.

Even today, Ron has vivid memories of being hurried into the air raid shelter at Parkside by his mother and can still recall the sound of the shrapnel hitting the outside. Just up the coast, between Ryhope and Sunderland at Leechmere, there was a huge anti-aircraft gun emplacement. Smaller batteries were built along the cliff tops at Seaham, and a military encampment established next to Seaham Hall to house the soldiers who manned the artillery positions. On Terrace Green, where the war memorial and famous "Tommy" statue now stand, a battery/observer post was erected, disguised as a public house called The Green Man. Ron told me that as they huddled in the Parkside shelter, they could hear the noise of the guns starting up and his mother would say, "There's Leechmere away, don't worry, they'll get them," to try to lift the children's spirits. Sometimes the guns were indeed successful in bringing down approaching enemy aircraft, but on the night of 16 February 1941, they were not.

Despite severe snowstorms, the Luftwaffe had for the second night running directed their attention to the mining communities of North East England. On the night of the 15th, mines had fallen at Seaham and Hawthorn, causing six people to suffer minor injuries, but there were no fatalities. As the air raid sirens began to sound the next night, accompanied by much muttering about "Another bloody false alarm!" or "Not two bloody nights in a row!", and no small amount of swearing, the good folk of Seaham Harbour dashed to the shelters. Many residents didn't have their own in their backyards or gardens, and not wanting to risk the short journey to the public shelters, simply took refuge in the subway at Lord Street, just near the railway line and at the bottom of Frederick Street.

The subway took a direct hit. Many of those sheltering were trapped and injured. A number of high explosives (HEs) hit Frederick Street. Four people lost their lives, and many more suffered injury. The next day, as Ron Toft came out of the school gates, two of his pals came rushing over to greet him and informed him that his old house in Frederick Street had been flattened. Boys being boys, the three of them went off to inspect the damage. The street was cordoned off by police, but Ron has never forgotten the sight of a wooden coffin lying on a pile of rubble. It transpired that the coffin contained the remains of the grandmother of the household who had passed away a few days previously, and who had been "laid out" in the upstairs room awaiting burial when the bombs hit.

A local newspaper reported:

> *"In one of the demolished houses was a woman who had died on Saturday and was laid out for burial. The body of Kenneth Green (8) was recovered from the wreckage… the boy was the son of Mr Arthur Green (30), who, with his wife Mary (29), his daughter Cerise (9) and his father Amos (55), suffered from cuts and shock. It was in this house that Mrs Mary Green (52), wife of Mr Amos Green, died on Sunday and was laid out for burial when the raid occurred. Her body has been recovered… It is feared that a woman and two children belonging to another of the demolished houses are still under the debris."*[15]

---

15   The *Sunderland Echo* Archives, 17.2.1941.

The trauma suffered by the surviving members of the Green family, having lost their grandmother, grandson, their home and all their possessions in the space of twenty-four hours, is unimaginable. The gap in Frederick Street where their house once stood remains to this day, now just grassed over, with no memorial and no indication of the horror which befell the street's residents on that bitter February night in 1941. Two hundred and fifty miles away, Jack was oblivious to the danger his family and friends were in; nor would he learn of the air raid until a couple of weeks later when he received a letter from Lydia enclosing clippings from the local newspapers.

In February 1941 Jack was sent off to No. 2 Electrical and Wireless School at RAF Yatesbury in Wiltshire, one of the many Initial Training Wings, for "square bashing," or basic training, which every new recruit, whether Army, Royal Air Force or Navy, had to endure, and for instruction in their allotted trade. Over the course of the war, this camp and the many others like it around the country (and indeed the Commonwealth) would churn out tens of thousands of young men and women ready to be sent off to their regiments, air force bases and ships to face the realities of combat.

Yatesbury was a harsh and swift introduction to the practicalities of service life in wartime, and to strict military discipline. For many of the young men, a fair proportion of whom, like Jack, were just boys, this was their first experience of being away from their families, and a fair few were desperately homesick. The dreadful food, the bullying by the drill sergeants, the physical training (PT) and cross-country runs in sub-zero temperatures did little to take their minds off the comforts of home.

The "Pre-Flying Training Syllabus" issued to all new aircrew cadets listed, in alphabetical order, the subjects the recruits would be expected to learn, and covered such essentials as aircraft recognition, drill and physical training, basic aeronautical engineering, hygiene and sanitation, principles of mathematics and "dead reckoning," the history and traditions of the Air Force, the laws of warfare and aerial combat, how to salute and how to use a rifle, principles of navigation, signals and even meteorology.

Among Jack Clyde's surviving possessions, there is a ragged navy blue hard-backed exercise book, the pages dog-eared and well-thumbed. It's a bit grubby, and the spine is broken now. On the inside cover there is a childish doodle, in pencil, of a Royal Air Force Cap Badge, with the words:

1125510
J. CLYDE RAF
7, CAROLINE ST
SEAHAM
CO. DURHAM

Written at the top of the facing page, in Jack's careful and neat handwriting, is the date, 26 February 1941, alongside the heading TECHNICAL WIRELESS NOTES (underlined twice, just for emphasis).

"ELECTRICITY – *All substances consist of various combinations of the 92 different ELEMENTS which constitute our universe.*"

Jack's training for Bomber Command had begun.

6

American Friends

For five long months Jack's days (and many of his nights) were filled with the rigorous and intense training required for a wireless operator. In every building and in every Nissen hut at No. 2 Electrical and Wireless School Yatesbury, hundreds of young men like Jack were crammed into rooms containing dozens of cubicles, almost permanently connected to their headsets and wireless terminals.

For the first time in his short life, Jack encountered men from all over the world – Canada, Australia, New Zealand, South Africa, even the Caribbean, India and Ceylon. As well as recruits from the nations of the British Empire, there were also a handful of English-speaking Poles and Czechs who had managed to escape from the invading Nazis. Due to the nature of the wireless operator's job, only those with a superb command of the English language were accepted for this role. By the end of the war, over 50,000 young men would have passed through the school.

Jack's notebooks record every aspect of his training, from basic physics, to the electronic functioning of a wireless set, Morse code, call signs, and a whole plethora of code words and code numbers. On each page there are meticulous circuit diagrams and mathematical formulae, detailed lists of technical instructions and operational procedures, all neatly written in pencil. The amount of information that a trainee wireless operator had to absorb and memorise was incredible. The technology was evolving all the time too. By the time a wireless operator flew with a crew on combat operations, some of the equipment upon which he had learned his trade was already obsolete.

Once the basics of wireless knowledge had been established, the operators would undergo training flights to allow them to put into practice all they had learned "on the ground." For aerial training, the old Proctor and Dominie aircraft were put into use, but the amount of aerial training the new operators received was very limited, due to the sheer numbers coming through Wireless School and the paucity of aircraft. For that reason, most newly qualified wireless operators would be sent to an RAF base for a period of twelve months or so in order to gain much-needed experience of an operational bomber station, without even setting foot on board an aircraft. As the war progressed, however, Bomber Command was losing hundreds of men every month; operators who came through Yatesbury in 1943 and 1944 were often not afforded that luxury and were thrown straight into aircrew training. On 22 June 1941, the war took on a new direction as the German invasion of Russia, codenamed Operation Barbarossa, got underway. Hitler seemed unstoppable, and Nazi domination of the entire European continent almost inevitable.

At the beginning of July, Jack was informed that he had passed his wireless operators' course, having only just scraped through his final exam with a mark of 40%. After a few days' leave back home in Seaham Harbour visiting Lydia, George and his father, Jack was ordered to report for duty at RAF West Raynham. He also had the opportunity to catch up with his best friend and next-door neighbour, Jimmy Thornton. Perhaps inspired by Jack, and keen to get in on the action, Jimmy had also enlisted in the Air Force, and, like Jack, had volunteered for Bomber Command, much to the horror of his mother. Jimmy was a grammar school boy and was therefore considered "officer material." He had been selected to train as a navigator.

Amongst letters and papers belonging to Edie Threadkell, the Clyde family's neighbour, there is a photo of the two boys stood together against the brick walls of the shared backyard at Caroline Street in their uniforms, with the white flash on their caps indicating that they were still undergoing training. Jack is just eighteen, Jimmy a year older. Edie kept this photograph of her two young neighbours on her sideboard for the duration of the war, and wrote to each of them regularly, especially her beloved "Jackie". Neither of the boys had any clue as to the trauma and the terror that lay ahead, nor that the chances of them both surviving the war would be negligible.

On 21 July 1941, Jack made the long journey to RAF West Raynham in Norfolk (a few miles from the quiet market town of Fakenham), to take up his first posting with 114 Squadron, as a ground-based wireless operator. The squadron, which had only just arrived at Raynham, had recently completed operations with Coastal Command, flying several missions attacking German shipping in the North Sea and the English Channel. The men and the rapidly ageing three-man Blenheim aircraft of the squadron had now been reallocated to Bomber Command.

For the first time, Jack found himself at the very hub of combat operations on a busy bomber base. Still two months short of his nineteenth birthday, this shy boy was thrown straight into the operations room, where he was required to relay messages and instructions to and from combat aircraft departing for raids over Germany. He soon became used to the frenetic radio activity, interspersed with long, pregnant pauses. Night after night Jack sat hunched over his wireless set, headphones on, finger hovering over his Morse code tapper, or twiddling his pencil around his fingers, doodling in the margins of his notebook, ready to transcribe messages from the returning Blenheim bomber crews. Frequently, no such messages were received. Jack would wait, staring up at the brass clock on the wall every few minutes, watching the second hand move around the dial, chewing the end of his pencil until he could feel the tiny splinters of wood on his tongue, desperately listening out for the crackle that signified radio contact had been made.

Silence.

In his early days at Raynham, Jack would often return to his bunk at the end of his long shift, visibly upset.

"Nothing further heard from this crew after take-off."

Almost daily, Jack or one or other of the wireless operators would have to relay this message to their superiors. Gradually, the tears that Jack had, at first, fought so hard to hold back subsided, replaced simply with a feeling of emptiness that stubbornly refused to go away.

While Jack was struggling to come to terms with the demands of his new role, the mood in the country, and in government, was changing. Subject to constant air raids, day and night, many citizens were becoming increasingly disillusioned with the war effort. In March 1941, a letter to the *Sunderland Echo*, signed only with the nom de plume "Bomber," gave vent to the frustrations experienced by countless civilians up and down the country. Under the headline "*Giving Germans Own Medicine*" the correspondent wrote:

"Sir – I consider the remarks of the Minister for Air, that heavier blows are to be aimed at Germany by the Royal Air Force, to be most heartening.

It is to be inferred that we can now attend to military objectives and yet make the Germans pay for wanton damage to our cities.

It is the only way. If bombing is ever to be outlawed the Germans must know what it means. It is time we started frightening them; Hitler is ever trying to ring the changes upon us, with secret weapons, submarine warfare, blitzes and the like.

Incidentally, before going in for greater bombing of German cities, let pamphlets be prepared showing in pictures what Nazi airmen have done, and saying 'Now it is our turn.'

Bomber"[16]

Increasingly, what people wanted was revenge. And who could blame them?

The British Government saw things differently. Although they had been desperate to avoid civilian casualties, it was very quickly becoming evident that the only means available of taking offensive action against Germany was by a sustained and unrelenting large-scale bombing campaign, initially targeting German industrial and military sites. The thinking behind such a campaign was that destruction of such targets would mean that crucial manpower and equipment would be diverted to defending them, instead of being utilised in the further expansion of the Reich. The Germans' capacity for production and distribution of armaments would be severely curtailed; this in turn would assist the Russians in halting the invasion on the Eastern Front. The British commanders also had their eyes on the long game; according to Air Marshal Arthur Harris, intensive aerial bombardment

---

16   The *Sunderland Echo* Archives, March 1941.

was "the only means... of preventing the Allied armies from suffering enormous casualties when they eventually invaded the continent."

In mid-1941, however, an Allied invasion looked, for the moment at least, a pipe dream.

By late summer, just as Jack was settling in at Raynham, RAF chiefs were already considering switching from precision bombing (attacking individual factories and industrial targets) to area bombing (attacking entire industrial towns and cities). Although Sir Arthur Harris has long been considered responsible for this change in policy, the decision had in fact been made long before he was appointed head of the Air Force in February 1942. That said, there can be no doubt that he was one of the strongest advocates of area bombing, nor that the policy was implemented whilst he was in charge. Harris would always deny, unlike the author of the letter to the *Sunderland Echo*, that he was motivated by revenge, or that area bombing was designed to break the morale of the German people. He pointed out in his 1947 autobiography, *Bomber Offensive*, that earlier attacks had been shown to have little effect on the spirit of the German civilians.[17] In the light of subsequent events, and the horror that unfolded on the ground, his comments are disingenuous at best. As the German armies swept into the Soviet Union at an astonishing speed, during the dark days of 1941 the end of the war seemed a very long way off, whatever the outcome. Then, on the other side of the world, an event took place which changed everything.

The United States Government, although openly assisting the British war effort with supplies of food, fuel and armaments, had been unwilling to become embroiled in a continent-wide war 3000 miles away, which had already begun to spill into North Africa. However, the hand of America was forced when

17 Harris, Sir Arthur, *Bomber Offensive*, Collins, London, 1947.

Japanese forces suddenly, and without provocation, launched a massive aerial attack on the United States Naval Base at Pearl Harbor, Hawaii, on 7 December 1941. A few days later, Japan's ally, Germany, declared war on the United States, and any difficulties President Roosevelt may have encountered in "selling" involvement in the European theatre of war to the American people quickly subsided.

At the Arcadia Conference on 21 December 1941, President Roosevelt and Prime Minister Winston Churchill met to discuss tactics. Naturally many Americans (including many military chiefs) wanted revenge on Japan first and foremost, but controversially their President agreed with Churchill that the main thrust of the Allied attack should be against Germany, as the largest and most powerful aggressor. It was decided that continental Europe should be invaded and the Nazis defeated at the earliest opportunity. Many in America were pushing for the invasion to take place in the summer of 1942, but the British, who had already been at war for two long years and were fully acquainted with the strengths (and weaknesses) of their foe, knew that such a tactic would be suicidal. In the event, no such invasion would prove possible for another two and half years after the two leaders' historic meeting.

With the Americans now committed to a war in Europe, plans were immediately implemented for the VIII Bomber Command of the Eighth Air Force to operate from bases in Britain. Unlike the Royal Air Force, the USAAF (United States Army Air Force) was part of the American Army and would remain so until 1947. In 1939, the USAAF was only the ninth largest air force in the world, and when it entered the war it still lacked enough aircraft and the necessary numbers of highly trained crews. What it did possess, however, were almost limitless industrial resources to build thousands of new aircraft, and a large, young, male population who could be quickly trained up to crew them.

The USAAF had two crucial assets: two technologically advanced, long-range heavy bombers, the famous B-17 (the Flying Fortress) and the B-24 (the Liberator). Each carried a crew of ten men. The American crews also had a lot of flying hours under their belts (although they lacked combat experience), which, as the war went on, would give them the distinct advantage over their less well-trained Luftwaffe adversaries.

The British and the Americans were not in agreement on every policy and tactical issue. One major area where they differed greatly, and one which would have direct implications for Jack Clyde's future, was the issue of area bombing. The Americans made it quite clear that they were opposed to area bombing on both military and moral grounds. From a military point of view, the USAAF chiefs thought that night-time area bombing by the RAF was imprecise, ineffective and greatly increased the risk of civilian casualties. At that time, when the navigational equipment aboard the average British bomber was basic to say the least, they were most definitely correct. After much debate, a strategy was agreed whereby the Americans would carry out precision bombing during daylight hours, and the RAF would continue to bomb targets at night.

The RAF's attempts at daylight bombing in the early days of the war had proved disastrous. The older Manchester, Whitley and Blenheim bombers were no match for the Luftwaffe's fighter aircraft, and lacked both the range and the payload to do any major damage. They also had a relatively low "ceiling" which made them sitting ducks for attacks both by flak and by fighters. The B17s and the B24s of the Americans were huge in comparison, could fly much further distances at much greater heights, and could carry huge payloads.

They were also very heavily armed, and when flown in tight formation, literally metres apart, less vulnerable to attack. Large numbers of aircraft flown in very tight formation, all dropping their bombs at the same time, resulted in a much more concentrated and therefore successful attack on a target. Finally, the American aircraft possessed the famous Norden bombsights, which allowed them to bomb with much greater precision. What the Americans did lack was combat experience.

By mid-1942, all down the east coast of Britain, and particularly in the counties of Norfolk, Cambridgeshire, Suffolk and Lincolnshire, new runways, hangars, barracks and administrative buildings were hastily constructed in anticipation of the influx of potentially tens of thousands of American airmen, groundcrews, support staff and hundreds of aircraft. Over 200 airfields were either adapted, taken over from the Royal Air Force, or newly built. At the height of the war, in 1944, there would be around half a million USAAF personnel stationed in Britain.

From his base at West Raynham, Jack was among the first to witness the arrival of the American aircrews. The vast bombers which began to fly into neighbouring bases at Shipdham, Coltishall, Downham Market and Watton were unlike anything he'd ever seen before. Terrifying, yet beautiful – the sort of machines which made Jack very glad indeed that they were on his side, and not in the hands of the enemy. The whole of East Anglia seemed to be teeming with Americans, but they were not the only visitors.

In the spring of 1942, Jack and the boys at West Raynham were informed of the imminent arrival of some VIP guests. The identity of the visitors was kept a secret until the very last moment for security reasons, but the base's residents had long had an inkling that something "big" was afoot. All the buildings on the base had been cleaned and painted, paths and roads swept, flowerbeds tidied and brasswork polished. Rumours spread around the base like wildfire.

"It's Churchill!"

"No, it's Harris and the Yank generals!"

"No, it's Clark Gable!"

It was none of the above. On a chilly April morning, Jack and the other ground staff were ordered to parade on the main square. The aircrews were instructed to await inspection by their aircraft. The base's top brass stood outside the entrance to the headquarters building, accompanied by a gaggle of invited press photographers and a Pathé news crew, complete with film cameras and microphones. Only the station commander, his immediate subordinates and the film crew knew the identities of the guests.

At eleven o'clock precisely, a motorcade swept through the gates and pulled up outside HQ. The men and women of RAF West Raynham were staggered to see a tall, slightly gaunt-looking gentleman, in full RAF dress uniform and cap, accompanied by a very well-dressed lady, wearing a hat at a jaunty angle, step out of the first motorcar.

"Bleedin' 'ell," someone hissed. "It's the King!"

Among Jack's treasured possessions is a set of six tiny black and white photographs, each about two inches square, which record in detail the visit of Their Majesties. At first, I thought perhaps Jack had taken the photographs himself but then realised that they were professional images, issued as a commemorative set to the staff of West Raynham as a morale-boosting memento of the day. Each photograph shows the King and Queen being shown around a different part of the base, chatting to senior officers and the aircrews. In one, the Queen is seen striding past a two-storey building painted with a camouflage pattern, the gable end of which has clearly been strafed with machine gun fire and is riddled with bullet holes. There's no information recorded on the back of any of the photographs, save for one. This picture shows Wing Commander J.F.C. Jenkins, DSO DFC, standing directly beneath his aircraft, leaning gingerly on a crutch, chatting to the King, with the Queen looking on. In Jack's neat handwriting there are the words:

"MISSING – Friday 27th March 1942. Reported safe 30th March 1942."

Why had Jack taken pains to label this particular photograph? Maybe the wing commander was a man he admired and respected, a hero. Perhaps Jack had been sat in the wireless room on 27 March, staring at that brass clock, desperately awaiting word from Jenkins and his aircraft, word that never came.

"Nothing further heard from this aircraft after take-off."

In circumstances far beyond his imagination, and for reasons he could never have contemplated, Jack Clyde would be destined to see King George again.

7

Unnecessary Railings

While Jack was getting to grips with his role as a wireless operator on a busy bomber station, there was no let-up for his family or the people of Seaham Harbour. Throughout 1941, the cities, towns and villages all down the North East coast were subjected to frequent air raids by the Luftwaffe, as the Germans, having suspended plans for any invasion of Britain, did its utmost to destroy British industry, military targets and, most importantly, civilian morale.

The air raid sirens would sound most evenings. How did people cope with that? It is difficult to imagine today the psychological toll that the constant fear of imminent death must have taken on ordinary people, whether they were being bombed by the Luftwaffe in Sunderland, or by the Royal Air Force in Düsseldorf. The anticipation when all was silent, the gnawing fear in the stomach at the first sound of the sirens, the sweat on palm and brow, the goose bumps, the hair standing on end, and sometimes the nausea and utter panic and desperation that true fear brings, children (and adults) often wetting themselves with sheer fright. Many citizens would swiftly gather their children and head straight to the nearest shelter, but equal numbers stayed in their beds and took their chances, as "air raid fatigue" began to set in.

In one of the heaviest attacks of the war up to that point, on the night of 9 April 1941, the ship-building ports of Tyneside, Hull and Sunderland sustained major damage. The famous Binns department store in Fawcett Street, Sunderland, a favourite of Jack's sister, Lydia, and the highlight of any shopping trip to "the town" as Seaham folk always referred to Sunderland (and indeed still do), was destroyed. There'd been a Binns in Sunderland since the late 1700s, and now all that was left of this fine family business was a smouldering pile of ashes, twisted metalwork and charred, blackened stone. There were heavy casualties throughout the North East, and a report in the *Sunderland Echo* of 10 April 1941 eloquently described the horror of the preceding evening:

> *"When the planes were at their height, the whole town was lit up with the glare, which acted as a magnet for the enemy planes which droned over the town in a more or less constant procession."*[18]

The incendiary bombing had clearly worked; hundreds of individual fires had been lit, each acting as a beacon and an aiming point for the German heavy bombers. Hundreds of homes and commercial premises were destroyed or damaged. Once again, local newspaper headlines played down the carnage, choosing instead to run with the headline *"11 ENEMY BOMBERS BROUGHT DOWN."*

18 The *Sunderland Echo* Archives, 10.4.1941.

Seaham had had a narrow escape, at the expense of its much larger neighbour. A large case of incendiary bombs had fallen in a field near Seaton Village, but had plunged into the soft earth and miraculously failed to explode. The mining town stayed in darkness that night, thankfully invisible to the Luftwaffe crews.

Greta Meek can still clearly recall the air raids on the town; her father was an air raid warden and would immediately reach for his tin hat as soon as the sirens sounded. Even the tiniest chink of light emanating from between a neighbour's curtains would attract his wrath, and the familiar command, "Put that light out!"

Her mother was an invalid, and had her bed set up in the lounge of their cottage. Greta's aunt (who later married her father after her mother's death) would read poetry to the whole family as they took shelter in the pantry, in a very loud voice so that Mother could hear it from her bed. The aunt flatly refused to use the air raid shelter, as her sick sister was bedridden, and she did not want to leave her alone in the house when the bombing started. A favourite poem was Tennyson's *Lady of Shallot*, perhaps selected because it was so lengthy and could therefore hopefully distract the children for the duration of the raid. Seventy-eight years later, Greta can still recite every word.

Seaham did not escape the attentions of the Luftwaffe for long. Just ten days after the Binns raid, a lone bomber attacked shipping lying off the harbour awaiting the tide, injuring a Norwegian sailor on the *SS Selvic*. Throughout the summer of 1941 there were minor skirmishes and incidents of houses and property being damaged by stray explosives, probably destined for Sunderland or Hartlepool. However, on 21 September 1941, the Germans launched another heavy attack on North East coastal towns. Twenty-five separate towns and villages were attacked, including Seaham this time, with deadly consequences.

That evening, fifteen-year-old Harry Sayers and his pal had just been to see a film at the Cosy Picture House, a few yards up the bank from the Mill Inn public house, in Seaham Colliery. Just before half past nine, as the boys made their way up the steep bank, past the pithead and the slag heaps and the rows of miners' cottages, the air raid siren sounded. Within seconds, Harry could hear the roar of aircraft very close overhead, followed immediately by the whistle of falling explosives. Harry instinctively took cover, diving through a gap in the low stone wall to his left, into the pit yard and landing on a pile of coal. Deafened by the explosion, he was showered in dust and debris as the Seaton Colliery Inn on the opposite side of the road took a direct hit. Despite being incredibly lucky to be alive, Harry recalled that all he could think of was what his mother would say when he arrived home in his brand-new mackintosh, filthy and covered in coal dust.

The occupants of the Seaton Colliery Inn were not so fortunate. The pub itself was destroyed by fire; the landlady and her friend were killed outright. Twenty people were injured, and several colliery cottages damaged. The A19 trunk road, which then ran through the centre of Seaham, was blocked by the rubble from the explosion for some hours. Some years after the war the inn was rebuilt and renamed The Phoenix. It's still there, in the same spot as the original pub, but is now home to a convenience store. All that remains of the pit yard (and indeed of the colliery itself), where Harry Sayers sought refuge, is the stone wall.

Just two months later, Jack Clyde's own family had a very narrow escape. Wednesday 12 November 1941 was a bitterly cold morning, with an icy wind that seemed to come straight in off the sea, buffeting the rows of terraced houses. Jack's father, John, had left for his shift at the pit some hours earlier and his little brother, George, was safely at school around the corner. At around twenty past nine, Lydia was sitting at the large table in the centre of the downstairs room of 7 Caroline Street, which served as kitchen, parlour, dining room and just about everything else, reading a letter from her husband, Jim, while she waited for the kettle to boil on the range. At that time Jim was based in the south of England, in the picturesque village of Abbotsbury near the Dorset coast, where he was being trained in mine warfare and serving with the Royal Engineers 565 Field Company.

With the letter Jim had enclosed a small black and white photograph of himself and a couple of his mates in uniform, all three grinning at the camera, standing "at ease" with hands behind their backs, in the rose garden of the pretty cottage where they had been fortunate to be billeted. Jim would later relate how they had spent hours during the summer of 1941 lying on the roof of the village church, ostensibly keeping a lookout for enemy aircraft, but more often than not snoozing in the sunshine, away from the gaze of their permanently annoyed corporal.

Lydia dropped Jim's letter on the table with a start when the air raid warning sounded. Daytime raids were quite unusual, and for that reason she immediately knew it wasn't a false alarm and dashed to the shelter. Moments later, as she sat down on one of the wooden benches which lined the walls, alongside Edie and Mrs Thornton, wondering if her house would burn down because she'd forgotten to take the kettle off the hob, there was the unmistakeable roar of aircraft engines overhead, followed a split-second later by the whistling scream of falling bombs and the crash of masonry. Lydia shut her eyes and braced herself, fingernails almost sunk into the wooden plank upon which she sat. And then... silence. No explosion, no sound of falling masonry, nobody crying or yelling. Lydia opened her eyes and wondered if she was going mad, if she had in fact imagined it all.

"That bugger Hitler! If that bloody kettle has boiled dry there'll be hell on!"

Lydia was never one to mince her words. Three large high-explosive bombs had fallen just a couple of streets away. Not one of them had detonated. Three people had suffered minor injuries, and several houses had been damaged. Because of the danger from the unexploded bombs, and the fear that they may have been fitted with time delay devices, the 250 residents of the surrounding streets were swiftly evacuated. Two of the bombs had ended up in a single house, one through the roof and one through the wall. The third had pierced the roof, attic and first floor of the house next door, ending up in the parlour. Mrs Dora Jefferies, who lived right opposite the damaged homes, saw the enemy aircraft swoop right down and then the bricks bursting out of the walls.[19] Harry Sayer, the young chap who had narrowly avoided death in the attack on Seaham Colliery, recounted how the air raid warden had gone to knock on the door of one of the bombed houses to assist the elderly chap who lived there to evacuate.

The old man refused to answer the door and wouldn't come out. The warden thought it best to enter the house in case the resident was injured. He discovered the gentleman sitting in his armchair by the fire, leaning over and raking the embers in the hearth with the poker.

"What's that?!" the warden exclaimed, observing a large shiny metal object resting by the fireplace.

"That? I dunno, son, it's just come through the wall."

After more than a little persuasion the elderly chap finally agreed to leave his home and was observed by Mrs Jefferies

---

19 The *Sunderland Echo* Archives, 11.12.1941.

being escorted out of the house, partly dressed, brushing dust and debris from his head, uninjured but clearly in shock.[20]

The final months of 1941 saw a great deal of enemy activity over this little corner of County Durham, with almost nightly raids by mid-December, but the Germans didn't have it all their own way. For every bombing raid that got through the defences and successfully attacked its target, a high number of Luftwaffe aircraft and their crews were lost, shot down by British fighters, hit by anti-aircraft fire from the coastal batteries, or became disoriented in bad weather and ditched in the North Sea.

On 9 December 1941, an invading bomber, a Junkers JU88D, was shot down off the coast of Seaham Harbour by one of the Hurricanes of 43 Squadron, piloted by Flight Lieutenant Geoffrey May. The crew, observer Fritz Bohme (the equivalent of a navigator/bomb aimer on a British bomber crew), pilot Ludwig Volk, wireless operator Fritz Schackert and mechanic Walter Lentfert were all killed instantly when their aircraft plunged into the sea. Their bodies were never found. This young crew had led somewhat charmed lives; Volk and his crew had already survived a crash in Holland in June 1941, and a forced landing in Sweden in the previous summer. On 9 December, their luck had finally run out.[21]

Neither Jack nor his brother-in-law, Jim, were allowed home on leave that Christmas; the constant air raids had made all non-essential travel difficult in any event, so it was a somewhat subdued little gathering that sat around the table at Caroline Street on Christmas morning, opening what few gifts they had. Lydia had rustled up some pancakes as a treat for breakfast, made from the dreaded powdered egg and a

---

20 The *Sunderland Echo* Archives, 12.11.1941.
21 Kracker Luftwaffe Archive, www.aircrewremembered.com/ Krackerdatabase, accessed 27.9.2018.

little milk, and spread thick with strawberry jam that she'd been saving for the occasion. Jack had sent a card and a new lace handkerchief for Lydia, and a small leather football for George. Jim had sent an enamel brooch for his wife and a board game for George, who was also thrilled to receive a new pair of football boots from his father, John. He never let on where they came from, and Lydia thought it best not to ask. John simply winked and tapped his nose. Lydia had already baked Christmas cakes and sent them off in tins to Jim in Dorset and Jack in Norfolk, along with a woollen scarf she'd knitted for her husband and a tank top for Jack. Lydia was forever knitting in her spare time, on those long dark winter nights. The wool from discarded garments would be carefully unravelled and re-knitted into something else.

After church, and visiting friends and neighbours, the family were joined by Edie Threadkell for Christmas lunch, and spent the afternoon playing board games and cards in front of the fire. As Lydia stood in the freezing outhouse in the backyard with Edie washing the plates in the stone sink afterwards, she allowed herself a few tears as she thought about Jack and Jim.

"Haway, pet, don't cry," whispered Edie.

Lydia was never one to mope about and quickly wiped her eyes with the corner of her apron, pulled herself together and simply got on with it, as she always did.

After the almost nightly raids of 1941, the New Year began quietly. There were no further attacks and the townsfolk began to breathe again, collectively wondering if the tide had begun to turn, whether the Luftwaffe bombing campaign was beginning to ease off. Repairs to damaged homes were affected, and the expansion of the new housing estates at Parkside and Deneside continued at a pace, in order to provide accommodation for the many families whose houses had been rendered uninhabitable. Lydia was thrilled with a surprise visit from Jim (who'd been given a week's leave at very short notice) on the occasion of her twenty-first birthday on 21 January 1942, and the young couple spent the evening at the Empire Theatre, followed by a day trip to Durham on the bus the following morning. Though he said nothing, as they wandered arm in arm over Elvet Bridge and up Sadler Street, pausing for a drink in the ancient Shakespeare pub, and headed towards the cathedral, Jim knew it was only a matter of time before he was posted abroad, very probably to North Africa, which was the main theatre of war for the British Army. He wasn't being trained to set and defuse mines for nothing, nor was there much demand for his unit's bridge-building, demolition and transportation skills in deepest Dorset. The hour was approaching. Neither of them could have any comprehension of the trials that lay ahead, nor of the horrors that Jim would encounter, which, though unspoken, would affect him for the rest of his days.

After Jim had returned to his unit in Dorset, following his all-too-brief spell of leave, Lydia and George and many of the other residents of the town threw themselves into "Warship Week."[22] In the autumn of the preceding year, the Government National Savings Committee had announced a series of Warship Weeks, to be held the following year. Towns and cities all around the country were encouraged to designate a particular week for fundraising, to "buy" a warship. Seaham's Warship Week was to take place between 7 and 14 February 1942. There was already an HMS Seaham, recently launched on the Clyde; the council had enquired about "adopting" the minesweeper and her crew but were informed that they would need to raise the enormous sum of £65,000 to do so. The acquiring of such a

---

22 Alexander, Les, *Seaham: A Town At War, 1939-1945*, Lighthouse Publishing, Billingham, 2002.

sum within the space of a week would be a big ask even today; in 1942 it was the equivalent of requiring the people of this small town to fork out around £2 million. Lord Londonderry, safely ensconced in his estate at Mount Stewart, and still writing bitter letters to anyone in government who would listen, was asked to contribute. The project was described by Mr Lee, the chairman of the Seaham War Savings Committee, as "the biggest financial venture Seaham has ever tackled." *Everybody* contributed. There were whist drives and dances, sports days and every sort of sponsored event imaginable. School children donated their pocket money, local businessmen donated what little profit they might have, housewives raked together a contribution from their housekeeping, and the miners' unions also weighed in.

*

So often our identities, both as individuals and as nations, are bound to our sense of place; a particular familiar landmark, be it a castle or a hill or a church or even a pithead, evokes a sense of community and belonging, a feeling of "home." These landmarks tie us to the land, helping to create within each of us our regional or national identity. We begin to see them as old friends, perhaps even as members of our families; bricks and mortar, yes, but so much more than that. In times of strife, these landmarks become symbols of spirit, of hope and determination. There is a famous old black and white photograph of St Paul's Cathedral in London at the height of the Blitz, its world-renowned dome towering above the smoke and the rubble, and the death and confusion which surrounds it.

For County Durham folk, our landmark, our talisman, the source of so much pride and affection, is Durham Cathedral.

For over a hundred years, every July, thousands of miners from colliery towns and villages all over North East England have gathered here with their banners for the traditional service which marks the beginning of the miners' gala, or as it is known in these parts "Durham Big Meeting," earning it the nickname of "The Pitman's Cathedral." As children, Jack, Lydia and George had been regular visitors to the annual miners' picnic at the racecourse near the river, which followed the religious service and the political speeches.

Entering the cathedral through the ancient Norman doorway, just as Lord Londonderry had with the German ambassador Von Ribbentrop in 1936, it is very easy to miss the Royal Air Force Memorial and stained glass window to the right, as one's attention is automatically drawn to the vast nave and the towering columns to the left. The window depicts an airman in his flying jacket, facing away from the viewer, gazing upon a mist-shrouded cathedral, and references one of the most famous episodes in the cathedral's more recent history.

On the night of 28 March 1942, 234 Royal Air Force Wellington and Stirling bombers had dropped around 400 tons of bombs, including 25,000 incendiary devices, on the medieval German city of Lübeck, a port on the Baltic coast. The raid was meant to be a show of force, a demonstration of the capabilities of Bomber Command, and the first time the Area Bombing Directive issued to the RAF in February 1942 had been implemented, to horrific effect. Lübeck had been chosen as a target because of its many medieval timbered buildings, which burned like tinder under the incessant deluge of incendiaries. The plan had been to replicate the method of bombing which had destroyed Coventry. It worked. Over 300 people were killed in the firestorm which resulted, and more than 15,000 were made homeless. Such was the intensity of the fires that the bells of St Mary's Church melted. In a savage turn of events, four Christian religious ministers (three Catholics and a Lutheran) were arrested by the Nazi authorities after the raid, tried and sentenced to death. They were beheaded on 10 November 1943 in Hamburg. Their crime? To explain the Lübeck raid as a "trial by ordeal" in their sermons, which the authorities interpreted as unacceptable criticism of the Government, intended to undermine morale.

In direct response to the attack on Lübeck, the Luftwaffe launched a series of bombing raids on historic British cathedral cities. These were nicknamed the "Baedeker Raids," because they targeted sites of cultural and historical significance picked out from the series of famous old travel guides. The first raid took place on 23 April 1942, targeting Exeter. Canterbury, Bath, York and Norwich were also bombed, the latter twice, along with small towns of no strategic importance such as Cowes, King's Lynn and Poole. Every one of the cathedrals survived, but there was heavy damage to the city centres and substantial loss of life. Over 1600 civilians were killed, even more injured, and 50,000 homes destroyed or damaged.

On the night of 30 April, a force of some thirty-eight German bombers passed over the North East coast and carried out raids on Newcastle, Sunderland, South Shields and Jarrow.[23] Seaham was spared this time, but a number of bombs were also dropped in the vicinity of Durham, which was much less heavily defended than the industrial towns and cities of the region. Four fell near Carville, on the outskirts of the city, others at Beamish village (including one with a timer device that exploded later in the day, killing eight people); a few miles to the north, an unpopulated area by a bend in the River Derwent was heavily bombarded, and two bombs fell at Finchale Priory, which perhaps had been mistaken for the cathedral. Many believed that the Luftwaffe had been aiming

---

23 www.bpears.org.uk/Misc/War_NE, accessed 25.2.2016.

for Durham that night, but for some reason had missed their target. However, it was a bright moonlit night, and the cathedral is hard to miss; it towers above the peninsula in the River Wear and is visible from miles around. Some local residents, including the chief air raid warden, George Greenwell, had recounted that a mist had suddenly and miraculously descended upon the city, rendering the target all but invisible to the marauding German aircraft. Many local people attributed the fog to divine intervention, perhaps on the part of the cathedral's resident saint, Cuthbert, and it became known as "St Cuthbert's Mist;"[24] whatever the cause, Durham Cathedral was spared that night, and it is this event which is so beautifully depicted in the stained glass window above the RAF Memorial.

In early May 1942, Jack arrived home on leave, full of talk of the visit of the King and Queen to West Raynham. Lydia noticed an immediate difference in him; fifteen months in the Royal Air Force had transformed her bashful younger brother into a slightly more confident young man, full of chatter, amongst friends and family at least. He looked taller and had filled out a little and was never without a packet of Player's Navy Cut cigarettes in his pocket. His cheeks still flushed with colour and his pale blue eyes were still cast to the ground whenever he was addressed by strangers or young ladies.

Jack showed his little bundle of photographs of the King and Queen to Lydia, to his father and to George, and relayed the story of the rescue of Squadron Leader Jenkins a hundred times. He popped next door to see Edie, then called upon the Selby family to check up on his good pal Tommy who was serving with the Army in the Far East, before

---

24 Dufferwiel, Martin, *Durham: A Thousand Years of History and Legend*. Edinburgh and London: Mainstream Publishing (1996), pp. 167-169.

visiting Mrs Thornton, to enquire as to the wellbeing of his mate Jimmy. He was somewhat envious when he learned from Mrs Thornton that Jimmy had already completed his ground-based bomb aimer's training and had begun flying training operations on the Short Stirling bombers. Jack had just three months to go before he completed his year of wireless operator's training at Raynham and was desperate to get airborne.

While Jack was at home, the final figures for Warship Week were announced. The generous people of Seaham, many of whom had very little to give as it was, had raised the staggering sum of £101,691. HMS *Seaham* was theirs, but cash was not all the Government was after. All around the town, the streets reverberated with the noise of iron railings being sawn off and removed. The council had issued a notice on 13 April 1942 that with effect from 20 April:

> "… all *unnecessary iron or steel railings, posts, chains, bollards, gates, stiles etc. in the Seaham Urban District Council area will be collected for use in the National War Effort in iron and steel works and foundries.*"[25]

A list of affected streets and buildings, which included all of the town's schools, was set out, and the hope expressed that "owners will be prepared to make a free gift of their railings etc to the nation but property owners and others whose interests are affected by the removal and who desire to claim compensation may obtain the appropriate form from the Clerk of the Council."

Everyone rallied round to do their bit, and whether as a result of patriotism or not wanting to be shamed by their neighbours, not one of the residents whose homes were

---

25 Seaham Urban District Council Public and Official Notice 13.4.1942.

directly affected would have dreamed (or dared) of making anything other than a free gift of their "unnecessary railings."

As Jack boarded the train at Seaham station to head back to Raynham for probably the very last time, Lydia waved him off as usual. Next time he came home, he would be an airman.

8

Airborne

In the first half of 1942, Hitler's grip on Europe had tightened. German U-boats based in the French ports of La Rochelle, Brest and St Nazaire were causing havoc in the North Atlantic, the Arctic Ocean and the Mediterranean, as well as much closer to home, in the North Sea, the Irish Sea and even the Channel. Hundreds of ships belonging to the Royal Navy and the Merchant Marine were damaged or destroyed every month, and the death toll spiralled. Ships were being sunk faster than they could be built; around Britain, in the shipyards of the Clyde, the Tyne and the Wear, in Belfast, Liverpool, Southampton and in Bristol, workers (many of them female) toiled around the clock in the most horrendous of conditions to build warships of all classes – cruisers, minesweepers, battleships – to replace those that had been lost.

Hundreds of thousands of German, Polish, Ukrainian and Russian Jews had already been murdered by the SS death squads in the East, and on 20 January 1942, the upper echelons of the German Government had met at Wannsee, to discuss the "Jewish problem." It was there that the policy of systematic, industrialised extermination, promulgated by Adolf Eichmann, was officially adopted. The "Final Solution," designed to rid the Reich of "the stain" of Judaism, quickly began to be implemented; the first transport of French Jews to Germany commenced on 27 February, and the first so-called Eichmann Transport on 26 March began taking Jewish families – men, women and children – to the gas chambers of Auschwitz and Birkenau.

Thousands of miles away the war also raged in the Far East; in the week that the people of Seaham were rallying around to raise funds for "their" warship, Japanese forces, buoyed by their successful invasion of Burma two weeks previously, launched a swift and brutal attack on the British Colony of Singapore, which had been left to its fate by the British fleet. The remaining British forces surrendered to the Japanese on 15 February; the subsequent occupation of the tiny colony and the atrocities committed by the Japanese against both the military and civilian populations – of all nationalities and creeds – is remembered as one of the most vicious episodes of the war in the East.

For the British Government and the Allies, the only effective way of "taking the fight" to the Germans remained a sustained campaign of combined strategic and area bombing of targets within Germany itself. It was simply too soon to even contemplate an invasion, as the Nazis remained indefatigable on mainland Europe, despite having been compelled to call off the proposed invasion of Britain. But chinks in the Nazi armour were beginning to show; the Allies had already gained supremacy in the air after the Battle of Britain, and Hitler's decision to march into Russia had both vastly overcommitted his ground troops and diverted much-needed resources from the campaign in Western Europe.

In early 1942 Air Marshal Arthur Harris had alighted upon the idea of the "thousand-bomber raid". The plan was to assemble a huge force of 1000 bombers and send them out in a single operation, to attack just one German city. The purpose of such a raid was twofold: firstly, as a demonstration of Allied aerial might and capability, and secondly, to achieve maximum destruction. The difficulty was, however, that Bomber Command had only 400 aircraft, and not enough experienced crews to fly them; Harris sought to boost the numbers by requesting help from the conversion and training units, and from the commanders of Coastal Command and Flying Training Command. The head of Coastal Command, Sir Philip Joubert, immediately offered 250 bombers, and Flying Training Command offered another fifty, but most of these weren't suitable or were too old. After calling in favours, Harris finally managed to assemble sufficient numbers. However, he faced opposition to his plan from those within the RAF who thought his scheme simply too dangerous; such a concentration of aircraft would surely be sitting ducks for the Luftwaffe, and there were grave concerns about the risks of mid-air collision.[26]

If the raid was to be a success, new tactics were required, and it was around this time that the concept of the "bomber stream" was introduced. This allowed huge numbers of aircraft to fly along a pre-set route, at the same speed, towards the target (and away from it once the bombload had been dropped). Each squadron was given a timeslot, and each of its aircraft would take off at very short intervals; each aircraft was given a particular height range, to minimise the risk of collision. The timeslots were all carefully co-ordinated so that the bombers could all fly out at their specified time to form

---

26 Middlebrook, M. and Everitt, C., *The Bomber Command War Diaries*, Pen & Sword Aviation, Barnsley, 2014, pp. 269-271.

part of the "stream" of aircraft from other squadrons. These new tactics, combined with the recent introduction of the Gee navigation system, made it much easier for the bomber crews to determine their precise location within the stream, and their position in relation to other aircraft within it. This was very different to the tight "formation flying" favoured by the Americans for their daylight bombing raids. It was hoped that the stream could pass through the least possible number of German radar areas, known as "boxes." The individual controllers of these boxes, who ordered the Luftwaffe night fighters to intercept the incoming bombers, only had a small number of fighter aircraft at their disposal, which meant that they could probably only co-ordinate around six interceptions an hour. The idea was to ensure that the bomber stream passed through the least number of boxes, in the shortest possible time.

Previously, around four hours had been considered the right sort of timeframe for a raid; in other words, one would expect around 100–200 aircraft to pass over a target in the space of four hours, which cannot be considered a particularly concentrated attack. Harris now came up with a revolutionary plan. A thousand aircraft would attack a target in a window of just ninety minutes. Again, concerns were voiced about the risk of collisions, but Churchill and Harris considered that the ends justified the means.

Just as the plans were about to be implemented, the Admiralty pulled the aircraft promised by Coastal Command, on the grounds that their bombers would be better employed in facing off the U-boat offensive. Harris found himself short of over 200 aircraft, which meant that he was forced to rely on inexperienced crews barely into their training. Forty-nine aircraft with only "pupil pilots," with no operational experience whatsoever, and many more with very minimal proficiency, were called upon to take part in what some commentators have referred to as "Harris' massive public relations exercise." There was significant disquiet from some quarters of the RAF at the thought of sending so many untrained crews to take part in such a raid, but Churchill indicated that he was prepared to allow for the loss of around one hundred aircraft and their crews, a massive casualty rate of 10%.

Harris originally planned to attack Hamburg, but bad weather over three successive nights forced him to opt for his second choice, Cologne, which at that time was the third biggest city in Germany. On the afternoon of 30 May 1942, orders were sent out for the dispatch of all 1047 aircraft at Harris' disposal. Six hundred and two Wellingtons, 131 Halifaxes, eighty-eight Stirlings, seventy-nine Hampdens, seventy-three Lancasters, forty-six Manchesters and twenty-eight Whitleys took off; these included 365 aircraft from the training units, with their crews made up of instructors and half-trained pilots, many of them still in their teens. According to official Bomber Command records, 868 aircraft bombed the main target.

The raid was considered a huge success; German records showed that 2500 separate fires were started and over 3300 buildings were destroyed, and thousands more damaged. Due to the design of the city, there was no firestorm as there had been in Lübeck or Coventry, and fatalities were around 480, with another 5000 souls injured. Around 45,000 German citizens were left homeless, and a fifth of the population fled the city. This "success" was not without cost, however; Bomber Command suffered its highest losses of the war so far, with forty-one aircraft and their crews failing to return. Miraculously, the rookie crews of the training units lost proportionally fewer men than the more experienced crews.[27]

---

27 *Ibid*, p. 270.

Buoyed by his success in Cologne, Harris once again summoned the host, and 956 aircraft were despatched to attack the industrial city of Essen in the Ruhr Valley on the night of 1 June 1942. This operation was an unmitigated disaster due to low cloud, which meant that the crews could not locate their target, and many other towns and rural areas were bombed by mistake. Thirty-one bombers were lost. Harris was undeterred, and boosted by aircraft from Coastal Command, after Churchill demanded they be made available, 960 aircraft attacked industrial targets, including the Focke-Wulf aircraft factory, in the northern city of Bremen, in the space of just sixty-five minutes. For the people of Bremen, those sixty-five minutes must have felt like a lifetime.[28]

Although much more successful than the operation on Essen, the efforts of the bomber crews were once again hampered by cloud which obscured the target for most of the duration of the raid. The aircraft factory sustained heavy damage but was not destroyed, and residential areas appear to have borne the brunt of the damage. Forty-eight bombers and their crews were lost including, this time, many of the young crews from the training units. The combination of old, barely serviceable aircraft from these units and the lack of flying experience meant that these brave boys faced much stiffer odds than their more seasoned, better-equipped colleagues.

In one of the buildings which houses the excellent Yorkshire Air Museum, on the site of the old Elvington airfield which formed part of 4 Group Bomber Command, there is painted on the ceiling a representation of a thousand-bomber raid. It is difficult to comprehend such numbers until one walks beneath them and gazes upwards; the painted silhouettes seem to go on forever. Such vast numbers of aircraft would not be

---

28 *Ditto.*

employed in a single raid again until the Battle of Normandy and the Invasion, two years later.

Jack Clyde knew that things were about to change for him; desperate to play his part, and keen, like so many of his young colleagues, to "give Hitler a bloody nose," he passed the slow summer days at West Raynham anxiously awaiting news of his next posting and the commencement of his aircrew training. June turned into July which turned into August, and still there was no word. Jack began to wonder if perhaps he'd been overlooked, if his name appeared on a list which had slipped down behind a filing cabinet in Whitehall, or been accidentally discarded by a careless WAAF at HQ; however, he was simply too shy to raise the matter with his superiors at 114 Squadron, and so he waited.

He need not have worried; on 2 August, Jack was issued with his orders to report back to No. 2 Signals School on Wednesday 26 August 1942, to begin his training as a Bomber Command aircrewman.

Jack's personal effects include a small, grubby, buff-coloured card, a little dog-eared now, and ragged around the edges. It bears the title "ROYAL AIR FORCE – FLYING CLOTHING CARD" as well as Jack's name, rank and service number. It is date stamped "16th August 1942 – Accounts Section RAF Station West Raynham." On the back appears a list of rules and regulations, including:

> "4. *Articles lost on active service through the exigencies of the campaign, or whilst actually flying, or destroyed in a flying accident, will be replaced free.*"

How generous.

Inside, there's a list of every piece of kit with which Jack was issued during his time with Bomber Command, the date he received them and the date they were returned. Next to each item appears Jack's unmistakable signature. In readiness for his departure to No. 2 Signals School, Jack was issued with the following items:

Boots, flying, knee	1 pair
Socks	1 pair
Gauntlets, flying, left hand	1
Gauntlets, flying, right hand	1
Gloves, silk	1
Suits, flying, collars	1
Suits, flying, inner	1
Suits, flying, outer	1
Goggles	1 pair
Boots, mosquito	1 pair
Wets	1 pair
Spectacles, anti-glare	1 pair
Helmet, flying, Type B (without mask, oxygen)	1
Masks, oxygen, Type D	1
Masks, microphone, Type E (oxygen)	1
Receiver, telephone, head, Type C	2

As instructed, Jack (and all his gear) reported for duty at No. 2 Signals School (Air Operations Section) on 26 August, just two weeks before his twentieth birthday. He received a pay rise and was soon in receipt of the princely sum of five shillings and sixpence a day.

By now, the war was entering a new phase, as German tanks and ground forces prepared to enter Stalingrad, and Hitler announced the formal annexation of Luxembourg. The expansion of the Third Reich appeared unstoppable. In Vichy

France thousands upon thousands of Jews were rounded up for transportation and execution – a pattern repeated across all the occupied nations of Europe. The Allied governments, through their intelligence sources, were becoming aware of what was going on in the concentration camps, although perhaps even they did not comprehend the huge scale of the extermination programme. Reports of frequent massacres of civilians by Nazi troops in Eastern Europe also began to filter through. Now, more than ever, the need for direct and swift action against the Reich was evident to all.

The Royal Air Force once again stepped up its efforts to recruit volunteers for Bomber Command, both amongst new conscripts and among the more experienced fighter pilots, many of whom had fought in the Battle of Britain, and who were now being retrained to fly heavy bombers. The fact was, though, there was no real shortage of pilots; it was gunners, navigators, wireless operators and bomb aimers who were required. By the autumn of 1942, aircrew numbers were significantly boosted by the arrival of No. 6 Canadian Group. Production facilities had been set up in Canada to build Lancaster bombers, to supplement the numbers of aircraft being produced here. These Canadian Lancasters were then flown, via Newfoundland, Greenland and Iceland, to Britain. The contribution of the Canadians during these dark days cannot be overstated.

As a result, huge numbers of young men were passing through the various Bomber Command training schools. Because of this, actual flying time for the trainee aircrews could be somewhat limited and was confined to the oldest and almost obsolete Dominie and Proctor aircraft, or "retired" Whitleys and Blenheims that were long past their best and no longer considered operationally serviceable. There simply weren't enough "spare" aircraft around.

As soon as he began flying, every trainee airman, regardless of whether he was a pilot or a rear gunner, a wireless operator or a navigator, was issued with a logbook, in which he had to record details of every flight – the serial number and type of the aircraft, the name of the pilot, the time of departure and return, the purpose of the flight and the amount of "flight time." Jack's logbook – a standard-issue RAF blue hard-backed notebook, in which he carefully divided each page into columns with a ruler and pencil – records, in his meticulous handwriting, his very first flights.

Jack had barely had time to deposit his belongings in the battered wooden locker next to his bed in the barracks when he was summoned to the airfield. After a very basic safety briefing, he boarded Dominie 5928, with Flight Lieutenant Wheldon at the controls, and by five past two in the afternoon was airborne, for the first time in his RAF career. In the company of an instructor, Jack was shown how to put into practice the ground training he had received over the last eighteen months or so, which began with radio tuning and reception.

After an hour-long flight, Jack was sent up again with Wheldon, for what was known as "air experience." This appeared to consist of nothing more than the very experienced Wheldon taking great delight in terrifying his young charge, swooping and diving and rolling the aircraft until Jack was sick into his handkerchief. After fifty minutes or so of "experience" they finally touched down on the runway. As he staggered out of the aircraft, his eyes still watering and with vomit all down his flying suit, Jack wondered if perhaps he'd have been better off volunteering for the infantry. Wheldon just laughed and shouted across to the group of waiting boys:

"Right then, chaps, who's next in line to lose his dinner?"

Over the course of the next two months, Jack flew almost every day, sometimes twice, as his aircrew training intensified.

After learning the basics, on 21 September 1942, he moved onto the Proctor training aircraft, where he worked relentlessly on radio tuning, learning how to take bearings, and transmitting in various conditions and circumstances, including where the aircraft had to make a controlled approach through cloud with visibility at a minimum. Sometimes the flights lasted only half an hour, sometimes longer, but never more than seventy-five minutes, due to the number of men requiring training and the lack of aircraft. When he wasn't flying, Jack was in the classroom, learning more about the aircraft he'd be flying on for real, how to repair a radio set in the event of malfunction or battle damage, and the various codewords which he had to memorise to cover every conceivable situation and emergency. Every step, every instruction, every circuit diagram, every scenario was carefully noted down in pencil in his exercise book and committed to memory.

"X195 – am wheeling in aerial, preparing to land at…"

"X556 – shift to normal frequency"

"X607 – am about to send callsign on my present frequency"

"Distress – dinghy, dinghy prepare for ditching – SOS x 30, WJKX x 5 15 seconds & repeat until ordered to ditching position"

The training was delivered with the express purpose of ensuring "that the pupils are fully conversant with the job before them". Jack even wrote this down in his notes.

At the beginning of October 1942, Jack moved on to the No. 3 Air Gunnery School, to complete the final part of his training. Every wireless operator was required to undertake additional training as an air gunner, so that they could take over control of the aircraft's machine gun defences should the upper or rear gunner be killed or injured. On 12 October, Jack began flying on the Botha aircraft, and for the first time met up with the team of Polish and Czech training pilots, many of whom had already "done their bit," and much more besides, in the Battle of Britain. Jack and his fellow trainee air gunners were totally in awe of these seasoned combat veterans and were terrified of getting things wrong and incurring their wrath. Despite Jack's lack of Polish, and some of the pilots' lack of English, there was no mistaking their anger when targets were missed repeatedly. Some swear words are simply universal. In the company of Sergeants Franczak, Balakowski and Poludwiak, Jack amassed a grand total of only eight hours' air firing practice, before being deemed fit to be let loose with a bomber aircraft's machine guns.

Amongst Jack's papers there is a postcard-sized black and white photograph of him, a portrait. On the back of the photograph, there appears a date stamp – 9 December 1942. He's seated, looking slightly into the distance, calm and resolute. His pale eyes shining, a tiny, unruly wisp of dark blonde hair protrudes from beneath his cap, which no longer bears the white training flash. On each arm he wears the three stripes of a Royal Air Force sergeant on his chest, just above his left breast pocket, a brevet, with the letters "AG" (Air Gunner), adjacent to an embroidered silver wing.

9

Penny's Prangers

Bonds of friendship and brotherhood can be formed at many points over the course of a lifetime. Often, they will begin in the schoolyard, perhaps during a kickabout with a battered old football, or during a game of tag. Sometimes emotional ties form years later, the result of shared experience in lecture halls and warm pints in seedy student bars, at university or college, or perhaps while learning a trade and getting to grips with the lot of the apprentice. Usually, relationships develop with those who are "like us," of similar social backgrounds, or who share a common interest or hobby, those in whom we see something of ourselves, reflected back.

The war changed all that. Men found themselves thrown together with others from all walks of life. Oxbridge graduates now rubbed shoulders with the sons of farm labourers and miners; particularly in the Royal Air Force, more weight was given to a chap's aptitude and abilities than the school he had attended, or who his father was. It would be wrong to say that there was no place for distinctions of class – the command structure of the RAF was still very much the domain of the middle and upper classes – but for probably the first time, anyone with the necessary skill, determination and courage – the "right stuff" – could progress. Consequently, lifelong friendships were made between men who, prior to the war, because of their social circumstances, could never have expected to meet, let alone forge deep and lasting ties. Nowhere was this more apparent than among the crews of Bomber Command.

After a spell of leave at the beginning of December 1942, Jack was instructed to report for duty at 24 Operational Training Unit (OTU) at Honeybourne, Worcestershire, to commence his operational training. On 23 December, some two months after his last flight, Jack was finally airborne again, this time in one of the OTU's Avro Ansons, in the company of Flight Sergeant Norvell and his crew. The training was intense, but again, due to lack of resources, Jack's flying time was very limited. He was allowed only two flights in December, but in January 1943 the pace of training and the frequency of flights increased. On 13 January, Jack experienced night flying for the first time. Within just four months, he would be taking part in night-time bombing operations for real.

The very next day Jack moved on to a nearby base at RAF Long Marston, in Worcestershire. That afternoon in the briefing room, Jack and the other young men of the OTU were informed that they were to commence their training on the Armstrong Whitley twin engine bombers, which required a crew of five: a pilot, a co-pilot (who was also the navigator), a bomb aimer, a wireless operator and a rear gunner. With its large rectangular wings, the Whitley was functional rather than aesthetically pleasing, and was often nicknamed "the flying barn door." Having been introduced in 1937, many of

1. Lydia Clyde and Jim Groark, 1938

2. New RAF recruit Jack Clyde, 1.2.41

3. "Penny's Prangers" June 1943 L-R Singh, Cox, Clyde,
Pennicott, Tann, Phillipson, Bradshaw

4. Tail Gunner Bill Bradshaw

5. Navigator Reg Cowles

6. "Skipper" Reg Pennicott

7. Leo "Titch" Groark (seated), RAF Melbourne

8 Cramped conditions on board a Halifax; the wireless operator sits directly beneath the pilot, with the flight engineer standing to the rear (Image courtesy of IWM)

9. Almost home – the Seaton Ross windmill was a welcome sight for returning 10 Squadron crews

the Whitleys in use in the training units were already well
past their best; at worst, some of them were barely serviceable.
Accidents and fatalities in the OTUs were commonplace.
Before the war had run its course, 8115 young men would
perish in training accidents, destined never even to reach their
operational squadrons or to experience combat operations.
Jack was not encouraged when he learned that his first flight
in the Whitley would be with Flight Sergeant Death at the
controls.

After an hour or so in the company of Death, Jack was
introduced to his second pilot of the day, Pilot Officer Reg
Pennicott. Eight years older than Jack, and an estate agent
by profession, Pennicott had an air of calm professionalism,
the confidence of a man who had seen and done it all. He
was already a successful businessman, very well-to-do, and a
regular competitor on the motor racing circuit at Brooklands.
When it came to flying bombers, however, Pennicott was as
an inexperienced as the rest of the crew. The son of a butcher
from Berkshire, he was a grammar school boy, well established
in his chosen career when war broke out. He had recently
married a young nurse from the East End Maternity Clinic
in Stepney. Jack was completely in awe of Pennicott and was
visibly nervous as he climbed on board the Whitley, his breath
forming small clouds in the bitter night air. Pennicott was a
man who noticed everything and gave Jack a reassuring pat on
the shoulder.

"Clyde, isn't it? Don't worry, Clyde, I haven't got a ruddy
clue what I'm doing either."

Over the course of the next month, Jack flew almost daily,
always in the Whitleys, frequently with Death and Pennicott,
but also with Flight Lieutenants Rawstorne and Nash, and
even with Squadron Leader Pestridge, of whom he was
terrified. By mid-February, Jack had amassed thirty-nine hours

of daylight flying, and over thirty-six hours of night flying time in the Whitleys. It was during this time that Jack became great friends with a small, dark-haired lad with a strong Norfolk accent, by the name of Roy Tann. A navigator, Roy was a quiet sort of boy with a dry sense of humour from the tiny village of Forncett End. He and Jack got on famously and spent many an evening playing cards in the Sergeants' Mess.

During such intense training, it was natural for bonds to begin to develop between those men who flew together frequently. A pilot might have a favourite rear gunner or bomb aimer with whom he seemed to develop a natural rapport; a navigator might begin to develop a particularly good working relationship with one wireless operator over another. So, the bomber crews began to form; by the time the next stage of training was due to begin, the matter of "crewing up" was already more or less settled.

"Crewing up," the process by which the Bomber Command trainees were divided up into individual crews, ready to complete the final part of their training before being sent on to operational units, was not an exact science. More often than not, the men would be told to report to the mess hall or even a hangar and divide themselves up into crews, without any official interference. This meant that men who had flown well together during training naturally gravitated towards each other, while those who hadn't got on could look for crews to whom they were better suited. Of course, there was always the fear that, like the school football team, you would be the last to be picked, but there was frequently a crew who would be one man short, so gaps were easily filled.

Tom Davidson, a Halifax flight engineer with 466 Squadron, told me how, on arrival at RAF Acaster Malbis, the pilots were all standing in the doorway of the mess watching all the other crewmen come in, eyeing up their potential crew members. Tom spotted one chap, a young Australian pilot. He recalls thinking, *I hope this fella picks me!* He immediately made eye contact; the pilot came straight over and introduced himself as Pat McGillis, and asked Tom to be his engineer. Pat was just nineteen. In that moment a friendship was made that would last for seventy years.

Jack, always so shy and quiet, was concerned that he wouldn't be good enough, that no pilot would want him on his aircraft. As he walked into the hangar back at Honeybourne, he wondered if he was bold enough to wander up to a pilot and ask to join his crew. All the airmen were given cups of tea on arrival, and, wandering through the throng, teacup and saucer in hand, he rehearsed in his head a little speech he had made up. In the corner of the hangar, he spotted Pennicott deep in conversation with Roy Tann, and one of the bomb aimers he'd flown with a couple of times, Londoner Ken Cox, a quiet, anxious sort of lad who had originally trained as a navigator. Pennicott looked up and began beckoning furiously to Jack.

"Where've you been, Jack? Thought I was going to have to find myself another WOP!" he exclaimed as Jack breathed a sigh of relief and joined the little huddle. Roy grinned at him. "Come on, Jack, you're officially one of Penny's Prangers now!"

Just then rear gunner Bill Bradshaw, a nineteen-year-old Ulster farm boy with film-star good looks and a ready smile, from Newcastle in County Down, appeared and nervously tapped Pennicott on the shoulder. He was welcomed into the group immediately. The Pennicott crew was almost complete.

The Allied air chiefs had, at the Casablanca Conference in January 1943, decided to utilise all available heavy and medium range bombers for a major offensive against Germany, with the express purpose of weakening industrial capacity and undermining the morale of the German people. The campaign was underpinned by three main aims. Firstly, by targeting industry, the Allies hoped to destroy the supply of armaments, aircraft, ships and tanks to the military. Secondly, they knew that sustained attacks on German cities would draw the Luftwaffe away from the Russian front, and give the Soviet ground troops a better chance of driving back the invasion. Finally, and perhaps most importantly, the prospect of a weakened Germany would allow an invasion by Allied forces at the earliest opportunity. It was only now, with the involvement of the Canadian Air Group and the huge numbers of American aircraft now stationed in England, that the Allies had enough resources to even contemplate such a campaign. Arthur Harris and the Royal Air Force top brass planned to use massive numbers of aircraft – usually between 500 and 800 bombers, supported by fighter escorts – in each individual attack.[29]

Harris was informed as early as 4 February 1943 that the policy was now to completely obliterate the major German industrial and port cities of Hamburg, Bremen and Kiel. A "Plan B" was put in place in case these targets could not be reached due to inclement weather conditions; other German industrial centres, naval bases on the Atlantic coast of France, and even Berlin itself were identified as legitimate targets.

Of course, none of these plans came as a surprise to the Third Reich; Hitler and his generals knew exactly what was coming and had been anticipating attacks since the British had gained air supremacy after the Battle of Britain. Boosted by slave labour, by March 1943, German aircraft factories were producing 700 fighters *per month*. Around 70% of these were allocated for defending Germany, and the Western Front, from attack by Allied bombers. The Germans knew the industrial

---

29 Cooper, Alan, *Air Battle of the Ruhr*, Airlife Publishing, Shrewsbury, 1992, p. 21.

Ruhr area in particular, being only around 300 or 400 miles from the British mainland, and therefore well within the range of the British bombers, was vulnerable to attack. Air defences were ramped up significantly; awaiting the bomber crews were around 930 heavy guns, over 3000 light and medium guns (all of which were quite capable of taking down an aircraft), almost 400 searchlights and over 1600 barrage balloons, as well as almost a million men of the Anti-Aircraft section, most of whom were civilians[30] (all German men aged between eighteen and sixty were eligible for call-up to the Home Guard flak units; as the war progressed, even younger children and the elderly were pressed into service).

Initially the German defences struggled to cope with the sheer numbers of incoming aircraft, but very quickly they introduced larger artillery, including 88mm and 105mm cannons, capable of hitting targets at heights of over 30,000 feet. If your aircraft was hit by a thirty-two-pound cannon shell, you had most definitely "had it".

As well as the hordes of Luftwaffe night fighters, and the attentions of the flak units, the pilots of Bomber Command also had searchlights to contend with. Once an aircraft was caught in the main beam, or "coned", the surrounding search beams would also begin to track it, so it was almost impossible to escape. A coned bomber was then easy pickings for the night fighters and the anti-aircraft guns; in the glare of the light it was easy for crews to become disoriented. Aircrews feared the blue lights above them all; the German technology evolved so that these larger lights could actually "lock on" by radar to an approaching bomber. If that occurred, there was little chance of escape.

In mid-March 1943, as the bomber campaign was growing in strength, Jack and the rest of the crew were sent

---

30 Ibid, p. 22.

on detachment to 10 Operational Training Unit (Coastal Command), to gain more experience of "real" flying in an operational environment, and where they would also, potentially, be exposed to fire from enemy aircraft and ships. Flying the five-man Whitley V bombers again, for the first time the crew took part in lengthy exercises, sometimes flying eight, nine or even ten hours a day. In just three weeks, the crew amassed almost seventy-two hours' flying time; worryingly, only an hour and a quarter involved flying at night.

Day after day the crew took off, usually mid-morning, and performed their various air tests, navigational exercises and sea patrols. Part of their task involved looking out for wreckage and life rafts from downed aircraft, but also attacking any enemy submarines sighted. On several occasions their patrols took them as far south as the Bay of Biscay, seeking out U-boats which had slipped out, unnoticed, from the Nazi submarine bases on the French Atlantic coast. Frequently the wily U-boat commanders would "take cover" beneath Spanish fishing vessels, but the crews of Coastal Command soon became wise to their tactics. Any fishing vessel which aroused suspicion could expect a "calling card" from Bill Bradshaw; a short burst of fire into the water from his twin Browning machine guns about 200 yards in front of the boat usually had the desired effect, with the disgruntled fishermen turning back for their home ports, thereby depriving any sneaky U-boat captain of his cover.

Bill, just two months older than Jack, had originally signed up to be a pilot; he went all the way to Canada to undertake his pilot training but failed the course. Wanting to get into the thick of the action as soon as possible, he decided instead to train as a rear gunner, because the course was only a month long. Consequently, Bill was one of a very few rear gunners who held the rank of pilot officer. Pennicott immediately took him under his wing (literally and metaphorically) and over the coming months the two would become very close. Bill was a very useful chap to have in the crew; in the event of an emergency, he could take over the controls of the aircraft.

Jack's logbook records every one of those Coastal Command flights:

"23/3/43 11.35 Whitley T-Z9285 P/O Pennicott (Duty: W/Op) A/S sweep – Loops, QDMs, fixes. Flying time 8:35"

It wasn't all plain sailing, but that was the point. On two occasions the crew were compelled to return to base, once with an unserviceable gun turret, another with engine trouble. The crew needed to learn how to cope when things went wrong with an aircraft and had to prepare for every eventuality. Equally, they needed to learn to work together seamlessly as a team, each man performing his own job to the best of his ability and trusting his crewmates to do the same. However, Jack and the boys knew that the old battered Whitleys could only teach them so much. They had already been pencilled in for operational duties with 10 Squadron in North Yorkshire, and 10 Squadron flew Halifaxes, not Whitleys.

The Halifax was never as popular or as "glamorous" as its rival, the famous Avro Lancaster. Even today, whenever the subject of Bomber Command is raised, people still automatically mention the Lancaster. That aircraft is ingrained in the national consciousness, rather like the beloved Supermarine Spitfire, probably as a result of its association with the Dambusters raids, and the films of the 1950s and '60s which commemorated the exploits of the famous 617 Squadron, and in later years as part of the Battle of Britain Memorial Flight. Air Marshal Arthur Harris loved the Lancaster and loathed the Halifax. The larger Lancaster was (and is) considered by many to be the superior aircraft, due to its speed and greater bomb capacity; the Halifax couldn't carry a 4000-pound "cookie" bomb, for example. Just never mention that to anyone who actually flew a Halifax. After some initial problems with the design of the tail, which led to a high number of fatalities, an aircrew's chances of survival were slightly greater if they were in a Halifax rather than a Lancaster; the Lancaster's central spar made it extremely difficult to bale out if the aircraft was hit. The Halifax was also structurally stronger, designed to break into sections in the event of a crash-landing, which saved the lives of many a crew.

In reality the Halifax played an equal part in the vast majority of Bomber Command operations, and was very much the "workhorse," despite the fact that Harris despised it. The fact is, without the Halifax, Bomber Command would have achieved very little.

By the time Jack and his crewmates began their heavy bomber training, several variants of the Halifax had already been produced. They knew that they would be flying one of the Mk II versions, although designs for a superior Mk III, with Hercules engines replacing the Merlins, were already well underway.

One of the two remaining Halifaxes on British soil, *Friday 13th*, lovingly restored and cared for, can be found at the Yorkshire Air Museum. One cannot fail to be impressed by the sheer size of the beast. It is *enormous*. The wingspan is vast, the four Bristol Hercules engines huge; thoughts automatically turn to the crews of these aircraft, many of them just boys. The inside of the aircraft seems so much smaller than one would expect, a sort of Tardis in reverse. Access is by means of a ladder and small door behind the port wing. The somewhat cramped interior is anything but luxurious – bare metal mainly, painted pale green, across which run miles of cables, pipes and wires. A single rudimentary Elsan toilet (basically a bucket with a lid) constitutes the bathroom facilities. At the nose of the aircraft, almost on the underbelly, is a large perspex bubble, where the bomb aimer would lie on his stomach, trying to visually identify the target, before pressing the button which released the payload. The pilot sits high up, on the left, with the radio operator's position tucked into a cubbyhole beneath him. All the crew's posts are situated on the left of the aircraft, with just enough space for one man at a time to walk to the rear. There are several steps to negotiate, and the atmosphere on board is incredibly claustrophobic.

Behind the pilot, facing in the opposite direction, is the flight engineer, with his panels of controls, dials and fuel gauges. A drop-down seat is located on the wall of the fuselage just opposite, though in reality a flight engineer was usually kept so busy that he barely had time to sit down once the aircraft had taken off. A drop-down seat was also available for a passenger (usually a trainee pilot learning the ropes, or a Special Operations Executive agent who was to be dropped by parachute behind enemy lines).

On the other side of the wireless operator's position, and further towards the front of the aircraft, is the navigator's table, his maps and charts and calculations spread out before him, his compasses and navigation equipment mounted onto panels at eye level. A double drop-down seat accommodated both the navigator and the bomb aimer, until it was time for the latter to take his position in the nose. The bomb aimer would normally provide assistance to the navigator, as he had little to do until the aircraft began to approach its target. There is so little room that the navigator sat almost "knee to knee" with the wireless operator.

Further back, on the "backbone" of the aircraft, is the mid-upper gunner's position; he would have to lift up an access hatch which doubled as his seat once he was in position, climb up into a harness and sit in his perspex bubble, ready to swivel round the aircraft's four Browning machine guns in case of attack by Luftwaffe fighters. Constantly on the lookout for enemy aircraft, and with a 360-degree view, he couldn't allow his concentration to lapse for a single moment. Then, right at the far back of the aircraft, far away from the rest of the crew, with whom he could only communicate by intercom, was the "tail-end Charlie" or rear gunner, in the most isolated, vulnerable and awkward spot from which to escape in the entire aircraft. At his disposal were four Browning machine guns, each supplied with 2500 rounds of ammunition (around two and half minutes' worth). The rear gunner's position is incredibly cramped, and its occupant would sit there for hours at a time, his knees tucked up towards his chest, unable to stretch out or move around. The turret is too small to store belts of ammunition; instead, the bullets were fed into the turret along a hydraulic track positioned in the main body of the aircraft. Many gunners never fired a single bullet in anger; there was no point wasting valuable ammunition unless an enemy aircraft was spotted approaching and was within range. As most bombers would be targeted by enemy fighters approaching from the rear, the rear gunner was incredibly vulnerable. He was also at risk from bombs falling from higher aircraft. Several aircraft arrived back at their bases with their rear turret (and their rear gunner) missing, sheared off by a falling bomb. At the height of the Bomber Command campaign, a rear gunner would be lucky to survive five missions.

It would be wrong to place more importance on any particular crew role, or indeed to downplay any other. Each crew member was essential to the functioning of the aircraft, the successful execution of its mission and the survival of his comrades.

At the beginning of May 1943, the Pennicott crew were on the move yet again, this time to 1663 HCU (Heavy Conversion

Unit) at Rufforth in Yorkshire. Right in the heart of the 4 Group Bomber Command stations, the HCU trained crews on the heavy bombers – the Halifaxes and Lancasters – which formed the backbone of Harris' area bombing campaign. The four-engine Handley Page Halifax was substantially larger than the Whitley, and carried a crew of seven; on 3 May, the Pennicott crew acquired two new members.

Mid-upper gunner Freddie Singh was an Australian, immediately marked out by the dark navy-blue uniform of the Royal Australian Air Force. His great-grandfather had gone out to Australia from India in the middle of the nineteenth century as an indentured servant, and the family had eventually settled in Queensland. With his dark, wavy hair, thin moustache, dazzling smile and sharp wit, Freddie had a wisecrack for every occasion, yet was still somewhat reserved. His somewhat aloof nature was sometimes mistaken for standoffishness, and some members of the crew felt that Freddie never really "fitted in". Perhaps he was homesick for Queensland; perhaps he felt that his surname and heritage marked him out as a "colonial" in the eyes of some of his fellow airmen, and that he was looked down upon as a result. Wherever the truth lay, the other members of the Pennicott crew adored him.

The remaining crew member, flight engineer George Phillipson, could not have been a greater contrast to Freddie. At thirty-three, Cockney George was the eldest member of the crew by far with a wife, Ethel, back home at Upton Park in the East End of London. They had already lived through the worst of the Blitz, and George was keen to do his bit. Tall and stern-looking, with a hangdog (and occasionally sceptical) countenance, George had served his time as a motor mechanic in heavy industry before enlisting in the Royal Air Force and volunteering for Bomber Command, although when war broke out he had been working as a clerk at the local coal merchant's yard. George kept his own counsel and spoke little about himself or his family. Many flight engineers were older than the rest of their crew, as men with years of experience in engineering who had the ability to understand the workings of complex machinery (and more importantly, who knew how to fix it) were much sought after by RAF recruiters. There wasn't anything that George couldn't take apart, mend and reassemble.

The crew barely had time to get to know their new members; in less than twenty-four hours Pennicott (always called Penny by the crew) and his men were already airborne in a Mk II Halifax, practising flying on three and then only two engines. The following day the crew went up with an experienced pilot, Squadron Leader White, who demonstrated three-engine circuits and landings. The fact that so much attention was focused on flying with reduced engine capacity was surely a sign of things to come. After only four days, which included only one practice bombing run, Jack and the boys switched to night-time training, which consisted mainly of taking off and landing the aircraft in the dark, and a single bombing run. Incredibly, by 14 May, just eleven days after arriving at the HCU, the crew were considered operationally ready.

"Penny's Prangers" had flown a Halifax at night (in training conditions, with no opposition, and not under enemy fire) for a grand total of thirteen hours.

10

Home Fires Burning

Lydia hadn't heard from Jim in a while. His letters had become sporadic, and she would receive nothing from him for weeks on end. Every morning she would wait for the postman, her stomach flipping at the familiar rattle-swoosh of the letterbox and the sound of the mail landing on the doormat. Some days the postman would walk right past. Silence. Lydia's heart would sink and she'd busy herself with her chores – blacking the kitchen range, polishing the brass fender on the hearth for the fourth time that week, or wondering how she could make a decent family meal with the rations they had left – and she'd try to think of something else.

Yet those mornings when a pile of buff-coloured envelopes scattered themselves behind the front door seemed, somehow, worse. She could hardly bring herself to pick them up in case she was to be disappointed again, or in case they bore bad news. Wiping her hands on her apron, and brushing back the hair stuck to her brow, she would sort through the envelopes, unconsciously holding her breath, looking for Jim's familiar flowing handwriting. Jack was not the best correspondent, she knew that, but as she saw him every couple of months or so, the absence of letters from him was bearable. Jim was usually much more diligent.

Lydia hadn't seen her husband since early September 1942, just before he had set sail for the desert war in North Africa. He had been allowed a brief spell of leave prior to embarkation, and Lydia had travelled up to Scotland to spend a couple of days with him. How the precious minutes had flown by, as if in the twinkling of an eye; neither of them could bear to speak of what was to come, and their conversation skirted around the very distinct possibility that they might never see each other again. Lydia shared news of relatives and neighbours and the constant air raids, while Jim regaled her with his usual witty jokes and amusing tales of his mates' escapades in training, in an unsuccessful attempt to raise her spirits. Some words remain best unspoken; some conversations are better left unsaid.

The battle in North Africa had already been raging back and forth for two years prior to Jim's departure. Following the destruction of the Italian 10th Army forces by the British at Sidi Barrani at the end of 1940 during Operation Compass, Hitler had dispatched his Afrika Korps to North Africa in 1941, to try to reinforce his Italian allies and prevent any further loss of territory. Led by the legendary German General, Erwin Rommel, the "Desert Fox", German troops engaged the Allies in a number of battles across Libya and Egypt, resulting in the famous Battle of El Alamein in October 1942, when British troops under the command of General Bernard Law Montgomery defeated Rommel's men and chased them into Tunisia.

Jim had sailed first for Algiers, as part of the Eighth Army invasion force known as Operation Torch. His troop ship had left the port of Algiers in the deep of the night, in order to avoid the attentions of enemy spotter planes and U-boats. As they made for their disembarkation point at Bone, in modern-day Tunisia, the ship was hit by a torpedo. Panic reigned, but Jim barked at his comrades to get back to their posts until such time as they were given orders to abandon ship. That order never came; badly damaged, they somehow managed to limp to the nearest port at Bougie, from where Jim and his company of Royal Engineers were transported eastwards, up to the front line at Souk-el-Arba.

Jim never told Lydia about this incident; she had learned of it only when queuing at the fruit shop on the corner of Sophia Street some weeks later. Arthur Conn, the husband of the lady behind the counter, had been on the same ship. Jim had not wanted Lydia to worry unnecessarily. He had recently received word from her that she was expecting their first child.

*

On the evening of 15 May 1943, as Jack and the boys celebrated completing their final day of training on the Halifax by heading to the local pub to sink a few pints, Lydia and her friends had been to see John Mills and Noël Coward in the classic wartime melodrama *In Which We Serve* round the corner at the Empire Cinema, at the rear of Church Street.

Lydia had been cheered by the arrival, that morning, of a long-awaited letter from Jim, announcing news of his promotion to corporal, and enclosing a photograph of him standing next to a captured German sappers' truck, full of mines and switches and triggers. Jim would later describe this vehicle as "a godsend", as it allowed him and the men of his unit to learn precisely how the Nazi troops assembled their mines; it was his task to walk through the German minefields with a rudimentary metal detector and a sharp stick, retrieving the mines and then disarming them. It was incredibly dangerous work, and several of his colleagues were blown up in front of him. Lydia was, of course, oblivious to all of this. Jim made sure of it. He was an intelligent and articulate young man, who soon caught the attention of his superiors; within a short time of arriving in North Africa, he had been given the task of instructing other troops in mine warfare.

Now heavily pregnant, and tired by the evening's excitement, Lydia had decided to have an early night. After saying goodnight to Edie, who had popped in from next door to check on her, as she usually did, Lydia hauled herself slowly up the steep and narrow staircase. Although still only mid-May, the evening was mild and calm. She pulled shut the blackout curtains and slid up the sash window a little, to allow the cool evening air to pour into her room, along with the sounds of laughter and music from the Volunteer Arms public house around the corner in Frances Street, before sinking into bed.

As Lydia was drifting off to sleep, the new photograph of Jim propped up on her dressing table, several hundred miles away at a Luftwaffe base in Soesterberg, Holland, a large force of German Dornier bombers were preparing to take off.

At around two o'clock in the morning, Lydia was awoken with a start by the now familiar scream of the air raid siren. Already she could hear shouts from the street below from the air wardens yelling at the town's residents to get to the shelters. Pulling the curtain to one side, she could see that the streets seemed strangely illuminated. An advance force of German aircraft had dropped parachute flares to light up the night sky, so that the bomb aimers of the rapidly approaching Dorniers could try to pick out their targets – the docks and the collieries of the Durham coast. Nazi propaganda leaflets, detailing heavy

British losses in the Royal Navy and the Merchant Marine, fluttered down onto the pavement, ultimately destined for a use that Hitler had not intended, in the backyard toilets of the town.

Seconds later, observers Tom McNee and Billy Whitelock, from their position on top of the tower of St John's Church, suddenly noticed a huge parachute mine drifting towards the corner of Adolphus Street and Sophia Street, barely 300 yards from where Lydia was sitting on the edge of her bed, trying to pull on a dress over the top of her nightgown. Within a matter of moments, a massive explosion ripped through the streets.

A "whooshing" sensation was followed by a deafening noise as Lydia was showered in glass from the blast, although the curtains saved her from injury from the larger shards. It was over in a split second. In the darkness Lydia felt that her heart would stop. Shaking, she quickly realised that she hadn't been hurt. Unable to hear properly, she could feel tiny fragments of glass everywhere – in her hair, all over the bed covers and in the folds of the garment she had been trying to slip over her head in the moments before the explosion.

As she lowered her feet to the floor, she felt the glass crunch beneath her bare toes. Coughing and spluttering in the dust and debris, yelling, "George, *GEORGE*! Are you alright, George?" Lydia made her way gingerly to the top of the staircase, grabbed hold of the sobbing George who'd been sleeping in the tiny box room next door, and began tentatively making her way down the stairs, one hand on the banister, the other sliding down the wall, feeling the familiar pattern of the wallpaper against her fingertips.

In the street, Lydia leant against what was left of the front door and tried to catch her breath. Her father, John, who'd been sleeping in the downstairs room, had already made his way outside and was trying to comfort George and Mrs Thornton.

Amid the shouts and screams and chaos, and the howling and barking of dogs driven mad by the blast, Lydia heard someone calling her name. She was unable to work out where the voice was coming from, though it seemed familiar. As she gathered her thoughts, she realised she could hear Edie's voice, coming from the staircase she had just descended. Edie was shouting, frantically searching for her. In the darkness and confusion, amid the smoke and the dust, Edie and Lydia had somehow managed to pass each other on the narrow staircase of the tiny terraced cottage. Edie's home was miraculously untouched, with not a single window broken; shockwaves from the bomb blast ricocheted off every other house, zig-zagging a path of destruction down the street.

"I'm alright, Edie, I'm here, I'm here! Edie!"

Edie grabbed hold of Lydia with one hand and grasped the collar of George's pyjamas with the other and frogmarched them both through the rubble to the nearest shelter. She was terrified, both that the baby was going to come early, and that the air raid was not over, but as usual she did not let her own feelings show.

As the first pale streaks of dawn began to light up the town, the scale of the destruction soon became evident. The beautiful Presbyterian Chapel at the corner of Sophia Street had been almost demolished, save for a single painted rear wall. Houses in Adolphus Street and Sophia Street were destroyed, but the worst of the devastation was in Viceroy Street, where several homes had been flattened, and many more rendered uninhabitable. In this poor and densely populated area, casualties were high. Two perished in Adolphus Street, six in Sophia Street and nineteen in Viceroy Street. Another seven of the town's citizens died of their injuries in hospital. A further forty-two were seriously injured. Several families were trapped in the rubble of their homes, including the Corkhills.

For thirteen hours, rescuers dug through a solid twelve-foot mass of debris to try to reach the family. Eventually, they were able to create a "tunnel," through which the local doctor was able to crawl to administer morphine to a severely injured young woman, Mary Kelly. Nineteen-year-old Mary's injuries were so severe that she died in hospital a short time later. The rescuers were able to retrieve seven-year-old George Corkhill from the remnants of his home; this poor boy was the only survivor of a family of six.

George Meek and his family had dashed into the above-ground shelters at the opposite side of the Londonderry Yard, immediately opposite the little row of ambulance drivers' cottages, as soon as the siren had sounded. George recalled that the bomb fell within a very short time of the warning being sounded; his father had instructed them to open all the windows as they fled, and theirs were the only windows in the row of cottages to be spared. As the mine exploded, George's elder brother, Fred, jumped on top of him in the shelter and covered him with a blanket, to shield him from the blast. The sight of hundreds of dust-covered people, many of them very badly injured, some of them sobbing, walking or being carried in a long procession past the Londonderry Yard to the temporary shelter at Camden Square School, lived with him to the end of his days.

Over a hundred families were left homeless, and plans were put in place to rehouse some of them in the old miners' cottages in New Seaham, which were due to be demolished as part of the slum clearance programme. Churches, homes, schools, shops and business premises – very few of the buildings in that part of the town had been left untouched by the blast. In neighbouring Sunderland, the devastation was many times worse; over a hundred high explosives fell on the town, killing seventy-five people and injuring hundreds more. A parachute mine, of the same type that had decimated Viceroy, Adolphus and Sophia Streets in Seaham, left a crater forty feet deep and ninety feet wide when it exploded near the town's fire station.

The Luftwaffe raiders did not escape unscathed. Contemporary reports record that one of the Dornier bombers was shot down by an RAF Bristol Beaufighter from 604 Squadron, stationed at Scorton in North Yorkshire, around fifteen minutes after the attack on Seaham. The crew were killed outright when their aircraft plunged into the sea. The body of the twenty-three-year-old pilot, Unteroffizier Karl Roos, was found washed up at Blackhall Rocks a few miles down the coast, some days later, and the corpse of another of his crew, Mitteldstadt, was picked up out at sea. The other two crewmen, Kaber and Richter, were never found.

When the all-clear sounded, and after gathering a few belongings, Lydia and George were sent to stay with Lydia's aunt in Emily Street, at the opposite side of St John's Churchyard. John Clyde refused to vacate his home, preferring instead to remain there to begin the clearing-up operation, and to protect the family's possessions from the very real threat of looting. Despite the close-knit nature of the community, then, as now, there were always those who sought to make a profit from the distress of others.

11

The Gathering Storm

Oblivious to the chaos in which his family were caught up at home, Jack arrived at his new base on the afternoon of Sunday 16 May 1943. RAF Melbourne, a few miles from York, was the home of 10 Squadron and looked exactly the same as every other base he'd visited – the same two-storey control tower, the same large khaki-painted hangars and ammunition store, and the same jumble of administrative buildings and accommodation blocks, surrounded by farmland and pockets of woodland. Beyond, there was constant activity on the three runways as thirty-six of the base's crews took off and returned in endless procession, practising formations, bombing, fighter affiliation and "Bullseye" exercises (a simulated night raid against British towns and cities, to prepare the crews for what was to come).

The air was filled with the constant roar of the Halifaxes' Merlin engines, and Jack had never seen anything quite like it. Momentarily dumbfounded, he and the crew stood in awe, trying to take in everything that was going on around them. In the distance beyond the tree line, the broken sails of the long-abandoned windmill at Seaton Ross, the nearest village to the base, were clearly visible. A sentinel on the horizon, the windmill would achieve iconic status for the returning aircrews over the coming months, welcoming them home from their trips to hell.

10 Squadron was (and is) one of the RAF's oldest and most esteemed squadrons. The squadron motto, "*Rem Acu Tangere*," means "hit the mark." Formed in 1915, as part of the Royal Flying Corps, when aviation was still very much in its infancy and the life expectancy of a pilot around eleven days, the squadron had moved into its new purpose-built home in Melbourne in August 1942. By the end of October, the three runways had been completed and the base was fully operational. When the Pennicott crew arrived there in May 1943, it was home to some 1500 aircrew, groundcrew, WAAFs and ground support personnel.[31]

There was one familiar face amongst the hundreds of RAF men and women stationed at Melbourne: a young man also from Seaham Harbour, Leo Groark. Leo was the younger brother of Jim, Jack's brother-in-law. Leo was already an "old hand" at Melbourne by the time Jack arrived. Known to all and sundry as Titch, due to his diminutive stature, Leo could usually be heard before he could be seen, his deep voice and unmistakable laugh well known to aircrew and ground staff alike. Always with a joke and a twinkle in his eye, he was a real favourite, and much loved by "his" aircrew, flight engineer Tom Thackray and pilot Doug Evans, and their men. Leo and Jack could not have been more different: Jack, shy and cautious, Leo the life and soul of the party.

---

31 MacMillan, Ian and King, Richard, *From Brooklands to Brize: A Centennial History of No 10 Squadron Royal Air Force*, 10 Squadron Association, 2015.

"Wheeeyy, look who it is! Jackie Clyde! What are you doing here?"

Six other crews had arrived at Melbourne that day, including that of Squadron Leader Hartnell-Beavis; a total of nineteen crews would be posted in during the month of May 1943 alone.[32] Losses had already been significant. One of the squadron's worst nights of the entire war, 1st - 2nd October 1942, had seen the loss of four out of the five crews detailed for an attack over Demark; three were flying on their first mission. However, training accidents could also prove fatal, and two crews had been killed when they crashed just beyond the airfield.

In accordance with nonsensical RAF regulations, the boys were split up for "billeting" purposes. Pennicott – at that time the only officer in the crew – was housed in rooms next to the Officers' Mess; the NCOs – Jack, Roy Tann, Bill Bradshaw, Freddie Singh, Ken Cox and George Phillipson – shared digs and ate in the Sergeants' Mess. From the outset this caused some disquiet among the crew who would have much preferred to room, and eat, together. Their accommodation, in hastily constructed corrugated iron Nissen huts, was cold and draughty. When it rained, the noise was deafening. Such was the rate of fatalities, a new crew could turn up at its accommodation to discover that it still contained the personal possessions of a crew killed the day before.

There were no operations that first night, nor any for the next week. This break in bombing activity gave the Pennicott crew time to adjust to their surroundings before their first operation. Of course, they could have been called upon at any time; operations were only announced on the day they were due to take place. The tension of awaiting the announcement of the crews rostered for that night's operations must have

32 National Archives AIR/27/144 10 Sqn Diary, May 1943.

been unbearable. As soon as the announcement "the bus will be running tonight" was made over the tannoy, the news spread around the base like wildfire and was inevitably met by cheers from the aircrew and groundcrew alike, while plans would be made to head into York on the coach provided, or to Seaton Ross to the Blacksmith's Arms. The tiny village pub was the hub of the crews' social lives, and soon became known to all and sundry as "The Bomber's Arms."

As Jack and the boys headed over to the Sergeants' Mess for a few pints that Sunday evening, forty-five miles away at RAF Scampton, nineteen Lancaster bombers from 617 Squadron were undergoing their final preparations for what would ultimately become one of the most famous military operations of the entire war.

Three waves of aircraft, led by Wing Commander Guy Gibson, Flight Lieutenant Joe McCarthy and Sergeant Townsend, embarked upon a top-secret mission to destroy the Mohne, Eder, Sorpe and Ennepe dams. These four dams on the Weser and Ruhr rivers supplied hydroelectric energy for a number of power stations in the Ruhr industrial area. Armed with the now-legendary bouncing bombs designed by scientist Barnes Wallis, the nineteen crews faced a dangerous and technically difficult task, which required precision bombing from the suicidal height of just sixty feet. The Mohne and Eder dams were successfully breached; the Sorpe was damaged but not breached; and the Ennepe was not attacked.

Historians have argued about the success of the raids ever since. At the time, it was said that the German Government fully expected further raids on the dams to render them completely unusable; no further attacks came and by the end of September 1943 the dams had been repaired by huge numbers of German civilians and enslaved workers. Air Marshal Arthur Harris had never been in favour of the raids in the first place and thought the whole project a "hare-brained scheme." However, every bridge for thirty miles beyond the Mohne dam was destroyed, and buildings were damaged by the deluge as many as forty miles away. Twelve war production factories were destroyed, and around a hundred more were damaged. Thousands of acres of farmland were under water. Coal mines, steel plants and armament factories all down the valley ceased production for weeks. In addition to the success "on the ground," the raids were presented as an enormous propaganda victory, forever remembered in the 1954 film *The Dambusters*. Of the 133 men who had set out from Scampton that night, fifty-three were killed and a further three captured. It is estimated that around 1300 died in the Ruhr Valley – German civilians, POWs and enslaved Russian labourers. Guy Gibson was awarded the Victoria Cross, but was killed on 19 September 1944, after a raid on München Gladbach.

News of the raids on the dams quickly filtered through to the other Bomber Command stations and must have been a huge boost to morale. However, if Jack, Penny and the boys were itching to get a share of the action, then they were in for a long wait. Jack's logbook records that after arrival at Melbourne, he and the crew flew only three times before their first operation. Due to operational requirements, and the sheer number of crews, the boys amassed only six hours' flying time together in the Halifaxes between their arrival at Melbourne and their first raid. Just after lunch on 18 May, they were allowed an hour in Halifax N-DT541, practising fighter co-operation. That same night, they hoped to put into practice all they had learned so far with their first "Bullseye" operation, but they were recalled to base after fewer than four hours in the air.

In the meantime, Jack had received word of the Seaham air raid from his sister, Lydia. She told him that she and

George were going to stay with their aunt, at least until after the baby had arrived. Their father was staying put in the house in Caroline Street, and Jack was informed that he should go there first when he next had some leave. As he sat on his bed and reread Lydia's letter, his fingertips automatically strayed to his mother's wedding band. Jack lay back on the rough woollen blankets, closed his eyes and thought of the little house in Caroline Street, and tried to imagine it, now windowless, the family's furniture and possessions covered in dust, debris and shards of broken glass. For the first time since he'd left Wireless School, the tears trickled down his cheeks. Desperately worried about his family, and especially Lydia, Jack set about his tasks with a renewed sense of purpose and a steely determination to see the job through, for their sakes.

After a break in the weather, on 23 May 1943, twenty-one crews from Melbourne were detailed to bomb Dortmund, joining 805 other aircraft from other squadrons, in three waves.[33] Jack and the boys were not included this time, but Penny was. That afternoon Penny had been informed that he would be flying on his first operation, as "Second Joe" (second pilot) in the crew of Flight Lieutenant Wood. A brand-new pilot with no operational experience would usually join an experienced crew for one or two missions, essentially as a passenger, before being allowed to take the controls on a bombing operation with his own crew. Most of the crews who took part in the Dortmund raid that night had "Second Joes" on board. At around 10.30pm the first crew took off, followed by the remainder, at roughly five-minute intervals. Of the twenty-one crews who departed from Melbourne that night, the Squadron Operations Book records that:

---

33   National Archives AIR/27/144 10 Sqn ORB, May 1943.

*"Seventeen crews attacked this target reporting a successful raid
and moderate opposition. Sgt. Watson had an encounter with
enemy fighters, his aircraft sustained heavy damage. Squadron
Leader Baird abandoned the mission due to failure of his
intercom. The crews of Sgt. Denton, Sgt. Rees and Sgt. Hine
failed to return from the mission."*[34]

Jack and the boys anxiously awaited news of their skipper's
return. The pilot of his aircraft, Wood, reported very stiff
opposition, heavy flak and very intense searchlight activity.
Three aircraft and twenty-two men were lost – including the
newly engaged Flight Sergeant Denton. His aircraft had been
carrying a second pilot, Sergeant Inglis, and was shot down
over the target area. Sergeant Rees' aircraft had been attacked
and brought down by a night fighter, crashing in the North
Sea; only the pilot's remains were ever recovered, washed up
on a beach the following July. Sergeant Hine's aircraft had
crashed into the Zuider Zee in the Netherlands; the bodies
of two of the crew, the navigator, King and the rear gunner,
Baggaby, were never found.[35] This story was repeated across
many squadrons; a total of 216 RAF aircrew were killed in the
raid, and sixty-one were taken prisoner. Hundreds of German
civilians died, thousands more made homeless. Penny was left
under no illusion as to precisely what would be required of
him and his crew, nor of the mortal danger that awaited them.

Despite the losses, the raid on Dortmund was considered
a huge success by Harris and the Air Force top brass. The
German Deputy Führer, Goebbels, wrote in his diary:

---

34   National Archives AIR/27/144 10 Sqn ORB, May 1943.

35   MacMillan, Ian and King, Richard, *From Brooklands to Brize: A
      Centennial History of No 10 Squadron Royal Air Force*, 10 Squadron
      Association, 2015, p. 127.

"The night raid by the English on Dortmund was extraordinarily heavy. Probably the worst ever directed at a German city. Reports from Dortmund are horrible. We have received reports from Bochum and Dortmund indicating that morale was lower than ever before... we must recognise that people in the west are gradually beginning to lose courage. The fires were under control by the afternoon, destruction, however, is initially total. Gauleiter Hoffman informed me that hardly a house in Dortmund is habitable."

There were no operations again the following night, but on 25 May, eighteen crews from Melbourne were detailed to attack Düsseldorf. Once again Jack and the boys waited for the call; once again Penny flew as a second pilot without them. The Station Operations Book records another successful raid, with sixteen of the eighteen crews bombing their targets. Thankfully all crews returned home safely that night; two had returned early with technical problems.[36] Two days later, on 27 May, eighteen crews were instructed to attack the industrial city of Essen. The boys were convinced that they would get their turn this time, especially now that Penny had done his two "practice" trips, but still they weren't required. Two more crews were lost over Germany, those of Flying Officer Rawlinson and Warrant Officer Price. Two airmen had managed to bale out and were taken prisoner, but the rest perished.[37]

As May 1943 drew to a close, Bomber Command redoubled its efforts; over the next five months or so, the bombing of the Ruhr would be utterly relentless. Jack and the Pennicott crew would find themselves in the thick of it.

---

36 National Archives AIR/27/144 10 Sqn ORB, May 1943.
37 *Ibid.*

12

The Shape of Fear

At around eleven o'clock in the morning, on 29 May 1943, word was received at Melbourne (via Group HQ) from Bomber Command Headquarters in High Wycombe of the plans for that evening's operations.

By the time the target was revealed to the crews assembled in the briefing hall at Melbourne, 4 Group's navigation team had already calculated the distance, time of attack and the fuel each aircraft would require (taking into account the distance to the target, route home, weight and size of the aircraft and its bombload). A subsequent message would be dispatched to the group confirming how many waves of aircraft would be sent, the time between each wave, and the number of aircraft required from each squadron. Of course, everything was weather-dependent; there was little point in sending out crews to attack targets if there was clear weather over Germany, if they were then unable to find their way home due to fog or blizzards.

Jack, Pennicott and the rest of the crew were notified just before lunch that they would be flying their first operation that evening. They had spent an hour that morning carrying out air tests on another Halifax, *V-Victor*. A couple of the lads were cock-a-hoop, excited to be finally given the chance to take the fight to the Nazis. Penny gave them a rousing pep talk but having already witnessed what would be involved, he didn't believe a word of what he told them, even as the very words left his mouth. Every one of them was nervous, apprehensive, perhaps even a little terrified, though of course they did not show it. Jack picked over his lunch with his fork, his appetite suddenly gone. No one said much until a bomb aimer from another crew began to relay in lurid detail his latest encounter with a WAAF from the Operations Room, which seemed to lighten the mood temporarily.

At the same time the groundcrews sprang into action. Each individual bomb was armed by the fitting of a fuse by the squadron armourers, having already had its "fins" slotted in, before being loaded onto trolleys and driven out onto the airfield to be loaded into each aircraft. The larger bombs, some of which weighed over 1000 pounds, were hoisted up by portable cranes and hung on hooks inside the bomb bay. All of the bombs had to be very carefully aligned; failure to do so could have fatal consequences for the crew. A very experienced "bombing-up" crew could load as many as fifteen aircraft in two hours. It was hard, physical and highly dangerous work. For the coming operation, four of 10 Squadron's Halifaxes were "bombed up" with two 1000-pound bombs fitted with time delay fuses, designed to explode some hours after the initial raid, to cause maximum damage and casualties. While the bombs were being loaded, other members of the groundcrew team "belted up" the machine guns with ammunition – 10,000 rounds for the rear gunner, 2000 for the mid-upper gunner.

Cameras loaded with film were fitted to each aircraft so that the bomb aimer could take the required photographs to show "bombs away" over the target.

There existed between aircrew and their groundcrew a very special bond indeed, and they often socialised together. Lifelong friendships were formed, as in the case of Leo Groark, Tom Thackray and Doug Evans. The safety of the aircraft, the success of the operation and ultimately the lives of the airmen depended on the skill, technical knowledge and professionalism of these men. There were ten groundcrew members for every aircraft, each with a different trade and with responsibility for a different part of the aircraft. The preparation of each of 10 Squadron's Halifaxes took around three hours and was an intense and extremely thorough process; even an ostensibly very minor defect could mean that a mission had to be aborted or could result in the loss of the aircraft and the death of the crew.

The engines would be run, the wireless, navigation and all electrical systems tested, and the hydraulics checked to ensure that the flaps and gun turrets were working properly. Once the aircraft had been thoroughly checked and found to be in good operational condition, the tankers would drive out to the aircraft to fill the fuel tanks with the precise amount of fuel specified by HQ – not a drop more, not a drop less. The aircraft was then ready to be handed over to the aircrew.

In the early hours of the morning, the groundcrew would assemble and wait anxiously for news of the return of "their" aircraft and crews. Once the aircraft was on the ground and the crew safely disembarked, the engineers and technicians would teasingly give the airmen hell if any damage had been sustained to their aircraft. It was very rare for an aircraft to return without sustaining at least minor damage, from flak, tracer bullets or cannon fire. Doug Newham, a 10

Squadron Navigation Leader in 1944, remembers that many groundcrews felt that they were simply "loaning" their aircraft to the bomber crews for their operations.

The female map clerk, often known as the "map queen," would issue individual crews with their maps. Rather like a librarian, she was in charge of thousands of maps and charts which she would have to locate in the blink of an eye, without the use of computer records. She would be one of the first people on the base after the Squadron Leader to be aware, roughly, of the target location. Once maps had been issued, crew members headed over to the parachute store, usually manned (or rather womaned) by WAAFs, to collect parachutes, dinghies and life jackets. Each parachute had its own logbook and had to be inspected, repacked, logged and signed for by the packer. Pilots were issued with a special seat-pack parachute which they actually sat upon in the aircraft. Other crew members' 'chutes were stowed away on board the aircraft; they were simply too large, too heavy and cumbersome to allow free movement within the cramped confines of the aircraft, and so were not worn until bale-out was imminent.

After an "operational supper" of eggs, bacon and beans, Jack, Penny, Roy, George, Freddie, Ken and Bill and sixteen other crews filed into the briefing room for their very first operational briefing. All briefings were conducted in secret. The map was hidden by a curtain, the windows were shuttered, and once everyone was inside, the doors were locked, guarded by RAF police. Once the briefing had begun, no one was allowed access, and no one was allowed to leave until it had been completed. Penny had of course flown two missions earlier that week as "Second Joe," so he knew what to expect. Perhaps this made it easier for him. Perhaps it made it worse. The more experienced crews knew full well that they would be headed for targets in the Ruhr Valley, and precisely what that entailed; as the Squadron Leader pulled back the screen to reveal that night's target, there was much murmuring and groaning amongst the assembled men, as well as a fair few swear words muttered under the breath. "Not bloody Happy Valley *AGAIN*."

Wuppertal.

The Air Ministry had labelled the Ruhr area "The Weapon Smithy of the Third Reich." A small part of that area, the town of Wuppertal itself, was set in the Wupper Valley, between steep granite cliffs, and at that time had a population of around 400,000.[38] Originally an amalgamation of two smaller towns, Barmen and Elberfeld, it lies about fifteen miles southeast of the city of Essen, and is roughly the size of, say, Coventry or Sunderland. Wuppertal wasn't a large industrial city like its neighbour but was important because it was home to many small factories which manufactured essential components for tanks, guns and aircraft engines. By May 1943 Wuppertal's population had been boosted by significant numbers of slave labourers, brought in from the concentration camps or enslaved from Eastern Europe to work in the factories, as well as a number of refugees who had fled those parts of the Ruhr Valley devastated by the "Dambuster" raids two weeks previously.

It later transpired that the crews of neighbouring 76 Squadron, based at Linton-on-Ouse, who were also to take part in the attack, had been informed by their own intelligence officer that part of their aim was to "catch" (i.e. kill) these thousands of refugees. This caused some disquiet among a few of the crews, who were not certain that bombing civilian refugees was what they had signed up for.[39] If that

---

38 Cooper, Alan, *Air Battle of the Ruhr*, Airlife Publishing, Shrewsbury, 1992, p. 81.

39 Hastings, Max, *Bomber Command*, Michael Joseph Ltd, London, 1979 p. 249.

was indeed one of the aims of the raid, rather than just an intelligence officer's bluster, then it was kept from the crews of 10 Squadron.

The route that the crews were required to take was shown on a large-scale map standing on the small stage at the front of the hall, red tape marking out their intended path. Jack sat and listened intently, taking it all in but as usual saying nothing. Roy carefully noted down the map co-ordinates in his navigator's notebook, and he and Penny then went over them together. Each crew was allocated an aircraft – Penny and his men were informed they'd be flying Y-JD109, callsign *Yorker*, an aircraft they had not flown before. The roll was called, followed by an intelligence briefing, which dealt with potential defences and the nature of any opposition the crews might encounter. The briefing concluded with a weather report.

Before each operation, aircrews had to empty their pockets of anything which might be of value to the enemy should they be shot down – money, personal letters and the like. All of these items went into a personal bag, and then each bag went into a larger sack for each individual crew. Frequently the boys would give letters to their groundcrew or a favourite and trusted WAAF, to be posted to their families and loved ones in the event of their non-return.

Penny's crew, along with those of Wood, Williams, Hellis, Beveridge, Wade, Dunlop, Belcher, Mellor, Clarke, Sutton, Brunton, Cox, Skerratt, Pinkerton, Thackray and Squadron Leader Hartnell-Beavis, all made their way to the locker room to get "kitted up" in their flying gear. Amongst an old pile of photographs belonging to Jack's sister, Lydia, there is a photograph of Jack in his flying suit, standing beside one of the buildings at Melbourne, half smiling, squinting into the sun, his shadow cast onto the wall behind him. Clad in his bulky suit, the fur collar up-turned, his white flying scarf wrapped around his neck and tucked smartly down the front, and still wearing his leather gauntlets and boots, he looks shyly at the camera, but every bit the experienced aviator.

Just prior to heading to the locker room to put on his flying suit and gear, Jack had quickly sought out Leo Groark. As usual, Leo had a joke and made some wisecrack, but Jack was even quieter than usual. He thrust into Leo's hand an envelope addressed to "Mrs Lydia Groark, 7 Caroline Street, Seaham Harbour, Co. Durham" and two metal door keys fastened together by a grubby piece of string.

"Here, take my house keys. Give these to Lydia if I don't come back."

Leo's face paled slightly as he took the keys and the envelope and stuffed them into the pocket in his overalls. He did his best to raise a smile.

"I'll give you them back in the morning, you daft bugger."

*

"The brave man is the fellow who recognises fear in himself, makes use of it, forcing it to be his servant while he remains master of his fate, refuses to be weakened by events, and with cool head and stout heart goes on with unswerving domination to achieve his purpose."

Reverend James Duncan,
Dawdon Parish Magazine, October 1940

How many of us can say that we have experienced true fear? We may have been terrified for a brief moment, but in the blink of an eye the danger passes, and all that remains is the recollection of that transient horror. The memory of that incident may, however, stay with us for a lifetime, haunting both our dreams and the quieter moments of our days.

What is the shape of fear? How does it manifest itself in each individual, in each set of circumstances? How do we use it, cope with it, hold it at bay, even conquer it? At what point does fear give way to acceptance, and the inevitability of one's fate?

The Reverend Duncan's description of "the brave man", written in the aftermath of the Ilchester Street air raid in August 1940, could have been composed to describe any one of the young men of the Bomber Command aircrews – men like Jack Clyde, Reg Pennicott, George Phillipson, Freddie Singh, Roy Tann, Bill Bradshaw and Ken Cox. When conducting interviews with Bomber Command veterans for this book, many of them revealed to me that the question they are most frequently asked is, "Were you scared?"

Perhaps this question says more about the person posing it than the person giving their reply. None of us can begin to even contemplate the numbing fear that these young men experienced, hour upon hour, night after night, when their lives were in mortal danger, and their survival dependent largely upon factors beyond their own control, not least a huge amount of bloody good luck. It is beyond our understanding. The aircrews lived with this fear night and day; every morning at breakfast in the dining hall, it was fed and reinforced by the sight of the empty chairs and untouched tables of the crews who had failed to return. For some of them, the question was not "if" but "when" they would meet their end, but others adopted a "Never-say-die, it'll never happen to us!" attitude.

"Failed to return." Three simple words, so understated, so typically British. No melodrama, no emotion, purely matter-of-fact, no hint at the last desperate moments of the men involved. In the operational records for each squadron, there is an entry for every operation, and every crew which took part. The entry gives a brief description of the target, for example,

"DUSSELDORF", the map co-ordinates, the bombload and the number of aircraft involved. The name, rank and position of every crew member are listed, alongside the serial number of the aircraft flown. Beside each crew, there appears a very brief description of the operation, defences encountered, and any damage they sustained on the trip. On almost every operational record appear the words, *"Nothing further heard after take-off"* or *"The crew of Flight Sergeant Smith failed to return."*

Jack and the boys knew only too well the odds they faced. A new crew had only a 20% chance of surviving its first five operations. To put it another way, only one crew in every five would still be alive after the first five raids of their tour. And there were thirty operations in a tour. The losses of men and aircraft were massive and unrelenting, day after day, month after month.

Doug Newham confessed that on some operations, while sitting on the field at Melbourne with his crew, awaiting their turn to take off, he'd be so tense that he had to get out of the aircraft, dash across the grass and vomit into the nearest hedge. Tom Davidson, a flight engineer on Halifaxes, serving with 466 Squadron, based at Driffield in East Yorkshire, confided that he would have regular nightmares about being burned alive. His greatest fear was that of colliding with another aircraft in those crowded chaotic skies. Mid-air collisions were commonplace, as were collisions between plummeting or out-of-control aircraft and other aircraft in the bomber stream. There was also an ever-present risk of being hit by the bombs dropped from another aircraft at a slightly higher altitude. Tom recalls distinctly the feelings he experienced when the duty crews would come around on a morning to clear the lockers of personal items belonging to those crews who had been lost during the night.

"That really got to me," he admitted.

After being kitted up in the locker room, Jack and the boys clambered into one of the transport trucks, driven by a young WAAF, who couldn't have been much older than nineteen. She greeted the crew with a smile and was full of cheery, if perhaps forced, chit-chat as she drove them out across the airfield to where their aircraft, *Y-Yorker*, was waiting for them. A few of the boys attempted the usual flirty banter, but their hearts weren't really in it. Jack sat in the back of the truck, in between Roy Tann and Bill Bradshaw, who had become his best mates over recent months. All were silent, Jack fiddling with his mother's wedding ring incessantly. Penny, business-like and as professional as ever, was discussing engine feathering with George Phillipson. The truck bounced over the rutted grass, and with a screech shuddered to a halt up alongside *Y-Yorker* just as the petrol tanker was driving away into the darkness. The last of the groundcrew were making their final technical checks, in a scene that was replicated right across the small airfield. Already the first of the aircraft was taxiing into position for take-off, with intervals of just a few minutes between each bomber's departure.

Jack climbed up the ladder into the belly of the aircraft and slid into the wireless operator's seat, directly beneath where the pilot sat. To his left was a very small window, covered by a canvass curtain; in front of him a small shelf-type desk, above which was mounted all the wireless equipment. To his right, on the double drop-down seat slightly in front of him, Roy busied himself with his maps and charts and testing the compass. In the mid-upper gunner's turret, Freddie was whistling as usual as he checked the hydraulics and his ammunition. Ken Cox, the bomb aimer, was up front, making sure the bombsights and camera were set up properly and that his calculations were all in order. George and Penny repeatedly revved all four engines, individually and in combination, in conjunction with the ground technicians. At the very back of the Halifax, some distance from the rest of the crew, Bill Bradshaw crawled into the cramped perspex bubble that was home to every Halifax rear gunner, the loneliest spot in the whole aircraft. For half an hour or so, the crew were so busy carrying out their various pre-flight checks, doing for real for the very first time all the tasks they had been trained to do, that the enormity of the task that lay ahead was briefly put to the back of their minds. All was in order, and the crew received their final instructions from the control tower to approach the runway.

At eleven o'clock precisely[40], the signal was given by means of a light displayed by the controller in a caravan at the edge of the airfield. Penny gave the four Merlin engines full throttle and *Y-Yorker* began to speed down the runway. In seconds the huge aircraft hauled her deadly payload and the seven young crewmen into the night sky. The last voice the crew heard was one of the WAAFs in the control tower; once they were airborne radio silence was observed. Leo and the other groundcrewmen watched every single one of their precious aircraft take off, in deadly procession, then retired exhausted to their bunks, ready to do it all again the next day.

When he awoke at dawn on 30 May, even before breakfast, Leo pulled on his overalls and dashed straight over to the stands where each of the aircraft that had taken part in the previous evening's operation stood, draped in tarpaulins, ready to be checked over by the technicians when they began their shift. He nervously turned over Jack's house keys in his pocket as he shouted over to one of his colleagues for news.

Two of the stands were empty.

Y-Yorker had failed to return.

---

40 National Archives AIR/27/144 10 Sqn ORB 29.5.1943.

13

Wings Over Wuppertal

Y-Yorker had soon been swallowed up by the darkness, she and her crew part of something bigger, yet entirely alone. She had climbed almost blind through the night, with only the glow and sweep of distant searchlights over Leeds, Sheffield and Hull visible; the blackout was in full effect, so there was very little in the way of visual landmarks available to the bomber crews, unless there was a particularly bright moon. Penny and the boys, and the other sixteen aircraft from Melbourne, had made their way south. Once they were up, visual contact with the rest of the squadron was virtually impossible at night in cloud or bad weather.

Seven hundred and nineteen Halifaxes and Lancasters had taken off from bases up and down the eastern half of England that night, in staggered departures.[41] It is hard to even imagine such vast numbers of aircraft, targeting one not

---

41 Middlebrook, M. and Everitt, C. *The Bomber Command War Diaries*, Pen & Sword Aviation, Barnsley, 2014, p. 394.

particularly large town. As each aircraft made its way to the Cottesmore Light assembly point at Orford Ness, a few miles east of Ipswich on the Suffolk coast, there was no radio contact with the ground bases. Jack and the other wireless operators would send a brief signal every thirty minutes or so to notify base of their position, but as they approached the target area radio silence was strictly enforced. As well as listening out for any change in orders or information on diversions on the way back, the operators would monitor radar screens, looking out for the approach of any enemy aircraft. If a Luftwaffe fighter came close, the wireless operator would be able to tell roughly where it was in position to the Halifax and would then warn the gunners to be on the lookout. Although they formed part of the huge "bomber stream", each crew acted independently, carrying out its orders, and focused on the task ahead. The code name for the target was *Sprod*, and zero hour (the time at which the bombardment was to commence) was 12.45am.

As *Y-Yorker* had reached her cruising altitude of 19,000 feet, the crew began to settle into their roles. George dug out the two flasks of coffee he'd brought with him and handed cups round to the crew. Freddie cursed as he tipped most of the hot liquid down his flying suit as they went through a patch of turbulence.

Although they had on their heated flying suits over their uniforms, the moment they removed their gloves it was bitterly cold. The suits themselves were notoriously unreliable, often overheating and singeing the occupant, as well as failing completely. The interior of the aircraft was not pressurised, so they had to keep their oxygen masks on at all times when flying at altitude. There was some heating on board the Halifax of course – Jack in his little seat beneath Pennicott was particularly cosy – but if the crew needed to move around the aircraft they quickly began to freeze. However, it didn't take much for the heating to malfunction, particularly at altitude when it was minus thirty degrees outside.

Unbeknown to the Pennicott crew, three of the aircraft from 10 Squadron had already turned back due to technical problems. The crews of Sutton, Pinkerton and Brunton had had to abort their mission before they even got over the enemy coast, but the thirteen remaining Halifaxes flew on.

Even as Jack and the boys had approached the Dutch coast, they could see the distant orange glow of fires on the horizon, signifying that many of those ahead of them in the bomber stream had already hit their targets and were heading for home. From his tiny side window, Jack could see very little. He poked his head out from beneath Penny's seat and asked if he could have a look up ahead.

"Alright then but be quick about it!"

And then it began, suddenly and without warning – the sweep of searchlight beams, scanning the night sky for the invaders, and the incessant noise of flak and anti-aircraft cannon shells exploding all around them. From silence to chaos in an instant. Tom Sayer, a Halifax pilot with 106 Squadron at the "next door" base to Melbourne, Pocklington, also took part in the raid on Wuppertal. Tom had joined the RAF as an apprentice before the war and had trained with the USAAF. He flew Blenheims initially, before moving onto Halifaxes.

"It was bloody awful, to put it mildly," he recalls. "There was so much anti-aircraft fire approaching the Ruhr Valley we could've got out of the aircraft and walked on it." As well as the threat of flak and anti-aircraft fire, the German night fighters were also lying in wait for them. Some bomber pilots adopted avoidance tactics, bobbing and weaving around to avoid the fire of the Nazi defenders, but not Tom – "I wasn't one for weaving around; it endangered nearby aircraft in the bomber stream, and it also took longer to reach the target. Best way was to just fly straight through it." For Tom, the hardest thing to deal with was seeing other aircraft being hit all around him, some exploding instantly, others falling out of the sky, leaving a trail of thick black smoke and flaming debris behind them. He remembers the groundcrew seeking him out the morning after the Wuppertal raid to ascertain the health of his crew, as there were so many holes at the front of the aircraft where they had been sitting.

By the time *Y-Yorker* was approaching her target in the Barmen district of the town, at around quarter past one in the morning, Wuppertal was already well alight. Although the Pathfinder aircraft had marked the targets with yellow flares, then red, then green, with the bomber crews having received instructions to aim for the red and green target indicators, in reality the extent of the bombing was such that the flare markers were neither visible nor necessary. Six hundred and eleven bombers would drop their high explosives on Barmen that night.

As Penny brought *Y-Yorker* into position to commence the bombing run, the sky around them was lit up almost like daylight. Ken, lying on his front in the bomb aimer's position, had the best view of all of the carnage that lay ahead, but he was fixed on his task. Poor Jack in his little cubbyhole could see nothing. Maybe that was just as well. In the rear gunner's position, Bill could see only the arcing searchlights, the puffs of flak exploding all around, and the seemingly endless procession of aircraft above, below and behind him. The noise from the engines, the thud-crump of exploding shells, and the vibration of the airframe as it was struck repeatedly by flak was utterly unbearable. That the crew would have to endure this a further twenty-nine times was almost beyond their comprehension.

Jack was sure he could hear his own heartbeat through his headphones. He thought about home, about Lydia and the imminent arrival of the new baby, about his father's fingernails, always black with coal dust. Most of all he thought about his mother. His mind was immediately flooded with memories of her putting out the washing in the backyard at Caroline Street as he made a den with the empty laundry baskets; of being told to play in the street even though it was dark as she struggled through labour with his little brother; the feel of her lips on his forehead as she kissed him goodnight. And the last time he ever saw her, pale and clammy in her hospital bed, the light gone from her eyes, skin the colour of candle wax and her lips tinged with blue, as she struggled to speak to his father. Instinctively, Jack began to sing quietly to himself the familiar words and tune his mother had taught him as a tiny boy.

> *"Ah went to Blaydon Races, 'twas on the ninth of Joon,*
> *In eighteen hundred an' sixty-two, on a summer's efternoon…"*

"Commencing bombing run." Pennicott gave word to the crew over the intercom, each man focused intently upon doing his job, and upon getting his mates out of this situation as quickly and as safely as possible. Fifteen miles short of the target (which isn't very far at all when flying at around 260 miles per hour) *Y-Yorker* flew into a flak barrage.

> *"Ah took the 'bus from Balmbra's, an' she wis heavy laden,*
> *Away we went alang Collingwood Street, that's on the road to*
> *Blaydon."*

An explosion of flak hit the upper gun turret, blowing out the perspex windows and causing the entire aircraft to shudder and vibrate. The temperature on board nosedived as ice-cold air poured in. Miraculously, evidenced by the choice Australian swear words and crashing and banging coming over the intercom, Freddie Singh was alive, well and bloody furious. Although he had a few cuts to his face, he had escaped major injury but crucially the mid-upper gunner's turret was rendered useless. This meant *Y-Yorker* had little means of defence against aerial attack other than Bill Bradshaw and his machine guns at the rear. If they were to be attacked by a night fighter from the front, the Pennicott crew had more or less had it.

Jack was utterly terrified, but kept on singing to himself.

"OH me lads! You should've seen us gannin'!
We pass'd the folks upon the road just as they wor stannin'…"

It was too late to abandon the mission; they were too close to the target, literally seconds away. Penny quickly told the crew to pull themselves together and focus on the job in hand. Freddie slid down into the main body of the aircraft. Covered in blood from a head wound, his injuries looked worse than they were as he climbed into the flight engineer's drop-down seat. The noise was deafening. Jack tried to concentrate on his radar screen, constantly scanning it for approaching fighters.

"There was lots o' lads an' lasses there, all wi' smiling faces…"

"Skipper," came the voice of Roy Tann in his soft Norfolk accent, over the intercom. "Skip."

"What the hell is it, Roy? We're a little busy right now, old chap."

"Compass is U/S, skipper."

"Bugger."

Within seconds, it was over. "Bombs gone" came the matter-of-fact statement from Ken up front.

"Gannin' alaaanng the SCOTSWOOOOD ROAAAAD...
To see the Blaydon Races!"

As Pennicott began to pull away from the target, Barmen was a mass of flames. The whole of Wuppertal seemed to be on fire. One pilot recalled, just after dropping his bombs and heading for home, two enormous explosions with flames 800 feet in the air, followed by massive smoke clouds which glowed red, lit from within by the flames below. Two hundred tons of explosives had been dropped, and the onslaught of high explosives and incendiaries, fanned by the winds that blew down the Wupper Valley, had caused a firestorm – just like those in Coventry and Lübeck. One fire alone spread over three square miles. From a military point of view, the raid was a huge success. A hundred and thirteen factory premises were damaged or destroyed, including two which made the fabric for parachutes for the Luftwaffe. The human cost was immense, with huge numbers of casualties. It is estimated that between 2500 and 3500 people died that night, most of them burned to death in the firestorm. Such was the intensity of the fires, there was very little left in the way of human remains. A further 2500 were injured. Almost 120,000 were made homeless. More still would die the next day during the rescue effort – Tom Sayer and several of the crews from Pocklington and Melbourne had dropped bombs with time-delay switches, primed to explode some six, nine or even twelve hours after the initial bombardment. Tom confessed that he has always found that very difficult to deal with; seventy-five years later, it continues to trouble him.

Five-year-old Heilgard Hacker[42], her elder sister, Waltraud, and her parents were away from Wuppertal at the

---

42 Heilgard married Ian MacNee, the grandson of Tom MacNee, the Seaham man who first spotted the descending parachute mine during the Seaham air raid on 16.5.1943.

time, in East Prussia where her father was stationed with the Wehrmacht. They first heard of the disaster which had befallen their hometown when a telegram arrived a couple of days later, to inform them that her father's mother had been killed. Heilgard recalls:

> "I was too young to know what that meant and I couldn't understand why Waltraud, who was seven years older than me, was crying most of the time. My father received compassionate leave and the family set out for Wuppertal. Waltraud and I were left with an aunt in Berlin and my parents continued on to Wuppertal.
>
> On the evening of the 29th May my Grandmother Elisabeth Stüting had been visiting a friend who lived in Paulstrasse. Whether she intended to stay overnight or go back home later nobody knows but when the air raid sirens sounded she was still there. All of the house occupants went down to the washroom in the cellar, which served as an air raid shelter in the majority of houses. The street received several direct hits and everyone in the cellar was killed.
>
> The next day rescuers found them all crouched together in the cellar where the firestorm had taken them. Their bodies were only half their normal size and absolutely unrecognisable. The only way my Grandmother could be identified was by the contents of her handbag which was laying beside her body. She was originally buried in an anonymous grave but as my parents were able to identify her belongings her grave was given a headstone which still exists in Barmen cemetery. The irony of it all is that my Grandmother's own house in Bahnhofstrasse survived the air raid unscathed."

Dr Elisabeth Stark was working as a GP on the night of raid. She recalled, in horrific detail, what occurred that night:

"… At about 11pm the air raid alarm sounded permanently and on the radio came the message that there was an air raid expected over Wuppertal. I quickly drove to the emergency centre in the Town Hall. I didn't even have time to close the main door of the Town Hall before I saw the 'Christmas Trees' which marked the target for the bombers. At the same time hundreds of bombers flew over Wuppertal-Barmen and started dumping their deadly load of bombs, incendiary devices, and phosphorous canisters on the town. My car, which I had parked in front of the building, caught fire immediately. The roof of the Town Hall was on fire. At the last minute the two schoolchildren who acted as messengers when the telephones failed were rescued from the second floor. We all fled to the air raid shelter in the cellar and started praying. The bombing was endless, the Town Hall was on fire, and then I gave the order to get out and try to reach the next emergency centre, which was about 500 metres away. We collected as many medical supplies as we could and tried to get out but every exit was blocked by burning material. We eventually broke a window and escaped through that.

Everywhere was burning. The houses that had not been destroyed by the bombs were on fire due to the incendiary devices and the phosphorous bombs, which prevented us from getting to the next centre. A strong wind came up which produced a firestorm. Barely 300 metres away the Birth Clinic had received a direct hit, although it had a large red cross painted on its roof and 30 mothers with their newborn babies perished in the flames.[43]

Twenty-one-year-old Marliese Burris was on her way home from an evening at the theatre with friends when the raid began.

---

43 Pogt, Herbert, *Vor Funfzig Jahren, Bomben Auf Wuppertal*, Born-Verlag, Wuppertal, 1993 (kindly translated by Ian MacNee), p. 69.

"All of a sudden a small boy appeared before us. He was naked and had multiple burns which he couldn't feel anymore. He had a birdcage in his hand, I couldn't identify the bird as it was burned to a crisp. We couldn't help him and in the next moment the gable end of a house fell on him and put him out of his misery, he didn't even cry out. I can still envisage him, even today."[44]

If Jack and the boys thought the worst of it was over as they wheeled away from their target, they could not have been more wrong. They faced intense flak defences on the return trip, especially as their route home took them over the heavily defended cities of Düsseldorf, Essen and Gelsenkirchen. There was a continuous belt of searchlights from Cologne at the southern end of the Ruhr to Dortmund in the north. The night fighters of the Luftwaffe – Messerschmitts mainly – patrolled the route, picking off the Halifaxes and the Lancasters as they tried to make for home.

As *Y-Yorker* approached Aachen, she was hit again, this time by a cannon shell from a German aircraft which had been stalking her for some miles. As the fuselage was raked with bullets, without her upper gun turret in operation *Y-Yorker* was powerless to defend herself. In his tail gunner's position, Bill Bradshaw could not see the enemy aircraft approach. With the upper turret's windows already having been lost on the approach to Wuppertal, the noise of cannon fire and flak shells exploding all around, it was virtually impossible for the crew to communicate with each other.

"PORT OUTER, PORT OUTER!" George Phillipson tried to yell to Penny. Jack, almost frozen with fear, remained in his seat, ready to send what might be the aircraft's final position to base in the event that Penny gave the order to bale out. Ken jumped up from his bomb aimer's position and took

---

44 *Ibid*, p. 33.

his seat next to Roy. Amid the chaos all around them, flames were clearly visible from the damaged engine.

Jack closed his eyes, certain that this was the end, his war over after just one mission. His voice trembled but grew louder.

"OH ME LADS…"

"Feather port outer, feather port outer!" screamed George, and Pennicott began to take the aircraft into a steep descent, towards the very anti-aircraft defences which were trying to destroy them, to try to extinguish the fire. With only three operational engines, a gaping hole in the upper gun turret, an interior temperature well below zero, an injured crewman and no working compass or navigation system, Jack and the boys were in dire straits.

Penny knew the lives of his crew now depended upon his skills as a pilot, and upon Roy's abilities to somehow find their way home in the midst of this hell on earth, using the old-fashioned methods of navigation – maps, pocket compass, sextant, visual landmarks and the star bearings from the astrolabe positioned above his head. Although there was a large compass just in front of Penny's knees, it was useless if he had no idea where he was in the first place, and he urgently needed Roy to give him a bearing to follow. This would have been difficult at the very best of times, let alone in the dead of night in a badly damaged aircraft, whilst under heavy fire, in cloudy weather. As *Y-Yorker* made for the less-populated and less well-defended Dutch border, Jack prayed that they would not be caught by a searchlight as they made their escape. To be coned at this point, at the height at which they were forced to fly, would have meant certain death.

As the Halifax battled on towards home, the glow of the firestorm they had helped to create began to recede until it was nothing more than a red smudge on the horizon behind them.

"Position please, Roy," requested Penny.

"Just approaching the Dutch coast, northwest of Groningen. We'll be over the sea in an estimated... six minutes."

"Can you plot a course to the nearest base in Kent?"

"West Malling."

"West Malling it is, then."

Although the crew breathed a collective sigh of relief as the unmistakable glimmer of moonlight on water came into view, every one of them knew the danger was not over. If anything else went wrong, if any more equipment failed, or if they came under attack again, Penny would inevitably have to ditch the aircraft in the North Sea; the chances of rescue would be very slim indeed.

At around four o'clock in the morning, just as *Y-Yorker* was about to make landfall over the Kent coast, the sudden thud-thud of anti-aircraft fire was unmistakable. Jack was furiously trying to make contact with base over the radio to warn them of their approach, to seek permission to land at West Malling.

"Bugger me, they're firing at us! Bloody Navy!" yelled Ken from up front.

"Alright, alright, settle down, everyone," came Pennicott's instruction over the intercom, calm and authoritative as usual. "Nearly there."

Jack had been able to make contact with Melbourne; they in turn had warned West Malling of *Y-Yorker's* approach. They weren't the only crew to land there that evening; other stragglers from the Yorkshire bases had been diverted to various airfields in the south of England due to fog and poor weather in the north.

Penny and his crew touched down at the Kent air base at quarter past four in the morning. They'd been gone just five and a quarter hours. In that time, thousands of German civilians had lost their lives. Thirty-three of the Halifaxes and Lancasters and their crews had been lost on the raid, twenty-two of whom had been shot down by night fighters.

Jack was still shaking as he sat in the truck which drove them from the aircraft to the debrief. The rest of the crew were ashen-faced and silent, mentally and physically exhausted from what they had endured. Bill whispered to Jack, "What was that song you were singing? You had your intercom on."

Jack's cheeks flushed crimson. He hadn't realised that any of the others could hear him. Embarrassed, his eyes were fixed on a clod of mud on the floor of the truck.

"Ermm, that's the 'Blaydon Races'. It's a North East tradition. My mam used to sing it to us when we were little."

Later that day, after a wash and shave and a short sleep, Jack recorded the following brief entry in his logbook, in his usual meticulous handwriting:

"Intense AA fire and searchlights encountered. Compass U/S on return, landed at West Malling."

The figure "1" appears in red ink next to the entry, to signify this was his first operation.

And that was it. No further details were given, no hint of the ordeal the crew had encountered, nor of their miraculous survival. A few days later, Jack pasted beneath this entry a newspaper cutting, which included a photograph of the Wuppertal firestorm, as seen from the air. The caption reads, "First Blitz on Wuppertal – a picture that gives evidence of the concentrated nature of the attack. Each 'bubble' of light is an incendiary bomb burning, the larger blobs indicating where fires are already beginning to develop." There is no reference in the article to the horror which had unfolded on the ground.

The Station Operations Book entry, compiled from Penny's report of their mission, gives a few further details:

"Bombed primary target at 01.20 hours from 19,000 feet on red/green marker flares. Visibility was poor, but a good number of fires were observed in the target area. Results of own bombing were not seen. Little opposition was experienced at target. Aircraft landed at WEST MALLING owing to bad weather at base. Aircraft was caught in a flak barrage 15 miles short of target, and compass, gee, were rendered u/s, perspex panels were blown out of mid turret and a hole made in cowling of port outer engine."[45]

At Melbourne, the stand usually occupied by Halifax S-DT787 *S-Sugar* flown by Flight Sergeant Clarke, a New Zealander, and his crew, remained empty. *S-Sugar* had taken off directly behind *Y-Yorker* the preceding night.

The Squadron Operations Book entry states simply:

"This aircraft failed to return from its mission, no message being received from it after it left base."

---

45   National Archives AIR/27/144 10 Sqn ORB 30.5.1943.

14

Innocence Lost

Which do we feel more keenly? Where lies the greater dread? In those circumstances of which we have no personal knowledge yet which, through rumour and speculation and the tall tales of others, torture our imaginations? Or the fear of the known, the expectation that only the exquisite pain of experience brings?

The raid on Wuppertal had, for Jack and the crew, been worse than any of them could have imagined. Even Penny, who had flown two additional preparatory operations, was shaken by their extremely narrow escape. The knowledge that each man had to endure that same scenario, that same stomach-wrenching fear a further twenty-nine times was a burden almost too great to bear. Halifax flight engineer Tom Davidson recounted how he had flown a staggering thirty-six operations:

"Thirty-six times we flew – and thirty-six times I was terrified."

Tom's perception of the dangers that lay in store for him and his crew had been intensified by bitter personal experience; he arrived at the family home in Gateshead on leave in November 1943, just two hours after his mother had received a telegram informing her that Tom's elder brother, Frank, was missing, presumed dead. Frank, a thirty-year-old Halifax flight engineer like Tom, had been serving with 419 (Moose) Squadron. He and his crew were lost in a raid on Mannheim on the night of 19 November 1943. Tom recalls how his mother, Ina, used to leave a place set at the table for Frank every time she went out, with a note saying where she was going, and what time she'd be home, just in case he turned up. The bodies of Frank and his crew were not found until November 1947, and they now rest in the Rheinberg War Cemetery in Germany.

Jack spent the next day hanging around West Malling chatting to the other wireless operators while the groundcrews there patched up *Y-Yorker*, so that she could be flown back to Melbourne for full repairs and made operationally serviceable once again. Jack's logbook records that the Halifax and her crew finally made it back to base just in time for tea on 31 May 1943. One of the first to greet the exhausted airmen on their return, after their own groundcrew, was Leo Groark.

"Jackie! Where the hell have you been? I've been making bricks here, man! Thowt I was going to have to tell your Lyd you'd copped it!"

Jack smiled shyly and said nothing. He didn't have to. Leo knew from a cursory glance at *Y-Yorker* and the dazed countenances of the crew just how lucky they'd been. He had seen those same expressions dozens of times before.

As the days grew longer, and the nights shorter, the combination of cloudless early summer evenings and the full moon saw the bombing campaign limited to minor operations for the first ten days of June. Every morning the anxious crews would await news of that day's schedule; every morning the men of 10 Squadron heaved a collective sigh of relief when word arrived that there would be no operations that night, and that they would be required to undertake training exercises instead. The Pennicott crew spent their nights in the pub and their days practising formation flying, constant take-offs and landings, performing air tests, air firing and bombing practice runs over the English countryside. On one such trip, and unbeknown to his superiors, Penny made a slight diversion and flew the Halifax at a very low height over the High Street in Ascot, right over his father's butcher's shop. Realising the identity of the culprit immediately, Pennicott Senior dashed out onto the street, still in his bloodied apron, waving his fist at the disappearing aircraft.

"Ruddy idiot!"

As he made his way back behind the counter, he announced proudly to the lengthy queue of waiting customers:

"That was my lad. Bomber Command pilot, you know."

Among papers which had belonged to Penny, and shown to me by his son Anthony, there's a piece of lined notepaper, about A4 size. A black and white photograph has been glued to the top of the sheet. Jack had a copy of the same photograph, which shows the crew, all wearing their life jackets and a sombre expression, standing in front of a Halifax, W7909 Z-Zebra. Underneath, the caption reads "PENNY AND HIS PRANGERS CREW OF Z, 10 SQUADRON." Below, Penny listed each crew member by his position in the aircraft, and each has written his signature alongside.

FROM L TO R

Mid-Upper Gunner	*FR Singh*
Bomb Aimer	*KR Cox*
Wireless Op/AG	*J Clyde*
Pilot	*R Pennicott*
Navigator	*R Tann*
Engineer	*G Phillipson*
Rear Gunner	*WHA Bradshaw*

Although undated, an examination of Jack's logbook and the squadron operational records reveals that this photograph must have been taken on 10 or 11 June 1943; these were the only dates that the Pennicott crew flew this particular aircraft.

On 11 June, Jack received a letter from his father. John Clyde wasn't one for writing letters, so Jack knew immediately that the subject matter must be of importance. He hardly dared tear open the small, grubby white envelope in case it bore bad news. He need not have worried. As he carefully unfolded the single page, a smile spread across his face. Roy Tann was sat opposite Jack, polishing his boots.

"What is it, Jack? A new sweetheart? Won a raffle? Or has this whole thing been a terrible mistake and they've offered you a desk job at HQ?"

"Better than that. I'm an uncle!"

The letter confirmed that, on 4 June, Lydia had given birth to a healthy baby girl, Lydia Moira. Mother and baby were doing well but would be staying on with Lydia's aunt until such time as the windows in the family home at Caroline Street had been replaced. Jack's younger brother, George, had been nonplussed at the new arrival.

"It's not very good looking, is it?" he'd opined, on being introduced to his niece.

Jack's excitement was suddenly cut short when Penny popped his head around the door and announced that they would be one of twenty crews detailed to take part in operations that night. On learning the news, Ken, the bomb aimer, promptly threw up, sick with nerves. Later that afternoon, after an hour or so of air tests, the crew attended the briefing meeting. Jack was praying it wouldn't be the Ruhr again, and his heart sank when, from behind the curtain in the briefing room, the target was revealed as Düsseldorf. Seven hundred and eighty-three aircraft were due to take part in the raid.

Penny and the boys headed off to the crew room to get kitted up, then waited in silence for the trucks to arrive to take them to the waiting Halifax. This time they had been allocated Halifax JD961, *R-Roger*, an aircraft they had flown several times that week in practice. The more experienced crews were full of chat and gallows humour, sucking on cigarettes and scattering fag ends among the shrubs; the newer crews looked on nervously, well aware that the odds were stacked against them.

At two minutes past eleven, *R-Roger's* wheels left the runway at Melbourne and the lumbering aircraft and its bombload rose up into the night sky, heading on the familiar route southwards over Lincolnshire, before making for the coast.[46] Jack, who could see nothing from the tiny window to the left of his wireless equipment, spoke to Freddie Singh up in the mid-upper gun turret over the intercom.

"What's it like up there, Fred? Can't see a damn thing here, pitch black. What can you see?"

"Well funnily enough it's night up here as well. Can see another Hali in front, think I can just make out another couple behind. Can see bugger all on the ground. Above, errmm… above us, only the stars, mate."

---

46   National Archives AIR/27/144 10 Sqn ORB 11.6.1943.

For the Pennicott crew, their second operation could not have been more different from their first, the raid on Wuppertal. As they approached their target, marked out by the green target flares dropped by the crews of the Pathfinder aircraft a few moments before, numerous fires were already visible, scattered around in the centre of the city of Düsseldorf. At sixteen minutes past one, Ken Cox announced on the intercom, "Bombs gone!" Penny held the aircraft steady for a minute or two so Ken could take his photograph of the bombs hitting the target, then wheeled away on a course for home. Although there was constant flak exploding around the aircraft, and the ever-present threat of searchlights, the opposition seemed so much less than that encountered over Wuppertal. Perhaps the crew, after their baptism of fire, were simply more mentally prepared.

Airborne for a little over five hours, the Düsseldorf raid had passed without incident for Jack and the boys. The relief was palpable as Penny guided them home, over the patchwork of fields of Norfolk and Lincolnshire. As soon as Lincoln Cathedral was spotted in the early glow of morning, the crew knew they were nearly home. The old windmill at Seaton Ross, within sight of the airfield at Melbourne and just visible in the morning drizzle, welcomed home every one of the twenty aircrews who had set off the night before; seventeen had successfully attacked the target, while three had had to return to base with technical problems.[47] This was becoming an increasingly unusual occurrence; at the height of the Battle of the Ruhr, it was rare for the squadron not to lose at least one crew for each operation flown.

After debrief and a very early breakfast, Jack recorded the following entry in his logbook:

---

47 *Ibid*, 12.6.1943.

"Little opposition encountered. Almost like a cross-country trip. (2)"

Other squadrons were not so lucky. Although the raid on Düsseldorf was considered highly successful, with vast areas of the city centre and industrial areas destroyed or badly damaged, it was not without cost. Thirty-eight aircraft and their crews were lost (mainly Wellingtons and Stirlings which had to bomb at a much lower level than the Halifaxes and Lancasters), almost 5% of the aircraft which had set out the night before. Such was the intensity of the bombardment the fires could still be seen as the raiders headed for home over the Dutch coast. As well as the destruction of a factory which made torpedoes and components for U-boats, and severe damage to other armament factories, some 50,000 homes were either destroyed or rendered uninhabitable, leaving 140,000 people homeless. Almost 1300 souls perished in the flames.[48] The fires were still burning a week later.

After a few hours' sleep, the boys were woken by an exhausted and grim-faced Penny; the crew had been rostered for another operation that evening. At the height of the Bomber Command campaign, it was not unusual for crews to be required to fly three or four operations in a week, sometimes on consecutive nights. The physical and mental toll on the airmen was enormous; in order to ensure that they did not fall asleep on operations, and in an attempt to aid concentration, the crewmen were frequently given amphetamines by the squadron medical officer to keep them awake. This was common practice on both sides; the rapidity of the German infantry and tank divisions' advance across Europe in the early stages of the war had been fuelled by

---

48 Middlebrook, M. and Everitt, C. *The Bomber Command War Diaries,* Pen & Sword Aviation, Barnsley, 2014, pp. 396-397.

Pervatin, amphetamines and many other chemical stimulants, including cocaine. Jimmy Thornton, Jack's best mate and next-door neighbour in Caroline Street, who served with 75 (New Zealand Squadron), once recalled how he was awake for three entire days until the effects of the drugs he'd been made to take wore off.

That evening, at five past eleven, the Pennicott crew took off once again in *R-Roger*, accompanied by sixteen other crews from Melbourne, bound for Bochum, part of a force of 503 aircraft.[49] The crews taking off from bases in Yorkshire, Lincolnshire, Norfolk and Suffolk were treated to a very rare and breathtaking display of the aurora borealis, not usually visible that far south. *R-Roger* had barely reached the rendezvous point when the anti-icing system on the aircraft failed, and Pennicott was forced to make the decision to return to base, along with the aircraft of Sergeant Morley, which had developed engine trouble very soon after departure. Although massively relieved, the crew knew full well that an aborted operation would not count towards their operational statistics, unless they had entered enemy airspace. No aircraft was allowed to return to base with its bombload – it was simply too dangerous to attempt to land an aircraft with thousands of pounds of armed explosives on board – and Ken safely jettisoned the payload over the North Sea after receiving confirmation from navigator Roy that they were in a safe position to do so, away from coastal areas and shipping.

From the reports filed by the returning crews the following morning, it seemed Jack and the boys had been spared a very rough trip. Flight Sergeant Fennell reported severe flak over the target, with as many as thirty searchlights working in three "cones". Sadly, the crew of twenty-year-old Gateshead lad Sergeant Innes had failed to return. Their aircraft was

---

49   National Archives AIR/27/144 10 Sqn ORB 12.6.1943.

shot down by a night fighter over Gildenhausen. The entire crew were killed. They had arrived at 10 Squadron in the same week as Jack; the Bochum raid had been their first, and only, operation. Their aircraft that night was W7909 *Z-Zebra*, the Halifax in the Pennicott crew photograph.

And then, for the best part of a week, normality prevailed, or at least some semblance of it. No operations were scheduled, and the Melbourne crews were rested. They were still kept occupied, however, and flew daily, on exercises and air tests, practising bombing runs and formation flying. Every night was spent in the mess or at the village pub in Seaton Ross, where many of the airmen would drink themselves to oblivion, hoping that their hangovers would subside by the time they were required to fly again the following afternoon. It was also a welcome opportunity for some of them to "come down," after several consecutive days of being administered amphetamines.

Jack wondered if he would be spared another operation before he began a spell of leave on 22 June; he was desperate to get back home and see Lydia, George, his father and the new baby. Bomber Command had other plans for him. On 19 June, Penny informed the crew just before lunch that they had been detailed for operations that evening; in the briefing hall the assembled crews were somewhat relieved to learn that their target that night would not be the Ruhr Valley, but Le Creusot, in Central France.

Le Creusot was an important industrial target, and home to the huge Schneider factory, considered to be the French equivalent of the Krupps factory in Essen. As well as heavy guns and artillery, the factory made railway engines, tanks and armoured cars; many of the workers lived "on site" in a company housing estate at one end of the premises. Its British equivalent would have been the huge Armstrong Vickers factory on the banks of the Tyne. Le Creusot had already been the subject of a heavy attack on 17 October 1942; that raid was only partially successful, with the majority of the bombardment striking the workers' housing rather than the factory itself.

A relatively small force of "only" 290 aircraft were detailed to attack the Schneider factory and the nearby Breuil steelworks, including sixteen crews from Melbourne.[50] Le Creusot is situated southwest of the city of Dijon and was much further than any of the crews had flown before. To attack under cover of darkness, on one of the shortest nights of the year, the crews had to depart from the bases in England at dusk. Just after ten o'clock, Jack, Penny and the boys took off from Melbourne, in a new Z-Zebra, JD202. In the last light of the summer evening they headed due south, this time flying the very length of England before heading out over the Channel at Littlehampton on the West Sussex coast, the rendezvous point. This was potentially a dangerous route as the French ports of Dieppe, Le Havre and the city of Caen were very heavily defended, and the crews flew in close formation, which they had fortunately been practising on the preceding two days.

It took the crew almost four hours to reach their target; Penny's report of the operation, delivered at the debrief on their return, records that they bombed the target at eight minutes past two in the morning, in excellent visibility. Many explosions and two very large fires were observed in the target area, with varying amounts of flak being encountered and fortunately only a single searchlight spotted.[51] Although one of the crews had a close encounter with a Messerschmitt ME109, which the tail and upper gunners shot down, Jack recorded in his logbook:

---

50 Middlebrook, M. and Everitt, C. *The Bomber Command War Diaries*, Pen & Sword Aviation, Barnsley, 2014, pp. 398-399.

51 National Archives AIR/27/144 10 Sqn ORB 19.6.1943.

"Flew in formation, no opposition encountered, landed at Tangmere with 2000 lb hang-up."

In other words, one of the aircraft's bombs had jammed and not been released. Returning to base with fused bombs on board was incredibly dangerous, particularly if the aircraft had been damaged by enemy fire en route. A crash-landing could spell disaster for the crew, and anyone or anything in the immediate vicinity. Tangmere wasn't a bomber station; it was home to the fighter squadrons and Spitfires who'd fought in the Battle of Britain, but on reporting their difficulty to their home base at Melbourne, Jack received orders for them to land at the fighter base, simply because it was the nearest place where they could land safely. It was already daylight when *Z-Zebra* touched down at the famous old airfield.

The raid on Le Creusot had been only a limited success; the attacking crews had been instructed to make a visual identification of their target rather than attacking areas marked by coloured flares. Only a fifth of the crews managed to hit the industrial targets, and many of the remaining bombs fell on residential or rural areas. No figures were ever made available for the number of French civilian casualties, but Bomber Command losses were very light, with only two Halifaxes and their crews being lost. One of them, that flown by 10 Squadron's Sergeant Watson, was *Y-Yorker*, the aircraft which had survived the Wuppertal raid with the Pennicott crew. Her luck had finally run out.

15
The Gates of Hell

Jack dug into his trouser pocket and pulled out the grubby piece of string to which his front door key was attached. Turning the key in the lock, he pushed open the door, still chipped and splintered and bearing the signs of damage from the bomb blast and sitting slightly off true in its frame. The house was empty. Jack felt a sudden calmness descend upon him as he stepped over the threshold into the familiarity and safety of "home". Nothing, and everything, had changed.

The family's possessions were all in their usual places: his father's tobacco tin and pipe on the windowsill; his late mother's best tea set in pride of place on the sideboard; one of Lydia's cardigans draped over the arm of his father's chair; and George's muddy football boots by the back door. The room smelled of fresh putty, the newly fitted windowpanes still bearing smudges and fingerprints, and criss-crossed with tape as a precaution against further damage. Jack pulled out a chair and sat down, elbows resting on the kitchen table, his chin in his hands. He wanted to absorb every detail of the room and the things within it, in an attempt to convince himself that this was his reality, that "normality" did indeed continue, away from the fear and chaos of his other life. For half an hour or so, he sat there, absentmindedly rubbing the fringe of the table cloth between his forefinger and thumb, or tracing the pattern of the lace doily under the fruit bowl with his finger, trying to arrive at some sort of reconciliation in his mind between the ordinary, everydayness of life at home and the extraordinary, terrifying things which he had witnessed. Although he might be able to *tell* his family of his experiences, he knew that he could never make them *understand*.

"Pull yourself together, Jack."

With that, he picked up his cap and the bunch of carnations he'd purchased at Sunderland station on his way home. He closed the door behind him and went off to inspect what was left of Sophia, Adolphus and Viceroy Streets, before making his way across St John's Churchyard to visit Lydia and the new baby at his aunt's home in Emily Street.

Unlike their colleagues in the Army or Navy, or indeed in other branches of the Royal Air Force, the aircrews of Bomber Command were given a week's leave every six weeks or so. Ron Toft, who was a regular visitor to the Clydes' home in Caroline Street, recalls that Jack often seemed to be at home, and remembers being somewhat overawed, and more than a little impressed, at the sight of him in his uniform. How quickly those seven days of leave would pass.

In the blinking of an eye, Jack found himself back at Melbourne with the crew. There was no backslapping, no enthusiastic greetings between crewmates this time; each of the boys had returned with a very heavy heart and a quiet, grim determination to see the job through.

In the Mediterranean, Allied forces were pounding German positions in Sicily in readiness for the forthcoming invasion; in North Africa, Jim, Lydia's husband, had received word of the birth of his daughter just after the Allied victory in the Battle of Tunis, but didn't know when – or indeed if – he would ever see her. He treasured a photograph of mother and daughter that Lydia had had taken at the photographic studio in Church Street and sent to him. "To Daddy, from baby Moira," was written across the bottom corner. That photograph was to accompany Jim through the darkest of times, and through some of the bloodiest battles of the entire war.

The tide was beginning, slowly, to turn.

American Forces in the Pacific had finally defeated the Japanese at Guadalcanal and German troops on the Russian front were struggling to make headway; Hitler had already given orders for their withdrawal from Kursk. However, the murderous persecution of the Jews continued, unrelenting; in June 1943, Heinrich Himmler, the head of the SS, had given orders for the Polish and Russian ghettos to be emptied of their inhabitants, who were to be transported to the extermination camps.

Against this background, the strategic and area bombing of German industries and cities continued apace, focusing of course on the Ruhr, and 10 Squadron were, as usual, at the heart of the action. While Jack and the Pennicott crew had been on leave, their colleagues had flown in raids on Krefeld, return trips to Wuppertal (or what was left of it), Gelsenkirchen and Cologne. Three crews had been lost: those of Sergeant Pinkerton, Flight Sergeant Geddes and Pilot Officer Peate, the latter two being lost off the Dutch coast.

After a day undertaking "local flying" exercises on 2 July, the Pennicott crew were detailed to take part in a raid on Cologne on 3 July. The air Battle of the Ruhr was at its height, and during July 1943 operations against German targets were mounted almost every night, subject only to the weather conditions. Crews would often be required to fly every other day or so, and sometimes even on successive nights. At nine minutes past eleven, Penny and the boys took off from Melbourne in JD202, *Z-Zebra*, on a "maximum effort" raid, with eighteen others of the squadron's crews.[52] Their target was the industrial area on the eastern bank of the Rhine.

Within an hour or so of departure, George Phillipson reported problems with the port inner engine; within another twenty minutes, just as the aircraft was approaching the coast of Holland, the engine cut out and neither Penny nor George could get it restarted. On only three engines, the aircraft could not gain enough height and was unable to climb beyond 14,000 feet, which would have made it an easy target for flak guns and night fighters. With the experiences of the Wuppertal raid still very fresh in the crew's minds, Penny elected to abandon the operation, wheeled the aircraft around and asked Roy to plot a course for home. Another crew, that of Sergeant Hepple, had also had to turn back after the hydraulics in their rear turret failed, which meant their rear gunner was locked in one position and unable to manoeuvre his guns to defend the aircraft should the need arise.

As it turned out, both Penny and Hepple had made the right call; the remaining seventeen crews reported very stiff opposition, with heavy flak, active Luftwaffe night fighters, and a great deal of searchlight activity. The crews of Cox and Wardman reported encounters with enemy fighters, causing Flying Officer Cox to jettison his bombload over Aachen, some miles short of the target.

---

52 National Archives AIR/27/144 10 Sqn ORB 3.7.1944.

Although the crews were not aware at the time, the night of 3/4 July 1943 was the first time the Luftwaffe implemented its new "Wilde Sau" (Wild Boar) tactics. Instead of night fighters taking off to protect their individual allotted "boxes" or areas of airspace, having been warned of approaching bombers by Fighter Control, the aircraft of the newly formed Jagdgeschwader 300 unit hung around over the target cities, targeting bombers purely by visual means, in the glow of the fires which raged around the cities, in the moonlight if weather permitted, or in the beam of searchlights. Concentrating on British aircraft leaving the target area, the night fighters could then "pick off" the departing bombers. Over the coming months this proved to be a hugely successful tactic for the Luftwaffe. Twelve bombers were shot down right over Cologne that night, although it is impossible to determine whether this was due to Wilde Sau or flak, which was particularly heavy that night.

Sergeant Wardman, in *K-King*, one of the aircraft for which Leo Groark and his groundcrew were responsible, had a very near escape with a Focke-Wulf 190 as they attempted to depart the target area. An enemy aircraft had been picked up on the "Monica" warning system, then spotted by Wood, the rear gunner, about 500 yards away. He fired a short burst at the Focke-Wulf and was convinced he'd struck the fuselage; the German pilot was seen to wheel away but then came in again, this time from starboard, and Wood gave him another blast of machine gun fire from close quarters. The Squadron Interception and Combat Report then records that *"the enemy aircraft dived away below and was not seen again. This aircraft is claimed as damaged. Rear gunner fired approximately 300 rounds. Enemy aircraft did not open fire."*[53] There's little doubt that the quick-thinking actions of Sergeant Wood saved

53 National Archives AIR/50/180(29).

the life of his crew; had the Luftwaffe pilot been able to fire upon the Halifax from such close range, it is unlikely that the aircraft would have survived.

Flight Sergeant Morley's crew weren't so lucky; the Operations Book states simply, *"Failed to Return."* Their aircraft had been shot down over Belgium. Morley, the pilot, was killed along with his mid-upper gunner, Sergeant Sadler; the remaining five crew members baled out successfully but were captured. Of the 653 aircraft which had set out the night before, thirty failed to make it home. The raid was considered to be a success; the target-marking by the Pathfinder crews had been very accurate. Twenty industrial premises and 2200 homes were flattened. Five hundred and fifty-eight people were killed, and some 72,000 made homeless.[54] For the citizens of Cologne, so much worse was yet to come.

The men of 10 Squadron enjoyed a brief respite from operations of five days or so. The days between operations were spent undertaking exercises of various sorts – the usual air tests, checking on the operational readiness of aircraft, especially those that had undergone repairs, and practice bombing raids.

On 9 July the crews were briefed for another "maximum effort" raid, with all twenty of the squadron's operational aircraft detailed to take part in an operation against targets in Gelsenkirchen, between Essen and Dortmund.[55] As soon as word spread that it was another "maximum effort" operation, Jack's heart sank, as he knew that he and the boys were bound to be required. This would be their fifth operation; if they could get through it unscathed, then they'd be considered an experienced crew, and the odds of their survival shortened.

---

54 Middlebrook, M. and Everitt, C., *The Bomber Command War Diaries*, Pen & Sword Aviation, Barnsley, 2014, pp. 404-405.
55 National Archives AIR/27/144 10 Sqn ORB 9.7.1943.

Roy was unnerved by the fact that they were allocated an aircraft they'd never flown before, not even in practice, *W-William*, JD199, and as they sat in the briefing hall that evening, awaiting the announcement of their target, he sat nervously flicking through his notebook. Penny kept a careful eye on each of his men; like so many skippers, he felt personally responsible for the welfare of his crew, both in the air and on the ground.

"Bet you a pint it's Wuppertal again," Freddie Singh whispered to Jack. He'd heard a rumour, on good authority, that they were headed back there, and Jack sniggered as the curtain was pulled back to reveal that their target that night would in fact be Gelsenkirchen.

"Cheers, Fred!"

Just before eleven o'clock that evening, *W-William* and its crew were airborne again, for what would transpire to be a fairly rough ride to Gelsenkirchen, in the company of 417 other aircraft. The two-man Mosquito bombers of the Pathfinder Force encountered a great many problems with their Oboe navigational equipment that evening; five Mosquito crews reported that it wasn't working at all, so they could not locate the target properly, and another dropped its marker flares in entirely the wrong place altogether, about ten miles away. As a result, the nearby towns of Bochum and Essen bore the brunt of the attack, although a few industrial areas in Gelsenkirchen were hit, almost by accident rather than design. Penny's report in the Operations Diary for that evening confirmed that they bombed the primary target (or at least what they thought was the primary target) at 01:26 hours, from 20,000 feet, in complete cloud cover. Almost poetically, he recorded that, "*An intense glow of fires was seen reflected on the clouds. Flak was severe and accurate over the target.*"[56]

---

56 *Ibid.*

So accurate in fact, that *W-William* took a direct hit. None of 10 Squadron's aircraft survived the trip unscathed, with eight sustaining significant flak damage. The sight and sound of flak shells exploding all around the aircraft must have been nothing short of terrifying; the vibration and shuddering of the airframe as the metal fragments tore through it is beyond comprehension. And then... the wait, the anticipation, while the extent of the damage was ascertained, the fear of hearing the order to bale out, and the terror that there might simply not be enough time.

Sergeant Fuller, mid-upper gunner in a Halifax named *Farouk*, after the King of Egypt (10 Squadron had had previous connections with the Middle East), recalled being given a "hot reception," with shrapnel damaging the cowling of the starboard outer engine, and a piece of jagged metal penetrating the side of the rear gun turret. He remembered hearing the loud "pinging" sound the shrapnel pieces made as they hit the aircraft, which he described in typical British fashion as "a very unpleasant experience."[57]

Incredibly, all the squadron's crews returned safely to base, although twelve other aircraft and their crews had been lost.

Rarely had the sight of Lincoln Cathedral, and the typically English patchwork of fields which encircle it, and which signified safety to the returning crews, been more welcome. After six hours and ten minutes, the Pennicott crew landed at Melbourne, only to be chided by their groundcrew for bringing the aircraft back in such a mess. Jack recorded in his logbook, in his usual understated manner:

"GELSENKIRCHEN. *Fairly heavy AA [anti-aircraft fire] around target area, 10/10 cloud cover whole journey, aircraft hit with AA.*"

----

57 Cooper, Alan, *Air Battle of the Ruhr*, Airlife Publishing, Shrewsbury, 1992, p.106.

There were no further operations planned for a couple of days, so the crews were given the Saturday night off. It was too far to travel home for one night, so Jack and the boys hitched a ride into York, where Penny treated them to a fish and chip supper, then had a few drinks in several of the city's watering holes. The next day, still considerably hungover, several of them attended the morning religious service, then did the same thing all over again. This time the crew confined themselves to the Sergeants' Mess, once the landlord of the Blacksmith's Arms in Seaton Ross had called "time." Sunday licensing laws were very strictly enforced, which meant that a lot of drinking had to be done in a very short space of time.

Andy Andrews, a 10 Squadron wireless operator like Jack, arrived at Melbourne in late July 1944; when I asked him what his memories of the base were, he just laughed and replied, "Rowdy nights in the mess!" He recalled the cigarette and pipe smoke, the laughter and chattering of the WAAFs, the gramophone blasting out the latest tunes, the rough and tumble, the fights and the non-stop drinking in particular.

All too quickly the weekend was over; by eleven o'clock on the Monday morning, Jack and the boys were airborne once again, performing air tests on *Z-Zebra*. As they landed just in time for lunch, Penny was summoned to see his commanding officer along with eighteen other pilots, and informed they'd be required for operations again that evening. There was barely a flicker of emotion among the crew this time, as he gave them the news. Later, in the briefing hall, their target was revealed to be Aachen, right on the border of Belgium, the Netherlands and Germany, some miles southwest of the Ruhr Valley. There was an audible sigh of relief when the assembled crews learned that, for tonight at least, they'd be avoiding Happy Valley.

At a quarter to midnight, and in bright moonlight which caused several of the crew some concern, the Pennicott crew took off in *S-Sugar*, JD200, another aircraft they had never flown before.[58] Such was the turnover of aircraft that crews could barely expect to fly the same Halifax more than a handful of times in the course of their tour. They had no choice in the matter; they simply took whichever aircraft was available and fully serviceable. Sometimes a crew would board their aircraft and in the course of their pre-flight checks a problem would be revealed. They would then hastily disembark and be shuttled over to one of the "spare" aircraft and start the whole process over again.

Strong tailwinds over the target meant that the first wave of bombers arrived more or less all at the same time, just moments after the Pathfinders had laid the target flares. As a result, 900 tons of high explosives and many 8000-pound "blockbuster" bombs were dropped in a very concentrated attack, which caused utter devastation on the ground. Almost 3000 buildings were destroyed, including the important Deutsche Phillips factory, and the cathedral, town hall and theatre were severely damaged. The raid was considered to be a successful one. Two hundred and ninety-four souls lost their lives that night, and it is estimated that 28,000 fled into the countryside. Of the 374 aircraft that took part in the raid (a relatively small operation, by Air Marshal Harris' standards), twenty did not return.[59]

Nineteen crews had set off from Melbourne; despite the excellent visibility which made the bomber stream clearly visible to the Luftwaffe defenders, all nineteen aircraft returned to base safely and without incident. Pennicott reported that *S-Sugar* had bombed the primary target at 02:04, and that scattered fires had been observed in the target

---

58 National Archives AIR/27/144 10 Sqn ORB 13.7.1943.
59 Middlebrook, M. and Everitt, C., *The Bomber Command War Diaries*, Pen & Sword Aviation, Barnsley, 2014, p. 407.

area; an "explosion with a big red flash" was noted. Moderate flak and searchlight defence was encountered, particularly on the outward journey.

Jack's logbook records:

> "AACHEN. Bright moonlight, target defences moderate, searchlights and flak active in Somme area on the way out."

The pace of the bombing campaign was unrelenting; although there were no operations that evening, the crew were once again detailed to take part in a raid the following night, their fourth in twelve days. Their target on 15 July 1943 was the Peugeot Motor Factory at Montbeliard in Sochaux, Eastern France, all the way down near the Swiss border. Again, there was much relief among the eighteen assembled crews that they would be avoiding the Ruhr.[60] The planned raid on the Peugeot site was unusual, in two respects. Firstly, only 165 aircraft would take part; secondly, only Halifaxes would be used. It was not a success. The town was a small one, and the crews of the Pathfinder Force had difficulty in picking out the factory from among the houses. Some of their marker flares fell around 700 yards beyond the industrial site. Only thirty bombs struck the factory, but another 600 or so fell in civilian areas. The damage to the factory was minimal, and production was unaffected. A hundred and twenty-three French civilians were killed and over 330 injured. The French casualties were buried in a mass funeral, each coffin carried to its grave on the back of a brand-new Peugeot truck. Some bombs also fell in Besançon, after an aerial battle between a Halifax and a Luftwaffe Dornier resulted in both aircraft crashing into the town, the Halifax coming down onto the main railway station. Aircraft further back in the bomber stream had mistaken the ensuing massive

---

60   National Archives AIR/27/144 10 Sqn ORB 15.7.1943.

explosion as the main target, and twelve crews dropped their bombloads on that unfortunate town.

The crews of 10 Squadron remained unaware of the chaos and civilian "collateral damage" on the ground. In his matter-of-fact way, Jack simply noted:

> "MONTBELIARD. Bright moonlight, no opposition, very nice trip, landed at Dunsford, shortage of petrol."

Not all the crews had the same experience, however. Five of the Halifaxes were lost, including two from Melbourne. At breakfast in the mess the next morning, there were two empty tables, and fourteen unused place settings. The aircraft of Sergeant Mellor was lost over Recey-sur-Ource, and Flight Sergeant Pyle's aircraft had also failed to return.

Many years later, the Halifax which had crashed into Besançon station was identified as JD211 – that of Pyle and his crew.

16

Wizard Prang

With a grand total of eight operations (two of which had been abandoned) under their belts, the Pennicott crew were now considered to have sufficient "combat experience" to allow another new pilot, Sergeant Bishop, to accompany them as "Second Joe" on their next raid, on 24 July 1943. Unbeknown to the aircrews of Bomber Command, even as they were attacking targets in the Ruhr Valley almost nightly, Air Marshal Harris had already formulated the plans for the next stage of the onslaught against Germany, codenamed Operation Gomorrah. As early as 27 May, two nights before Jack and the boys commenced their first operation to Wuppertal, orders were issued to the Bomber Group commanders to make preparations for a series of massive attacks on the German "second city" of Hamburg, which at that time was the Nazis' largest port, the site of numerous ship and U-boat construction yards, and home to 1,750,000 civilians.

Raids on Hamburg were nothing new; the city had been subject to ninety-eight earlier raids, but these had, by and large, been on a relatively small scale and of only limited success. The city had thus far avoided any substantial destruction such as that wrought upon Cologne and Wuppertal; originally intended as the target of Harris' "thousand-bomber raids," Hamburg had enjoyed a narrow escape when the plans were switched at the last minute due to inclement weather.

Hamburg was an easy target to identify, being sixty miles inland and on the banks of the vast Elbe river. Harris knew that "all" the Pathfinder and Bomber Command crews had to do was to pass over the coast near Cuxhaven and follow the wide silver thread of the Elbe before the docks and industrial areas on the south bank of the river came into view. However, the target was the north bank, the commercial and residential heart of the city.

Murmurs of surprise, and no great relief, had rippled around the briefing room when that night's target had been announced to the waiting crews. Anything to avoid the Ruhr. This was to be a "maximum effort" operation for 10 Squadron, with twenty-one Halifaxes rostered to join 770 other aircraft in the attack.

The raid on Hamburg was significant for another reason; it was the first time Bomber Command had used "window" on operations. Each aircraft was issued with several brown paper parcels, containing bundles of thousands of black paper strips backed with aluminium foil, 27cm long and 3cm wide, which were to be thrown out over the target area. If dropped in sufficiently concentrated amounts, the effect was to create "false echoes" and thereby confuse the German radar systems. Harris had been trying to get authority to use this new technology since late 1942 but had only just received permission in time for the Hamburg attack. The use of "window" didn't require any special training or equipment; any one of the crew could simply shove the bundles out of the aircraft at the appointed time. If done properly and according to plan, the effect would be to have the whole bomber force flying along, for a short time at least, in a metal cloud, bamboozling the Nazi defences.

Why was it necessary? The Luftwaffe radio monitoring stations were able to detect Jack's test transmissions several hours before he even took off. Although they lacked the technology to decipher what was being said, the fact that hundreds of wireless operators were transmitting at the same time usually indicated that a raid was imminent.[61] It was impossible for the Nazi radar operators to determine the precise target, but they would usually have a pretty good idea once the bomber stream was airborne, simply by observing the route that the aircraft were taking. To counter this, and to try to befuddle the German defences, decoy raids to less important targets by smaller numbers of bombers would often be undertaken. However, once over the coast of mainland Europe, the aircraft would be monitored and dealt with by night fighters as they passed through the "box" areas or pursued by the "Wilde Sau" pilots as they flew over their target towns and cities.

At ten minutes to eleven Penny and the boys took off from Melbourne, with Sergeant Bishop sitting alongside the skipper, for his first operational experience. The parcels of "window" were stowed near the door of the aircraft, ready to be shoved out by Jack and George when Penny gave the signal. In his logbook, Jack had carefully noted:

"Commence of the Battle of Hamburg."

---

61 Middlebrook, Martin, *The Battle of Hamburg*, Cassell & Co, London, 2000, p. 56.

The Squadron Operations Book records that *Z-Zebra* had bombed the main target at half past one in the morning from 18,700 feet, on red and green target indicators laid down by the Pathfinders. Penny had reported:

> *"Visibility was good and numerous fires were seen in the target area. Large vivid explosion flashes were seen at 0125 and 0135 hours. Two columns of black smoke were rising to 15,000 feet. Two large blocks of buildings were seen to disintegrate. Moderate flak was experienced and searchlights although very numerous were not troublesome."*[62]

All of 10 Squadron's twenty-one crews returned home safely that night, although Sergeant Lucas and his crew had a narrow escape after an engagement with an enemy Messerschmitt 109. Other squadrons lost a total of twelve aircraft and their crews.

From the date of the raid on Hamburg, the entries in his logbook hint at a change in Jack. His notes and descriptions of each raid suggested a growing confidence, almost an air of flippancy, and a cockiness totally at odds with his personality.

> *"Intense searchlight activity, slight AA – Wizard Prang!"*
> (In the RAF slang of the time, a prang was an operation or sortie.)

The more I began to delve into the experiences of bomber crews throughout the war, and the more veterans I interviewed, the more I began to realise that there were three possible explanations for this apparent change in Jack's language and behaviour.

Firstly, it is conceivable that Jack *was* becoming more self-assured as he settled into his role and became more familiar with the lot of the operational airman. He knew his own

---

62 National Archives AIR/27/144 10 Sqn ORB 24.7.1943.

trade as a wireless operator inside out; he trusted Penny, Roy, George, Ken, Freddie and Bill to fulfil their duties too. Each member of the crew knew full well that the lives of his mates depended upon his ability to do his own particular job. The crew had come to know each other like brothers within a very short space of time, and they functioned as one.

Secondly, there is no doubt that some men experienced a feeling of elation, an adrenaline rush after the completion of a successful operation and a safe return to base; a few enjoyed the exhilaration of operational flying.

The third, and most likely, scenario is that this was simply bluff and bluster, and an attempt to disguise what Jack and his crewmates were really feeling: a growing horror at the impact of their operations "on the ground" in Germany, coupled with the ache of fear and moments of pure terror, and the slow unravelling of the nerves which progressed exponentially with each raid. Psychological damage was suffered by so many of the young men of Bomber Command, to varying degrees. In its most extreme form, we would recognise it today by its correct medical diagnosis: post-traumatic stress disorder.

Halifax flight engineer Tom Davidson revealed that it had taken almost seventy years for him to be able to talk about his experiences; it was only after he had reached his early nineties that he felt able to open up about the things that he saw and the things he and his crew were expected to do. Another elderly gentleman confided, with some emotion, how he still has flashbacks to being in a bomber amid heavy flak and seeing his dead tail gunner with half of his face shot away. It would be wrong to say that every young man who flew with Bomber Command developed psychological issues, as that quite simply isn't the case; however, a great number struggled with crippling anxiety during their tours, and many had to live with the trauma for the rest of their lives.

Some still do.

It is a distinct possibility that the entries in Jack's logbook were an attempt to hide the fact that, like so many of his comrades, he was terrified for a huge part of the time.

One airman, Frank Hugo, recalled:

> "The bravado and boasting in the de-briefing but, later in the dark, the tears being shed into one's pillow... being very scared and frightened, but even more of showing it, and not being able to do the job properly."[63]

Such was the strain, that some men simply went mad in the midst of battle. Flying Officer Bob Lloyd, a Canadian pilot serving with 408 Squadron at RAF Linton-on-Ouse, described the mental impact on his crew:

> "My navigator lost his mind during our 26 November trip to Berlin. My mid-upper gunner got hit in the ankle with a 20mm shell on the same trip; he never flew again. My bomb aimer went absolutely wild over the target area on a later raid, to such a degree that we couldn't let him wear an intercom; the navigator had to drop the bombs. Then I finally got hurt, smashing my left femur, and the bomb aimer had to fly out the rest of his tour with another crew; he 'bought it' the first night out. They were as frightened as hell, but their morale was good. They flew until they couldn't fly anymore."[64]

Even by the end of the First World War, the psychological strain suffered by military aviators was clearly recognised. The

---

63   Cooper, Alan, *Air Battle of the Ruhr*, Airlife Publishing, Shrewsbury, 1992, p.136.
64   Middlebrook, Martin, *The Berlin Raids: RAF Bomber Command Winter 1943-44*, Viking/Penguin, London, 1988, pp. 317-318.

Royal Flying Corps pilots' days were famously described as "long spells of idleness punctuated by moments of intense fear", a narrative which has been used to illustrate the lot of soldiers, sailors and airmen at war on numerous occasions since. By 1918, psychologists were well aware of the cumulative effects of stress, identifying the three stages as inexperience, experience, then stress or burnout. However, in the inter-war years, several eminent doctors began to postulate the theory that some men had an underlying "weakness of character" and a predisposition to combat stress. This theory began to take hold, and from it developed the idea that psychological reaction to combat situations, and in particular aerial combat, was due not to illness caused by exposure to external situations, extreme fear, stress and trauma, but rather to a chap simply "not being up to it," or to put it more bluntly, cowardice.

By 1939, official RAF policy was beginning to reflect these beliefs, and "character defects" were emphasised as being the underlying cause in cases of mental breakdown. A Canadian academic, Allan E. English, described in his book on combat stress in Canadian members of Bomber Command, *The Cream of the Crop*,[65] how the response to such stresses and the development of psychological symptoms became the fault of the individual airman: "*Unlike a physical disability, their psychological complaint was as a result of their own inability to control their fear.*"

As early as January 1941, as many as 5% of all operational aircrewmen had developed psychological illnesses which were considered bad enough to merit admission to hospital; these were the recorded figures, so the actual number suffering was likely to be much higher. As the number of psychiatric casualties began to grow, at a time when there were already huge numbers of men being killed on operations, the

---

65   English, Allan D. *The Cream of the Crop*. Montreal: MQUP, 1996.

Air Ministry published a document known as the "LMF Memorandum," in September 1941. LMF was an acronym for "lack of moral fibre," the label given to those airmen who had demonstrated signs of combat stress, or who, in extreme cases, had simply refused to fly. The memorandum was specifically targeted at *"the members of aircrews who forfeit the confidence of their commanding officers in their determination and reliability in the face of danger in the air, owing either to their conduct or their admission that they feel unable to face up to their duties."*[66]

By 1942, one of Bomber Command's chief medical officers, Squadron Leader Reid, was arguing that "aircrew lacking in moral fibre" should be removed because of their "bad influence" on other members of the crew. Concerns were expressed that if a single member of the crew began to show signs of "LMF," it could unsettle and spread to the whole crew. Reid took the view that some men, "by virtue of their genes and upbringing," were more likely to suffer mental breakdown, were unfit to be aircrew and "should be treated without sympathy." Reid considered that officers were of stronger character than lower ranks, and better able to cope, which of course was complete nonsense.

Those who were labelled "LMF" were frequently treated incredibly harshly, and as cowards. Often those who could bear the strain no longer were publicly humiliated, and swiftly removed from their squadrons or transferred to menial ground duties such as working in the kitchens. However, there was very little consistency in the treatment of the men who developed signs of mental stress; there are extreme examples of men being court-martialled and imprisoned. Officers were required to resign their commissions; non-commissioned officers were

---

66 National Archive, AIR 2/8591/S.7.C(1), "Memorandum on the Disposal of Members of Aircrews Who Forfeit the Confidence of their Commanding Officers", 19.9.1941.

demoted to the lower ranks. From 1944, those found to be "lacking in moral fibre" could be sent to work in the coal mines or drafted into the army. However, it would be wrong to say that every man who developed psychological symptoms was treated in this way; the handling of an individual's situation largely depended on the attitude of a squadron's commanding officer and its medical officer. A fortunate few were dealt with sympathetically, being quietly moved to other duties or perhaps being transferred to an instructor's role at one of the operational training units. If signs of stress were spotted early, an airman, or sometimes an entire crew, would be sent off to the Aircrew Refresher Training Units at Sheffield or Eastchurch; these units were in fact disciplinary centres, where psychological issues were treated like offences. After a few weeks, the individual would either be returned to operational duties, if he had mended his ways, or be sent for groundcrew duties, or sometimes discharged altogether.

Jack's best friend and next-door neighbour in Caroline Street, Jimmy Thornton, flew thirteen operations with 75 (New Zealand) Squadron. He was unable to complete his tour due to being "bad with his nerves," following an incident when he was temporarily trapped in a burning aircraft. After a period of leave he was transferred to an instructor's position, and recommissioned. Jimmy was one of the lucky ones.

There is no doubt that the adoption of the policy of "LMF," and the treatment of those airmen who developed signs of psychological illness, marked one of the most shameful episodes in the history of the Royal Air Force, one which, quite simply, was covered up and not spoken about for decades. The threat of being labelled "LMF" was almost as fearful as flying operations against the enemy, and the policy was used to intimidate and stigmatise airmen who showed indications of combat stress. Any airman who was considered to "lack moral fibre" had his personnel file marked with a "W," to indicate that he was a "waverer" – in other words, a coward.

There was no consistency of approach; the risk of being labelled "LMF" didn't apply just to those who refused or who were unable to fly. There were instances of men being categorised in this way who, in the very early stages of training, quickly realised that flying wasn't for them, and who had a genuine fear of flying from day one. This was incredibly harsh when one bears in mind that every single one of these men was a volunteer. Unfortunately, no allowances were made whether you were an eighteen-year-old rear gunner six weeks into your training who was simply nervous of flying, or an experienced, battle-worn pilot with twenty-five operations showing signs of extreme combat stress. Andy Andrews, a wireless operator on 10 Squadron in 1944, recounted how his crew's bomb aimer had decided during training that he just wouldn't be able to cope with operational sorties, and he "went off with LMF." He was removed from the crew immediately, and they never saw him again.

Even those crews who returned early from raids with mechanical faults (particularly those that could not be replicated by groundcrews on return to base), or who had dropped their bombs too early on the periphery of the target area before heading for home, fell under suspicion. Jack and the Pennicott crew were aware of this; prior to the Hamburg raid, they had failed to complete two of their eight operations (20%) and were very much under pressure to perform. Although the reasons for their aborted missions were entirely genuine, the fear of being labelled "LMF" and being sent for retraining would have been at the forefront of their minds.

But why did the Royal Air Force top brass take such a hard line against psychiatric casualties? There is an argument that they had no choice. By late 1941, Bomber Command was already suffering from a shortage of manpower; it took many months to train a new crew and increasing numbers of crews were needed both for operational reasons and because of the extremely high number of combat deaths. Quite simply, men were being killed quicker than they could be replaced, and every single man was desperately needed. The brutal truth was, that for many Bomber Command crews, death came before many of them had any opportunity to manifest psychological problems. Those that survived were simply instructed to "man up" and get on with the task. Jack knew that he had to keep a stiff upper lip, a veneer of steely courage and unflappability, and be seen to be doing so, at all costs.

There was no let-up for the Pennicott crew; the very next night after the raid on Hamburg, 25 July 1943, they were informed they would by flying again, on another "maximum effort" operation.[67] Sitting in the briefing hall with nineteen other crews, having barely slept, the boys fully expected to be returning to Hamburg. Ever conscientious, despite his exhaustion, Roy had already begun to prepare his notes and maps for another trip to the port city.

"Tonight's target is Essen," the Commanding Officer announced as he whisked the curtain from the map on the stage at the front of the hall.

Bill and Jack glanced at each other in horror. Another trip to the dreaded Ruhr Valley. Freddie nudged Roy, gesturing towards Ken who had dropped his notes on the floor and was sitting with his head in his hands. Penny was becoming increasingly concerned about Ken; the mental strain of operations and anxiety about his family in London during the air raids were beginning to take its toll on the young bomb aimer.

"Keep an eye on him tonight, Roy."

---

67   National Archives AIR/27/144 10 Sqn ORB 25.7.1943.

By 22.45, Penny's Prangers were airborne once again in *Z-Zebra*, on their tenth operation, heading to the very heart of the German defences, and the giant Krupps armaments factory in Essen. Of the 705 aircraft that took part in the raid, 628 attacked the target. Jack and the boys arrived over the target area at 0057 hours and bombed from a height of 18,000 feet in hazy visibility. The factory and its environs were already well alight, smoke visible from over 150 miles away. The Squadron Operations Book contains Penny's report:

> *"Visibility over target was hazy but a concentrated area of fire could be seen with a pall of smoke up to 15,000 feet. A series of red explosions were seen before and after bombing. Flak was moderate and though searchlights were operating in large numbers they were not effective."*[68]

Like the crews of Bomber Command, it appeared that the Germans had been anticipating another raid on Hamburg, not Essen. Essen had already been the subject of five previous attacks; the Americans had been carrying out daylight raids (and suffering very heavy losses), and by dawn on 26 July 1943, 90% of the industrial area had been destroyed. Hitler's deputy, Goebbels, had reported that 800,000 people had been left homeless. Twenty-three aircraft were lost that night, including that of 10 Squadron's very experienced Squadron Leader, Johnny Hartnell-Beavis. Hartnell-Beavis and his crew had arrived at Melbourne on the same day as the Pennicott crew. Having successfully bombed the target, they were attacked by Luftwaffe fighters over Holland. Hartnell-Beavis gave the order to bale out, but only he and his wireless operator, Ray Smith, survived. The Squadron Leader was captured and taken prisoner of war, but Smith was taken in by various

---

68 *Ibid.*

Dutch families, and with the aid of resistance networks, over the course of the next three months he evaded capture and made his way back to England via Spain and Gibraltar.[69]

As *Z-Zebra* made landfall over the coast, the aircraft hit a patch of particularly violent turbulence. So relieved to be once again within sight of home, the crew barely seemed to notice as they were bounced around in their seats. Jack swore as he cracked his elbow against the metal aerial winder to his left. He flicked back the handkerchief-sized patch of canvas that passed for a curtain and peered out. The first grey-gold stripes of dawn were painted across the sky; slowly, the patchwork of fields, the toy-town jumble of towns and villages and the occasional glittering thread of a river began to shed the monochrome cloak of darkness and take on colour. England, emerging from the night, in all its thousand shades of green.

As Penny turned the aircraft slightly north, the boys began to look out for the familiar landmarks, as they always did.

"There's the Wash!" yelled Roy over the intercom, even though they all (with the exception of Bill, who was always the last to see anything due to his position at the rear of the aircraft) could see the broad expanse of water beneath them. Next Ken picked out the towers of Lincoln Cathedral, shortly followed by the Humber – distant merchant vessels, like tiny black diamonds, heading in and out of the busy port of Hull, clearly visible.

Far away to his left, Jack could just make out the black pockmarks on the landscape which signified the collieries on the eastern fringe of the Yorkshire coalfields. For a moment, he felt a pang of homesickness as he thought about the thousands of men – men like his father – who laboured deep

---

69 MacMillan, Ian and King, Richard, *From Brooklands to Brize: A Centennial History of No 10 Squadron Royal Air Force*, 10 Squadron Association, 2015, p. 129.

underground, their efforts unseen but as essential to the war effort as those of Jack and his crew. A different sort of hell, but hell all the same.

Finally, as *Z-Zebra* descended, the most long-awaited landmark of them all hove into view: the battered old windmill at Seaton Ross, its broken sails raised in crooked salute, welcoming home the Halifaxes of 10 Squadron once again.

Jack's report of the Essen operation in his logbook is, once again, brief but ebullient:

"ESSEN. *Intense searchlights, moderate AA – Good Prang!*"

As he boarded the train to Seaham Harbour the next day, at the commencement of some much-needed leave, his hands were still trembling. He began to whistle and thrust his hands deep into his coat pockets, just in case anyone noticed.

17

Purgatory

By the end of July 1943, of the eighteen other crews who had arrived at Melbourne with Jack and the boys just two months earlier, eleven had been lost. A handful of these men had survived and been taken prisoner of war, but the vast majority had been killed, torn to shreds by German bullets and shrapnel, burned alive as their aircraft exploded, or lost without trace, drowned in the icy depths of the North Sea. That was the reality, the long and short of it all. Survival was, so frequently, entirely a matter of happenstance. When it came down to it, whether an airman lived or died was not dependent so much upon his ability to do his job, or the efficacy of the equipment with which he was supplied, but was largely down to old-fashioned good (or bad) luck.

Doug Newham recalls the complete physical and mental fatigue of operational flying:

"I was always utterly exhausted when I got back. I would go into the Mess and collapse onto a chair, and I'd be sitting there in the dark, awaiting the return of my mate's aircraft which still hadn't come back. You always hoped for the call to say that they had landed at another base, but they rarely had."

After the chaos and exhaustion of flying on six operations in less than three weeks, sometimes on consecutive nights, the pace of the area bombing campaign suddenly seemed to slow down, at least as far as the Pennicott crew were concerned. Between 26 July and 24 November 1943, a period of 115 days, the crew flew only four operations. All Bomber Command crews were of course kept in a constant state of readiness, and would not know, from one day to the next when they would be required to fly. Although many men were mightily relieved not to be called upon, the waiting and long periods between raids shredded the already taut nerves of many more, particularly those who were a substantial way through their tours. For Jack, Bill, Roy, George, Freddie, Ken and Penny, there was simply no end in sight. Other crews were rostered for raids on Hamburg and Mannheim, on 2 and 9 August, but in the interim, there were no operations for 10 Squadron due to bad weather.

Ten operations down, another twenty to go – not even halfway through. No light, just an endless tunnel of fear and uncertainty.

Already within 10 Squadron, the Pennicott crew were beginning to develop something of a reputation, not for any particular skill under fire, nor for any particular feat of bravery, but for simply continuing to be alive. There were whispers in the canteen and in the mess, in the briefing hall and in the Blacksmith's Arms, that the Pennicott crew were blessed with that rare quality – luck. Ground staff and airmen alike began to refer to them as "a lucky crew." Airmen are notoriously superstitious (Doug Newham recalls his wireless operator always flew with a pair of his girlfriend's knickers draped over his radio; the crew were never sure whether it was always the same pair, or even the same girlfriend) and often in the kit room or even at breakfast, members of other crews would pat them on the back or tap them on the arm, hoping that some of the boys' good fortune would rub off. Jack and the boys hated that; as if they could somehow have a hand in the fate of their comrades, let alone their own. They would smile and nod politely, then Roy (it was always Roy) would mutter as soon as the departing crews were out of earshot, "Ruddy kiss of death, more like!" before tucking back into his eggs and bacon.

On 6 August, the boys had resumed their usual schedule of training flights and air tests, in good old *Z-Zebra*, JD202, which was fast becoming their "favourite" aircraft. *Zebra* had got them to Le Creusot, Cologne, Hamburg and Essen and back again safely, although not in one piece. Two days later on 8 August they were given a different aircraft, *T-Tommy*, to practise bumps and circuits (take-off and landing). Jack's logbook for that date simply states:

"Aircraft crashed – crew ok."

No other information is given, no further comment made. The flight time is given as twenty minutes; something went wrong with the landing gear on take-off and Penny had to crash-land at the nearest base. Although the incident was insufficiently serious to merit any mention in the Squadron Diary that day, Penny's Prangers' legendary luck was beginning to wear thin.

If the crew had been shaken up by that experience, they did not have time to dwell upon it. On the morning of 10 August, Penny received word from the Commanding Officer that they had been rostered to take part in that evening's operation. Rumours had circulated around the base all day when groundcrews were instructed to adjust the bombloads to allow for more fuel to be carried on the aircraft than usual. There were gasps and sideways glances aplenty in the stuffy briefing hall when their target was revealed. Not Essen, not the Ruhr Valley at all this time, but Nuremberg, much further east and much further south than any of the assembled crews had flown before. Greater distance entailed greater danger quite simply because it meant the aircraft would be over enemy territory for a significantly longer period, and even more vulnerable to attack or technical failure. While the Ruhr Valley was fraught with danger, it was a relatively short trip, and not far beyond the Dutch border; a raid on the southern and eastern cities of Germany could easily add on another two or three hours.

For the first time, the crew were not all flying together, which caused some unease. Roy Tann and Bill Bradshaw were both sick. Bill had a small piece of flak embedded in his arm, a souvenir from one of his trips, which had been troubling him. He had paid a visit to the station medical officer, the wonderfully named Dr Ponder, to see if he could try to remove the troublesome fragment of shrapnel. Unfortunately for Bill, Dr Ponder did not like the sight of blood, and his patient ended up fishing the fragment out of his flesh himself. Replacements for Bill and Roy had to be drafted in from other crews; Penny wanted someone he knew and trusted to be the "eyes" of the aircraft in the rear gunner's position, so Freddie Singh took Bill's position in the tail, while Sergeant Round took Freddie's usual place in the mid-upper gun turret. Sergeant Marsh filled in for Roy as navigator. Penny and Ken were wary of having to rely upon the skills of an unfamiliar navigator on such a long trip. However, by this stage in the bombing campaign, as a result of illness or injury or even death of crew members, crews were having to "make do and mend," and it became increasingly common for individual airmen to be rostered to fly with other crews who were short of numbers.

In the heart of the state of Bavaria, and then at the very end of the range of the British and American bombers, Nuremberg had (when compared to many other German cities) escaped relatively lightly up until that point. By the end of the war, it would be almost destroyed by Russian artillery and Allied bombing.

Nineteen crews took off from Melbourne that summer night, the Pennicott crew aboard JD202, *Z-Zebra*, as usual, with extra packets of sandwiches and flasks of coffee for their long and perilous journey. Pilot Officer Death, who had given Jack his first taste of flying at Wireless School, had recently joined 10 Squadron and he and his crew were also rostered to take part in this operation.

The Squadron Operations Book records that Jack and the boys were airborne at exactly 9.30pm, and headed south, then east, to take their place in the bomber stream with 652 other aircraft.[70] The advance party of Pathfinder aircraft had encountered difficulty marking the target areas due to low cloud, however by the time *Z-Zebra* arrived over Nuremberg at 1.07am, the cloud had dispersed a little. A large number of fires were already taking hold to the south and southeast of the city. The incoming bomber force encountered moderate flak defences over the target, but the crew were alarmed when they witnessed something they'd never seen before. Penny recorded:

"A new type of projectile was seen being fired, bursting at 17,000 feet and cascading like our own target indicators and emitting numerous white fragments."

---

70 National Archives AIR/27/144 10 Sqn ORB 10.8.1943.

At that time crews had been briefed about the possibility of a new anti-aircraft weapon, known as "scarecrow", so perhaps this is what Penny thought he'd seen. However, it was subsequently determined after the war that no such weapon actually existed and what the bomber crews were seeing was other Bomber Command or Pathfinder aircraft being hit before reaching their target, with their bombloads or pyrotechnic markers exploding mid-air.

For Penny's crew, the raid on Nuremberg passed largely without incident. Significant damage had been caused to the central and southern parts of the city, particularly in the Altstadt (Old Town); the Lorenzkirche, one of the oldest and largest churches, was very badly damaged, and over fifty ancient houses were destroyed. Elsewhere, a huge fire had broken out in the Wohird area. Five hundred and seventy-seven German civilians perished that night, crushed by falling masonry, burned to death in their homes or suffocated by the force of the explosions as they huddled in their cellars.

Jack diligently recorded the operation in his logbook upon his return, adopting the German spelling of "Nurmberg". The crew had finally landed back at Melbourne at six o'clock the next morning, some eight and a half hours after their departure. What an ordeal that must have been, particularly for Freddie Singh in his cramped and freezing position in the rear turret, trying to stay awake and focused in the darkness. Jack noted:

"NURMBERG. *Defences moderate, fair prang. A hell of a binding stooge!!*"

To translate the RAF slang of the day, a successful but very tedious operation.

Of the 653 aircraft who had departed the evening before, sixteen were lost, including that of Sergeant Dibben and his crew, of 10 Squadron, whose aircraft went into the sea off the French coast. Miraculously, he and his crew were rescued and taken prisoner.

The crew flew no more operations in August, despite the squadron taking part in raids on Milan, Peenemünde, Leverkusen, Nuremberg, Berlin and München Gladbach; Jack amassed no more than ten hours' flying time that month. After another week at home on leave, his logbook flying record was signed off at the end of the month by the new Commanding Officer of C Flight – one Flight Lieutenant R. Pennicott.

At the beginning of September 1943, the weather had not improved. Still Jack had to wait; the Pennicott crew were not called upon to take part in another operation until 15 September, some five weeks after their trip to Nuremberg. Patience grew thin and nerves ever tauter as the end of the crew's tour seemed interminably distant. The boys tried to distract themselves with various activities; Bill had recently become the proud owner of a Triumph motorbike and would often take Jack or Roy for a spin around the Yorkshire countryside. The more senior members of the crew occasionally went fishing in the Pocklington Canal that ran near to the airfield or would borrow a dog from one of the senior officers and spend hours playing "fetch." Many crews spent their free time drinking themselves to oblivion and chasing women; Pennicott was not a big drinker and made sure that none of his crew were either. Doug Newham recalls a party in the Officers' Mess one evening which went on until the early hours, and the squadron Medical Officer dishing out "horrible pink medicine" the following day to the hungover crews who were required to fly that night.

Discipline on the bomber stations tended to be fairly lax – what possible punishment could a commanding officer inflict upon a young man who was quite likely to be dead within the week? As a result, aircrews were given free rein to do as they pleased, but this brought its own problems, not least a massive increase in cases of venereal disease. Statistically, the young men of Bomber Command, with their "live fast, die young" mentality, were more than four times as likely to contract venereal disease as servicemen in other branches of the armed forces. Despite graphic slide shows and lectures by squadron medics, the problem became so great that at one time RAF chiefs considered threatening any man diagnosed with the condition with a ten-mission extension to his operational tour.

In 2018 I interviewed the indomitable Rusty Waughman, a Lancaster pilot with thirty operations under his belt. Rusty, a County Durham lad like Jack, was extremely candid. He revealed that his rear gunner had often said that the only thing that kept him going through his operational tour, and the only reason he managed to retain his sanity, was all the sex. So many young men found themselves in that vicious cycle of extreme fear, hard drinking and casual sex. For some, that's what kept them alive. Pennicott, who was a deeply religious man, ensured that his crew kept pretty much on the straight and narrow. The younger men of the crew – Jack and Bill in particular – were incredibly naïve, and the more senior, Penny and George, both had wives waiting at home. Ken Thomas, a pilot with 622 Squadron, recalls that his crew were "an unruly lot – I just let them do whatever they wanted really, within reason".

In the first week of September 1943, the crew were kept busy with exercises and air tests, practice bombing and moving aircraft around to different bases. A "weather window" on 5 and 6 September allowed raids to take place on Mannheim and Munich, but once again, "Penny's Prangers" found themselves surplus to requirements.

Pilot Officer Death and his crew were lost on the Mannheim trip; the buried remains of the aircraft and its crew were only discovered in 2016, in a farmer's field near Waldsee. On 31 August 2019, a ceremony was held in their honour at the crash site, and a memorial erected by local residents. Death and his crew now lie in the Rheinberg War Cemetery.

The weather closed in once more; low cloud, heavy drizzle and fog meant that no operations could take place for another week, and Jack found himself kicking his heels again. On 9 September he and the boys headed into York to celebrate his twenty-first birthday, after sharing slices of fruitcake baked and sent in a tin by his sister, Lydia. George had drawn him a birthday card, and Edie Threadkell had sent boiled sweets and chocolate. The boys made a bit of a fuss of him, as the youngest member of the crew, and Jack was mortified when the piano in the Sergeants' Mess struck up the old music hall tune "21 Today." He hated to be the centre of attention and blushed fiercely, with a shy grin. Upon returning to his bed that evening, slightly the worse for wear, he began to twist the gold band around his right ring finger, and wished his mother could have been there to kiss him on the cheek and say "Happy Birthday," just this once.

Less than a week later, Pennicott was notified that at long last he and his crew had finally been rostered for another raid. Although he did not admit it, he had concerns that some of the crew may have been a little "ring rusty;" they were all relieved when they were allocated *Z-Zebra* for their operation that evening, and even more so when their intended target was revealed to be the Dunlop rubber factory on the outskirts of the medieval town of Montluçon, deep in the heart of France. The Nazis had taken over the factory not long after the invasion, keen to utilise the technology and resources to make rubber wheels for Luftwaffe aircraft, and it was therefore considered an important industrial target.

At that time, Montluçon and its surrounds were known to be a hotbed of French Resistance fighters, led by an Australian woman named Nancy Wake. On 6 January 1943, a crowd of angry citizens had overpowered German guards who were co-ordinating the deportation of huge numbers of French men to Germany, to be used as forced labour in the factories of the Reich. All the men who had been rounded up for deportation managed to escape, melting away into the surrounding countryside. Nancy Wake went on to become the most decorated woman of the Second World War, passing away at the grand old age of ninety-eight in 2011.

Z-Zebra and her crew were airborne at precisely eight o'clock on the evening of 15 September 1943, in company with fifteen other crews from 10 Squadron.[71] The raid on the Dunlop factory was a relatively small one, by Bomber Command's standards, with "only" 369 aircraft taking part. Unusually, the RAF were accompanied on this occasion by five USAAF B-17s. Of the sixteen crews who had left Melbourne that evening, fourteen bombed the target successfully. Sergeant Culverhouse had had to abandon the mission due to severe icing on the wings of his aircraft. Penny recorded that *Z-Zebra* had bombed the primary target at 23.33 hours, in good visibility, from the very low height of 4500 feet. A large flame which had lasted around two minutes was observed, together with a cloud of oily black smoke rising to around 10,000 feet. Lack of ground defences, clear weather and accurate bombing from a low ceiling resulted in a very successful raid, and every building in the factory was damaged.

Jack recorded in his logbook, next to the target co-ordinates, written in pencil:

---

71 National Archives AIR/27/144 10 Sqn ORB 15.9.1943.

"MONTLUCON. *Wizard Prang! No opposition of any description.*"

Only three aircraft were lost; one of them was that of 10 Squadron's Sergeant Dunlop and his crew. Two of the crew survived the crash and were taken prisoner; a third, one of Jack's wireless operator mates, Sergeant Bilton, evaded capture and eventually, with the help of the Resistance, made his way back to England.[72]

The second half of September 1943 was an extremely busy one for the squadron, but again, the Pennicott crew were not required for operations. Four months since arriving at Melbourne, they still weren't even halfway through their tour. The purgatory of waiting for news, not knowing from one day to the next whether they would be called upon, played upon the nerves of the crew and tensions began to arise. Some of the boys, like Jack and Bill, were desperate to be rostered, just so they could get their tour over and done with; others, Roy and Ken in particular, were really beginning to struggle with anxiety, and were massively relieved when their services were not required. Penny had always adopted an "open door" policy with his crew, and (unusually for the time) he encouraged them to open up and discuss how they were feeling about things, to share their hopes and, more importantly, their fears. He was particularly fond of Bill and would frequently confide in him. Perhaps he saw something of his younger self in this polite, enthusiastic, highly intelligent young man with the winning smile; perhaps Bill, the only other member of the crew to have flown an aircraft, was the only one who really *understood* the responsibility that a pilot feels for his crew.

---

72 MacMillan, Ian and King, Richard, *From Brooklands to Brize: A Centennial History of No 10 Squadron Royal Air Force,* 10 Squadron Association, 2015, p. 130.

Although the crew weren't required for operational flying throughout September, they were airborne almost every day, taking part in cross-country training exercises, fighter affiliation and ferrying aircraft around. Things didn't always go smoothly, and no member of the crew was immune from criticism. Jack noted in his logbook on 17 September:

"Air test. Pilot had finger trouble, or maybe just one of those things."

10 Squadron was involved in operations on Modane, further trips to Mannheim and Bochum and two raids on Hannover. The latter of these, on 27 September, cost the squadron dearly. Of the eighteen crews sent out that night, three failed to return. The turnover of crews was huge, with different faces appearing at breakfast and in the mess almost daily. "Shiny Ten" had lost seven crews and eight aircraft in the space of just a month, and things were about to get a whole lot worse.

18

A Ticklish Business

As the days shortened and the nights began to grow damp and chilly, October began badly for the Pennicott crew.

On the night of 1 October, the crew were undertaking cross-country night flying exercises in *B-Beer*, an aircraft they had used in training on previous occasions. Little information survives as to what happened next, but it is evident that Jack and the boys had a very narrow escape indeed. First the port inner engine failed; as Penny and George stabilised the aircraft, both starboard engines cut out. After a hair-raising few seconds, miraculously Penny managed to restart one of them, and *B-Beer* limped back to base on two engines. Jack was clearly shaken up by the experience, which he described in his logbook afterwards as being "worse than an op." Perhaps the legendary luck of the Pennicott crew was beginning to wear as thin as their nerves.

Incidents such as this occurred so frequently that they did not merit mention in the official records kept by the Station

Commander; they were to be expected. Only when an aircraft suffered significant damage, or was destroyed, with its crew killed or injured, was a formal report made, as on 10 March 1943 when one of the squadron's Halifaxes had crashed near the airfield, killing all six crew members.

Within the week, Jack was flying operationally again. On the morning of 7 October, Penny was informed that he and his crew would be required, not for a bombing raid on enemy targets this time, but for a task which they had not undertaken before – minelaying.

As well as striking against military, industrial and transport targets in occupied Europe, since the very earliest days of the war the RAF had sought to attack German shipping belonging to both the Kriegsmarine (the Germany Navy) and the Merchant Marine. In addition to targeting Nazi warships and submarines in the North Sea, the Channel, the Mediterranean and the Atlantic, the plan was to disrupt the supply of goods, natural resources and raw materials coming into Germany, particularly from Scandinavia, and to interrupt the movement of men and equipment coming out. Bombing of the German and French rail networks had resulted in the need for more freight to be moved by sea. Mines were dropped, usually by bombers, near ports and harbours, docks and submarine bases, inland waterways, estuaries and even canals, as well as in busy shipping lanes. The Frisian Islands (codenamed Nectarines), off the coast of Holland and Germany, the area around Kiel and Rostock in the Baltic, and the submarine ports on the Bay of Biscay were all heavily mined.

The effect was two-fold: the destruction of ships (and their contents), and the diversion of thousands of military personnel who were tasked with trying to clear the mines. Minesweeping took up valuable time and human resources; preventing mines being dropped in the first place required the construction of hundreds of additional searchlights and anti-aircraft batteries, both on land and at sea, on floating platforms known as flak barges.

The European coastline was divided into sectors and given separate codenames, mainly names of trees and plants. Hence the dropping – or "sowing" – of mines, became known as "gardening", and the individual mines themselves as "vegetables". Different types of mines were given horticultural names too, such as "artichoke" or "aubergine". When we think of mines today, we perhaps have in mind the black, spiked spheres that bobbed around on the surface, so beloved of World War Two filmmakers. These were usually laid by specialist minelaying ships; those dropped by bomber crews were intended to be laid in shallow water, and had parachutes attached which allowed them to drift slowly into the sea. On contact with the water, the chutes would disengage, and the mine would sink to the seabed. The mines would be triggered by the magnetic interference from a passing ship (the mechanism could be set to detect larger ships, so that they didn't explode under every passing fishing boat) or by the acoustics from a ship's propellers. Cunningly, some of the mines also incorporated time delay mechanisms which allowed the explosion to be delayed until the fifth or sixth time they were triggered, thereby giving the enemy the impression that an area had successfully been swept clear of all hazards before detonating beneath an unsuspecting vessel. Fleets of bombers could drop more mines than could be laid by ship, and they could also reach areas that the Royal Navy simply couldn't get to.[73]

Each mine was around nine feet long, with a seventeen-inch diameter, and weighed around 1500 pounds. Due to the

---

73 I am indebted to Craig Smith for permission to utilise information on mining operations from his website at www.lancaster-ed559.co.uk throughout this chapter.

weight and size, bomber crews had to carry fewer mines than they would bombs on conventional overland raids, usually half a dozen, but sometimes only two.

Some aircrews considered minelaying operations to be an "easy pass," as they usually did not involve flying over enemy ground defences, and new crews were often rostered for minelaying for their first operation, to ease them in. In reality, "gardening" missions were fraught with danger, and many men and their aircraft were lost without trace in the icy waters of the North Sea, the Baltic and the Bay of Biscay. Wireless operator Andy Andrews, who joined 10 Squadron in July 1944, was shot down with Flying Officer Grayshon's crew on a minelaying operation over Kiel Bay, just off Stettin, on 14 February 1945. He recalls:

"We were tasked with laying mines in the German shipping lanes in Kiel Bay. The bomb aimer was in his position in the nose of the aircraft, locating the drop zone with the H2S. We were tagged by a Junkers 88, who crept up on us and flew directly underneath. He fired his 6 cannons straight up under the belly of the aircraft, bracketing the front where we were sitting. He hit the petrol tanks, and the port wing was a mess of flames. The pilot, who was sat immediately above me, was mortally wounded, and our navigator, who'd been sitting 'knee to knee' with me was killed outright. The aircraft was obviously out of control and the G Forces made it difficult to stand or even move. I managed to clip my parachute on and tried to move towards the escape hatch in the floor of the nose. I never got there. The aircraft blew up at 18,000 feet and I was knocked unconscious. To this day I don't know how I got out, but the nose must have come off and left a gap for me and the bomb aimer to fall through. Fortunately, I came to. Everything was silent as I had gone deaf. I was able to pull my ripcord and seconds later I hit the ground."

Andy remembers seeing his flaming aircraft streaking through the night sky like a comet above him. The pilot and navigator were both killed, but the rest of the crew managed to escape. They were incredibly lucky to have come down over land. A few miles further out into the Bay and none of them would have survived. The Flight Engineer and two gunners were picked up by the Danish Resistance and evaded capture, eventually making their way home via Sweden within days. Andy and his bomb aimer were rescued by a Danish family who got them to hospital. There two of the doctors introduced them to members of the Resistance, but they were betrayed to the German authorities by someone in the hospital. After three days being held captive in a cellar, they were "extracted" by the local Luftwaffe who treated them very well, before they eventually ended up in a prisoner of war camp near the infamous Dachau concentration camp. Andy remembers:

> "We were only a mile or so from Dachau. We could see the smoke from the crematorium chimneys. The smell was appalling."

Andy and his fellow prisoners were eventually liberated by American troops a couple of months later.

Just after half past eight on the evening of 7 October 1943, Jack and his crewmates took off from Melbourne in *Q-Queen*, aircraft Q-HX184, on their very first gardening operation, bound for the sea lanes off the northernmost edge of the Danish coast, codenamed "Hawthorne III."[74] Their relief at not having to fly straight into the enemy defences over, say, Mannheim or Berlin or Frankfurt was tempered with anxiety at the difficult and very technical nature of the task ahead, and the fear of attack by the flak ships of the Kriegsmarine, as

---

74   National Archives AIR/27/144 10 Sqn ORB 7.10.1943.

well as the Luftwaffe night fighters who patrolled the shipping lanes and harbours, eager to pick off any RAF bombers they sighted.

Roy, meticulous as ever, carefully plotted their course, and the crew, in company with four other aircraft (those of Pilot Officers Walker, Cameron and Ayre and Flight Lieutenant Trobe) from Melbourne, were soon heading out over the coast at Flamborough Head. At this point in the war, gardening operations only ever involved five aircraft, as quite often the main body of the squadron would be deployed on bombing targets on Germany on the same evening; a smaller force was also more difficult to detect. There was little for bomb aimer Ken Cox to do until Roy was able to inform him that they were over the target area; there was nothing to see, and in the dead of night, one patch of the North Sea looks identical to every other. Minelaying was extremely monotonous for the crews, but also technically very difficult. It wasn't just a case of flying over the general area, opening the bomb bay doors, pressing a button and hoping for the best; the precise location of where the mines were to be sown was decided in advance by the Admiralty, but it was then left to the RAF to find these spots, in the dark and without the use of the visual landmarks which bomber crews usually relied upon to help determine both their own position and the location of their targets. Many bomber crews found minelaying unsatisfactory from a psychological point of view, as they were unable to see the results of their efforts – no great explosions, no columns of smoke and flame, no burning buildings or ruined factories to be seen and reported upon. Ted Church, a rear gunner from 77 Squadron at neighbouring RAF Elvington, summed it up perfectly:

"... the minelayer, after going through the ticklish business of finding the exact spot, plants his mine and watches it disappear *into the dark waters. There is no explosion, no damage to the enemy – yet – and he cannot know for certain whether his mine will serve its purpose."*[75]

Sometimes aircraft from the Pathfinder Squadrons would assist the small group of bombers and drop a coloured flare over the intended destination. The level of concentration required by both navigator and pilot on a minelaying operation was incredible. As *Q-Queen* neared the intended drop zone, Roy notified Penny over the intercom; Penny then began to bring the aircraft down to the optimal height from which to sow the mines, an altitude of only 6000 feet. On some operations, aircraft had to fly at less than 1500 feet. A steady speed of 180 miles per hour was required (any faster and the parachutes attached to the mines could be ripped off, causing the mines to fall in the wrong place or to sustain damage on impact with the water), and Penny had to keep the aircraft at this altitude and speed for the entirety of their timed twelve-mile bombing run. When flying at such low heights, the slightest error on his part could quite easily have consigned his crew to a watery grave. They were often too low to bale out if anything went wrong; even if Penny was successfully able to ditch the aircraft, the chances of all seven of the crew being able to escape as it rapidly sank into the icy blackness were slim indeed. In those freezing cold seas, a man would be dead within two minutes. Even if he made it to one of the life rafts which every aircraft carried, the prospects of being spotted and picked up were virtually nil.

The requirement for low, straight flying over considerable distances also meant that gardening aircraft were sitting ducks for Luftwaffe night fighters, and there was always the risk of being spotted by the German Navy, or the searchlights of the

---

75 www.tailendcharlietedchurch.wordpress.com.

flak barges. Some mining operations were conducted very close to shore, where the crews would be exposed to fire from heavy anti-aircraft cannons; even heavy machine guns could bring down a bomber if it was flying low enough. If that wasn't enough, there was also the Sperrbrecher to contend with. This was a fleet of around a hundred ships, including modified merchant vessels, fitted with 20mm, 37mm, 88mm or even 105mm cannons, designed for escorting U-boats through minefields, which could be encountered virtually anywhere along an aircraft's route. These lethal vessels employed magnetic field generators which could detonate mines up to 500 yards away; however, due to the timing devices on the British mines many of the Sperrbrecher, and the U-boats they shepherded, were destroyed. Just a few days before the Hawthorne trip, three aircraft from Melbourne on a gardening operation had been attacked by night fighters, but all returned home safely

The Pennicott crew successfully planted their "vegetables" at ten past eleven that night, and headed for home, landing just after two o'clock in the morning. In his report Penny noted:

> "Mines laid as ordered at 23.10 hours, from 6000 feet, by navigational aids and pinpoint of coast. Visibility was good, with 3/10 cloud cover. No opposition encountered."

The mention of "navigational aids" was a thinly veiled reference to the new recently installed H2S mapping radar, which was a huge improvement on previous systems, as it allowed crews to "bomb blind" with accuracy and without the need for visual markers. All five crews returned to base safely; the operation was only a partial success, however, as Flight Lieutenant Trobe's crew had been unable to pinpoint the target area and had brought their vegetables back home with them. Unlike conventional bombing loads, mines were considered safe to be brought back as they would not detonate even if a crash-landing was necessary. They were also simply too expensive to be disposed of randomly in the middle of the sea, where they might pose a danger to British shipping. As for Jack, his logbook simply states:

"MINELAYING (DANISH COAST)."

He'd spent almost the entire trip bored witless, reading the newspaper, checking on his two pigeons and completing the crossword.

The squadron had taken part in raids on Kassel, Frankfurt and Hannover during the first week of October, as well as the two gardening sorties; miraculously not a single crew had been lost, although there had been a few particularly narrow escapes. On the Frankfurt trip, Sergeant Evans' crew had to abandon their mission as their navigator had somehow managed to puncture his oxygen supply line while sharpening a pencil; Sergeant Dean's crew were hit both by flak over the target and an incendiary bomb dropped by a higher aircraft; fortunately it didn't ignite and the quick-thinking crew quickly got rid of it down the flare chute. The raid on Hannover had got off to a very bad start when the flight engineer of one crew had been struck by a propeller while attempting to guide his pilot onto the perimeter track. Pilot Officer Cameron's aircrew sustained heavy damage to the undercarriage and flaps over the target. They crash-landed at Melbourne on return, and all survived. Cameron's navigator, Reg Cowles, was subsequently awarded the Distinguished Flying Cross for his actions that night.[76]

---

76 MacMillan, Ian and King, Richard, *From Brooklands to Brize: A Centennial History of No 10 Squadron Royal Air Force*, 10 Squadron Association, 2015, pp. 131-132.

Bad weather combined with a full moon meant no operations for the next fortnight. Jack kept himself busy with preparations for an exam on the new navigational equipment on 14 October. The break allowed crews to familiarise themselves with the H2S, as well as the usual round of training exercises and ferrying aircraft between bases. A full five weeks after the Montluçon raid, the Pennicott crew were finally rostered to take part in a further "maximum effort" operation on Kassel, on the night of 22 October.

As was now his usual habit, as soon as Jack heard that he'd be flying that night, he sought out Leo Groark amongst the other "erks" and handed him his house keys, to give to his sister, Lydia, in the event that he did not return. Jack and Leo had the exchange and return of keys down to a fine art now, and for Jack it had begun to be a ritual, a superstition; if Leo had the keys, he'd return safely. For his part, Leo was a nervous wreck for every moment that the keys remained in his possession, and he would constantly check his pockets to make sure they were still there. He feared that if the keys were lost, then Jack would be too. He had watched too many crews go out and never come back.

Jack never used to say much, but Leo would always shout after him as he turned to walk away, "See you in the morning, Jackie Clyde!"

If their first gardening sortie had been relatively straightforward, the Kassel trip could not have got off to a worse start for the Pennicott crew. To begin with, they were allocated *M-Mother*, M-JN948, an aircraft they'd never flown before, not even in training. *Z-Zebra* had suffered damage while on an operation with another crew and was undergoing repairs. At twenty-five past five in the afternoon, *M-Mother* hurtled down the runway and disappeared into the darkness. Almost immediately Penny sensed that something wasn't quite right with the aircraft, although he couldn't put his finger on it. He asked George to run through all his checks again, but all the various dials, gauges and indicators showed no evidence of any technical problems. The rest of the crew soon picked up on the tension in the cockpit, and there was very little in the way of the usual banter over the intercom. Even Freddie, who always had a witty remark for every occasion, was silent in the upper gun turret.

Jack and the boys took their place in the bomber stream over Suffolk and headed out over the North Sea at Southwold. As they approached the Dutch coast, the silence was interrupted as first Roy, then Ken, then George reported instruments malfunctioning. One after another – compass, GEE, H2S began to fail; then there were problems with the hydraulics and the fuel lines, which meant that Penny just couldn't gain enough height. The airframe began to creak and vibrate, and the cause of the problems was evident to all: ice.

"Sorry, boys, that's it for us this evening, I'm afraid. I'm aborting this mission, it's simply too dangerous to continue."

Although every man in the crew was mightily relieved, each knew that this operation would not be counted towards their tour, as they had not crossed over into enemy territory. To have continued would have been suicidal; if M-Mother hadn't been caught in searchlights and brought down by anti-aircraft guns due to her low altitude, there was every likelihood that the weight of ice on her wings would have caused her to go into a spin and nosedive into the ground at 200 miles an hour. The crew knew that Pennicott had made the right call, and in doing so, had saved their lives. Four other crews (those of Simmons, Dixon, Whitmarsh and Bullah) had encountered identical problems and had been forced to abandon their missions. After jettisoning both of their 1000-pound bombs in the North Sea, Jack and the boys headed for home. After a quick debrief, they were back in the Sergeants' Mess by ten o'clock.

Once again, it transpired that the Pennicott crew had had a narrow escape. Of the remaining fourteen crews who had gone on to attack Kassel that night, three had failed to return to Melbourne. Those of Heppell, Wilkinson and Plant all came down in the target area; only one man survived, Flying Officer Pyne, the bomb aimer of Pilot Officer Plant's crew, who was taken prisoner.[77,78]

The raid on Kassel was utterly devastating and was considered a huge success by RAF chiefs; that success came at a very high price for Bomber Command, with the loss of forty-three aircraft and their crews, out of a total force of 569 aircraft. On the ground, the scene was one of absolute horror. Still reeling from an attack earlier in October, the citizens of Kassel were confronted with a huge firestorm, the like of which had not been witnessed since the bombing of Hamburg the previous summer. The centre of the city contained many wooden medieval structures, which were simply incinerated. Almost 27,000 apartments were destroyed, and 120,000 people made homeless. Three thousand six hundred individual fires were reported, and massive damage was inflicted on industrial, public, military and police buildings, including the local Gestapo headquarters. The railway system was badly disrupted and most importantly, three Henschel aircraft factories where V-1 flying bombs were being made were seriously damaged. The German authorities had recorded 5599 dead, of which over 1800 were unidentifiable, burned beyond recognition in the firestorm. Thousands were injured,

---

77 National Archives AIR/27/144 10 Sqn ORB 22.10.1943.

78 MacMillan, Ian and King, Richard, *From Brooklands to Brize: A Centennial History of No 10 Squadron Royal Air Force*, 10 Squadron Association, 2015, p. 132.

and a further 3300 were unaccounted for, although it is likely that many of these had fled into the countryside.[79]

Upon reading the newspaper reports of the success of the Kassel raid, Jack was tortured by a complex and conflicting range of emotions, all too familiar to many Bomber Command crewmen: guilt that he had not been involved in a raid which had claimed the lives of twenty of his colleagues, and relief that he had not been responsible, on this occasion at least, for the deaths of thousands of German civilians, in the most horrific of circumstances.

The autumn weather began to deteriorate again, and as October turned to November, the Yorkshire airfields of 4 Group Bomber Command remained shrouded in mist, fog and drizzle for days on end. Even test flying and exercises were cancelled, and the crews were kept busy with "ground instruction" and lectures during the day, and drinking, attending the mobile cinema or dancing with the WAAFs in the mess of an evening.

Clearer weather was predicted for the night of 3 November, and eighteen crews were selected to take part in a raid on Düsseldorf. The Pennicott crew were not chosen; however, later that afternoon Penny collared Ken and Roy to inform them that they'd be flying after all, as Pilot Officer Cameron's navigator, Reg Cowles, was sick, and Wing Commander Sutton's crew was short of a bomb aimer. Neither was very enthusiastic about having to fly without their own crew but there was little they could do about it, and they looked upon it as an opportunity to tick off one more operation from their tour of duty.

That evening Bill, George and Jack went for a couple of pints in the Blacksmith's Arms with Alec and Ronnie from

---

79 Middlebrook, M. and Everitt, C., *The Bomber Command War Diaries*, Pen & Sword Aviation, Barnsley, 2014, p. 440.

their groundcrew, to try to pass the time; Penny had gone into York to catch up with some old friends from his training days, and as usual, Freddie did his own thing, complaining about the weather and playing cards in the Officers' Mess with a couple of fellow Australians.

The morning of 4 November dawned cold and misty. As the pale early morning sunlight began to melt away the haze, hundreds of airmen shuffled in and out of the canteen for breakfast. Amid the buzz of chit-chat and the occasional howl of laughter, the clatter of crockery and the scraping of chairs, the crashing of pans in the kitchen and the sound of boots on the concrete floor, Jack and the boys collected their plates of bacon and eggs, and their mugs of coffee and headed over to their usual table.

There, they sat in silence.

Roy's chair was empty.

19

Finest of Mortal Friends

Pilot Officer Cameron's crew, with Roy on board as stand-in navigator, had taken off just before five o'clock the preceding evening, in Halifax HX163, *L-Love*. Roy knew a few of the crew by sight but not very well; crews tended to socialise together and with their own groundcrew but did not really mingle with others. There was a constant flow of new faces into the squadron. Many of them would be seen in the mess perhaps only a handful of times and it was difficult to form friendships outside of one's own crew. Some men deliberately avoided it; what was the point of creating bonds, when there was every chance you wouldn't see a chap again?

Roy knew Reg Cowles, whose place he had taken, from their navigator briefings and lectures. Although Cameron was not keen on flying without his regular navigator, Roy Tann was very experienced and a safe pair of hands. And better than that, he was one of the "lucky crew."

L-Love's target that evening was the German industrial city of Düsseldorf. In company with seventeen other aircraft from 10 Squadron, Roy and the Cameron crew headed south towards the assembly point at the Cottesmore Light, where they joined 561 Halifaxes, Lancasters and the Mosquitoes of the Pathfinder Squadron and then out over the North Sea over the Sussex coast. The trip to Düsseldorf was a relatively short one but involved flying through some of the most perilous and heavily defended airspace in the whole of Germany. A diversionary raid on Cologne, designed to deflect attention from the main attack, was made by fifty-two Lancasters and ten Mosquitoes from 8 Group.

Under the weight of sustained bombing attacks throughout 1943, the Nazi authorities' record-keeping was starting to break down and for that reason it is difficult to determine precise results for the success or otherwise of the raid. Whilst there was extensive damage throughout the city, the numbers of buildings damaged or destroyed, nor persons killed, was not accurately recorded.

The Royal Air Force lost eighteen aircraft that evening. The 10 Squadron crews met with mixed results. Two crews had to return early due to technical problems. Flight Lieutenant Trobe's aircraft, *D-Dog*, had a very narrow escape indeed, after being repeatedly attacked by four different Luftwaffe fighters. Three of his crewmen were injured and his aircraft was badly shot up. Sergeant Mowatt, the mid-upper gunner, thought he'd shot down one of the attackers. The rear gun turret, hydraulics, intercom and radio were all rendered useless, and the fuel tanks damaged, causing two of the engines to fail. Sergeant Bisby, the wireless operator, had been severely injured yet still managed to repair the radio twice, while his colleagues tried to put out a fire on board. Somehow Trobe and his battered aircraft and crew were able to limp back home safely to Melbourne on three engines after Sergeant Bridge, the flight engineer, managed to get one restarted. Pilot Officer Dixon, in *P-Peter*, had been attacked by a Junkers 88, and he and his crew also had to get home on three engines after abandoning their mission.[80]

The raid was significant as being one of the few where a Victoria Cross was awarded to a participant. Flight Lieutenant William Reid of 61 Squadron managed to get his Lancaster and his crew home despite sustaining significant combat damage. His navigator had been killed outright and his wireless operator later died of his injuries. Both Reid and his flight engineer, Sergeant Norris, were injured on the way out to the target, which they still somehow managed to bomb successfully. On the way home the cockpit screen shattered, the oxygen supply failed and Reid began to lose consciousness. His flight engineer had to fly part of the way home (they were trained to take over in such circumstances) but Reid pulled round and succeeded in making an emergency landing in fog at RAF Shipdham, an American airbase in Norfolk, despite not being able to see properly due to the blood trickling into his eyes from a head wound.

At the same time, another of 10 Squadron's aircraft was also making for Shipdham, with very different consequences.

Roy and the Cameron crew had successfully completed their mission and were well on their way back to Melbourne. It is not known whether *L-Love* had suffered combat damage or if she had run out of fuel and had requested permission to make an emergency landing. Perhaps Cameron was injured or simply couldn't make out the runway in the fog and darkness

---

80 MacMillan, Ian and King, Richard, *From Brooklands to Brize: A Centennial History of No 10 Squadron Royal Air Force*, 10 Squadron Association, 2015, p. 132.

and misjudged his landing. At 9.16pm, less than an hour from home, *L-Love* plunged into the rich Norfolk soil and exploded on impact. The American fire and rescue crews were on hand almost immediately; one of the local Home Guard managed to pull the tail gunner Sergeant Winstanley free of the burning wreckage but he could not be saved and died from his injuries just a few hours later. Cameron and the remainder of his crew – Fielder, the bomb aimer, Hutton, the wireless operator, Williamson, the upper gunner, Eyre, the flight engineer, and their stand-in navigator, Roy – had been killed instantly.

Roy Tann was twenty-three.

The next morning, Jack, Bill, Penny, George, Freddie and Ken sat at their usual table in the canteen, unable to comprehend what had occurred. Penny had been informed of Roy's death in the early hours, and it was he who had had to break the news to the rest of the crew. Every time the canteen door squeaked open and then banged shut, they looked up from their untouched plates and cold coffee as one, expecting to see him burst through the door, late as normal, with his usual refrain, "You leaving that? I'll have it!" But Roy did not come. Across the canteen, Reg Cowles cut a lonely figure, sitting at his crew's usual table with the chaplain, simply staring into space, and occasionally glancing down at the six empty place settings which surrounded him.

It fell to Penny, as captain of the crew, to write to Roy's parents. Of course, the squadron Commanding Officer had to write the formal letter to notify them of their son's death in the first place, but he had thirteen other letters to write that day. Flight Lieutenant Harden's crew had also failed to return that night, although it would later transpire that three had survived being shot down over the target area and were being held prisoner of war. Penny later encouraged each of the boys to write to Mr and Mrs Tann too, and to share memories of

10. Aftermath of the 16.5.43 air raid on Seaham Harbour, showing bomb damage to Viceroy, Adolphus and Sophia Streets

11. Lord Londonderry (left) with Hitler and Von Ribbentrop, Reich Chancellery, February 1936

12. Sergeant Jack Clyde, just after completing his gunnery training, 9.12.42

13. The beautiful Friday the 13th, a reconstructed Mk III Halifax at the Yorkshire Air Museum

14. Extract from Jack's logbook, detailing the crew's first operation, to Wuppertal, on 29.5.43

15. "Endex Photograph" 8.3.43, the morning after the crew's last raid, on the marshalling yards at Le Mans. (Colourisation by Marina Amaral – image Author's own)

Standing L-R: Freddie Singh (Mid Upper Gunner), Jack Clyde (Wireless Operator), Reg Pennicott (Pilot), Reg Cowles (Navigator), Ken Cox (Bomb Aimer) George Phillipson (Flight Engineer), Ronnie Rudkin (Ground Crew).
Seated L-R: Bill Bradshaw (Tail Gunner), Alec Evans (Ground Crew), Tommy Hunter (Ground Crew), Norman (surname unknown, Ground Crew).
The Halifax in the background is A-Apple, which the Pennicott crew never actually flew

16. Jack carries the RAFA banner at the Seaham Harbour Armistice Day Parade, 10.11.1957

17. Old friends, reunited...

their precious son. He delivered the letters personally; as well as providing some comfort to the family, Penny hoped that the very process of committing their thoughts to paper would help his crew to come to terms with the loss of their friend and brother. He was a deeply thoughtful and incredibly generous man. Although the rest of his crew did not know it at the time, he had written to the widow of one of the squadron's pilots with whom he had been friendly and had offered to assume financial responsibility for her children's school fees.

Jack and the crew were sent home on nine days' leave a couple of days early. Lydia was surprised and delighted when she heard the front door open and Jack's voice shout upstairs, "Lyd? Lyd! It's me, I'm back early!"

She dashed downstairs to greet her brother but instead of the usual smiles and jokes, Jack was sitting in his father's chair by the window, his head in his hands, sobbing quietly. Lydia stood behind him and placed a comforting hand on his shoulder.

"What's happened?" she said softly.

"Roy. Roy's dead, Lyd."

*

Amid a maze of country lanes and hedgerows, of flat soft fields and huge horizons, there stands a small stone church, with an unusual circular tower. In front of this church, dedicated to St Peter, in the village of Forncett in Norfolk, lie the graves of many of the souls who, over the centuries, worshipped within its walls. The inscriptions on numerous headstones have all but disappeared, being worn away by time and season, so that only the odd letter is legible, the memory and the identity of the loved one who lay there now lost and forgotten several lifetimes ago.

Roy lies buried here. His final resting place is hard to find, among the rows of headstones of differing sizes and shapes and ages. The usual upright grave marker of creamy stone which signifies a Commonwealth war grave, carved with a regimental or squadron or naval crest, was not visible. After some time spent pacing up and down, stooping occasionally to read the dedications, I finally found him. His headstone had toppled over years ago, and lay flat, facing the heavens. Moss and lichen had begun to grow in the crevices of the carved inscription, which had almost been worn away by the wind and rain and frost of seventy-five winters, and the cream stone had turned to grey. There were no flowers, no rosebush planted at the base, no indication that Roy was remembered by anyone, anymore.

Finest of mortal friends, I'll not forget.
When war's a faded memory in the land
Which once stood tensely in the closing net,
I'll think of what is past – and understand.

Yours was the truthful voice among the lies,
Unshaken by the falsehoods that were rife,
You were the men with level, fearless eyes,
Who lived with death, yet still believed in life.

Laughter was yours, that held no bitter sting,
That bubbled up more quickly than the rest.
Your steady friendship was a sacred thing,
And I who held it, I was doubly blessed.
Decades of easy peace may go their way,
And tide and time will drift us far apart,
But you, who shared our savage Yesterday,
Will hold the highest places in my heart.

"To The Men Of My Squadron"

By Flight Lieutenant Peter Roberts,
RAF, 1944[81]

---

81 From *Take Off At Dusk*, by Flight Lieutenant Peter Roberts, Frederick Muller Ltd, London, 1944. Reproduced with kind permission of Tobin Roberts.

20
Paper Daddy

No more bombs fell on Seaham Harbour.

The air raid sirens began to sound less frequently, but the fear they had heralded never quite dissipated. There were no more fevered rescue attempts, no more digging through rubble to locate whimpering children and no more mass burials. The war had not gone away of course; the nature of it had simply changed.

Public mourning gave way to private grief. Up and down the soot-blackened terraces, behind the net curtains and beyond the thresholds of daily-scrubbed doorsteps, individual tragedies continued to unfold as parents and wives opened dreaded telegrams with trembling fingers.

"Regret to inform you…", that's how they began, a few sparse words which delivered a punch to the chest and a blow to the soul from which the recipient would never recover. Very occasionally there would be good news: a son or husband reported as missing, presumed dead, would surface in a prisoner of war camp, and then a different kind of agony would begin. In those dark days of the second half of 1943, there seemed no end in sight.

At Number 7 Stavordale Street, yards from where the first air raid of the war had destroyed part of Ilchester Street almost exactly three years before, Mr and Mrs Rochester had received word of the death of their son John, a sergeant with the Royal Corps of Signals in Greece, on 18 August. In the row of tiny miners' cottages which made up Australia Street, Seaham Colliery, Mrs Sarah Malkin received notification of the death of her twenty-seven-year-old husband, William, a sergeant in the Green Howards, during the invasion of Sicily on 5 August. Just around the corner in Doctors Street, the Bullimore family mourned the loss of their son Jonathan, a ship's cook on *HMS Limbourne*, sunk by Nazi U-boats in the English Channel, two days before his twenty-third birthday, on 23 October. In Polemarch Street, a short walk over the railway bridge from the Clyde family home, on 5 November, the widowed Mrs Moss received a telegram to inform her of the death of her only son, Albert. Albert had served as a flight engineer with 428 Squadron Bomber Command and had died in the same raid on Düsseldorf which had claimed Roy Tann and the Cameron crew. Like Roy, his aircraft had crashed in England, on the way home.

Sixty-three years before, an explosion at the local colliery had claimed the lives of 164 men and boys. Now, as then, there was barely a street which was untouched by grief and loss. For those families whose sons and husbands, brothers and fathers were held prisoner of war, the anguish never ended. Half alive, interminably distant, as ghosts within the walls of their own homes, their spiritual presence lingering, their physical presence longed for, with no hope of reunion. Letters and postcards flowed constantly between the imprisoned men and their families. Lots of Seaham ladies of all ages had volunteered to send regular letters to the town's prisoners of war. Edie Threadkell, the Clydes' next-door neighbour, wrote dozens. Amongst her personal effects is a postcard dated 12 August 1944, from a chap called Ernest Temple, written in pencil and bearing the stamp of the German military authorities. Edie was a friend of his parents who lived around the corner in Church Street and had known Ernest since he was a baby. Before he enlisted, Ernie had been the projectionist at the local cinema.

> *"Dear Edith,*
>
> *Just a card to let you know I'm still alive and kicking and think of you all occasionally. As you probably know, I'm a prisoner. I had a rough time in Italy, but things are better now thanks to the Red Cross. I met some Seaham men at this camp, so I have friends here.*
> *Best Wishes,*
> *Ernie"*

Mothers struggled to keep their absent husbands alive in the minds of their children; many who had perhaps been babies when war broke out had little or no recollection of their fathers; many more, conceived during a spell of leave, were yet to meet their daddies. Some never would.

On the mantelpiece, Lydia kept a large photograph of Jim in his uniform, which she would talk to every day, baby Moira in her arms. Moira would eventually come to refer to the photograph, when she learned to speak, as her "paper daddy".

Lydia hadn't seen Jim for well over a year. After the conclusion of the Battle of Tunis in May 1943, Jim had remained in North Africa with the rest of the Eighth Army, even as the Allies began to plan the invasion of Italy. Very intelligent, quick thinking and with an authoritative, no-nonsense manner, Jim had soon caught the eye of his superior officers and he had already been promoted to corporal. He was sent off on a mine warfare training course with his company sergeant and Regimental Sergeant Major. Jim learned quickly and passed with flying colours. Upon return to his unit, he was given the role of instructor, responsible for passing on his newly acquired knowledge to the rest of his company. Throughout the summer, now that the fighting in the desert was over, Jim was sent off to various units to train them in mine warfare – not just in the detection and rendering safe of these small but lethal weapons, but also in how to plan and lay out a minefield, and what sorts of mines should be used in particular circumstances, for example anti-personnel or anti-tank mines. It was ridiculously dangerous work, of which his family back at home had no inkling.

Jim soon became a valued and knowledgeable instructor, and was sent off with his RSM, a Geordie from Wallsend by the name of Armstrong, to train the Royal Corps of Signals in Constantine in Algeria. On arrival back at his unit, there was a letter waiting for him from Armstrong informing him that he'd been recommended for a commission. When the offer of a commission came, it was with an infantry regiment. Jim had no hesitation in declining, stating simply that he had absolutely "no intention of becoming cannon fodder," which must have raised a few eyebrows at Headquarters. Typical Jim. After five days' leave in Tunis, which he spent with lads from 213 Park Field Company, he received orders to assist in the clearing of a minefield just outside the city. There, in a field of maize littered with explosives, and due to the impetuousness of a young officer who wouldn't wait until Jim had completed his safety checks, he witnessed his friend and colleague Geordie Porterhouse being blown to pieces before his eyes.

So much worse was to come for Jim, horrors that he could never have imagined, and for which not even the desert war could have prepared him.

The battle for control of North Africa may have been won, but the Nazis still held sway over vast swathes of Europe, from the Atlantic coast of France in the west, to Norway in the north, and deep into Soviet territory in the east.

With the defeat of Italian and German forces in the desert campaign, and plans for the main invasion of France still being formulated, the Allied generals took the view that the best way to draw German troops away from the Eastern Front, where they had already suffered catastrophic losses, and thereby to give the Russians the best chance of victory, was to open up a second front in the Mediterranean theatre, by invading Italy, and then forcing the Germans who occupied that country to retreat northwards. Hundreds of thousands of Allied soldiers were already in the region, kicking their heels in units all along the North African coast, and Italy was the logical place to send them.

Allied troops had landed in Sicily in July 1943, suffering very heavy losses, and on the Italian mainland in September. The American Fifth Army, led by General Mark Clark, began its advance up the "toe" along the west coast, while the Eighth Army, led by Montgomery, made its way up the "heel" in the east, separated by the Apennine mountain range which runs the length of the country. The plan was to take Rome by the October, but the Allies made very slow and painful progress. The Italian Fascist dictator Mussolini had been arrested on the orders of the exiled King Victor Emmanuel in July 1943, immediately after the invasion of Sicily had begun, and the country descended into the chaos of civil war. The Italian Government capitulated on 3 September. Hitler, backed up by those Italian troops still loyal to the Fascist cause, poured his own men into the region to try to stem the Allied advance, in what quickly developed into one of the bloodiest and hardest-fought struggles of the war.

In September 1943, Jim had set sail on a troop ship from Tunisia bound for Taranto, in the very south of the country, in the second phase of the invasion. There was no prospect of any home leave; it was simply logistically impossible to send men back to Britain from North Africa and then require them to meet up with their units in Italy. Most men would not see home again until the end of the war, which, as autumn approached, must have seemed as far away as ever. Many, like Jim, had already been away for well over a year; all must have wondered if they would ever see their loved ones again. Jim's unit of Royal Engineers were sent in the advance party to clear roadways, construct bridges and clear minefields so that the main body of the force could then progress. From Taranto, they crossed quickly overland to Brindisi, then up the coast to the port city of Bari. They were subject to constant shelling and attacks from entrenched and experienced Nazi and Italian Fascist forces, over difficult and frequently mountainous terrain, in rapidly deteriorating weather.

Jim wrote letters home whenever he could, but these were sporadic and few and far between. When they did arrive, his words were always cheery and upbeat, with snippets of amusing stories about his mates and the places he had seen. The truth of what he had to endure remained unspoken. Sometimes small parcels would arrive, containing a little dress for Moira or a scarf or trinket for Lydia. Quite where Jim had managed to obtain such items Lydia was never sure. The Italian invasion received little coverage in the press back home, and all eyes were focused on the bombing campaign and the war in the East. Lydia struggled on her own at home, bringing up the baby by herself, looking after her father and little brother, George, while continuing to provide emotional and moral support to Jack. Roy's death had affected him deeply, and his sister had noticed him becoming increasingly withdrawn and unwilling, or unable, to talk about his time "away." Lydia was one of the lucky ones, though; she had a close network of female friends and relations to rely upon, not least her aunt and, of course, Edie. Some girls she knew were already widows.

Although the general populace was unaware, plans for the D-Day invasion were already well advanced. Even the workers of Seaham had their role to play. Just up the road from Caroline Street, and close to George Meek's cottage in the Londonderry Yard, Messrs Crompton and Harrison, Steel Fabricators, were contacted by government representatives to construct 600 steel booms. Mr Edward Crompton, one of the owners of the firm, related to the *Sunderland Echo* on 25 October 1945 how he was approached, in great secrecy, to make components for a job which was simply given the codename "Whale."[82]

"Special security measures were taken and no-one in Seaham knew what was afoot – not even the officials of the works. All we knew was that this job had to be finished by the end of March, 1944… with only five months to do it in, we worked night and day on this contract. All our units were electrically welded and to avoid infringing the black-out regulations we built a complete welding tent in the works, which could not be seen from above or from the ground.

Most of the finished articles went from the works by road. We had a fleet of eight- to ten-ton lorries which took our product to an unknown destination for assembly…"

---

82 The *Sunderland Echo* Archives, 25.10.1945.

For month upon month, day and night, George Meek could hear the constant clang of metal on metal, the high-pitched squeal of drilling and a never-ending parade of trucks rumbling in and out of the works yard. Neither he nor the workers of Crompton and Harrison knew that they had just built essential components for one of the most famous feats of modern engineering, the Mulberry Harbours positioned off the Normandy coast at Arromanches, without which the invasion on 6 June 1944 simply could not have succeeded. The Crompton and Harrison works still stands, now owned by Katmex Seaham Ltd. Steel is still fabricated there, seventy-five years later.

As Lydia and her family prepared for their fifth wartime Christmas – this time with both Jim and Jack absent – a distinguished visitor arrived in Seaham on 18 December, his tall but now slightly gaunt and stooped figure immediately recognisable. The townsfolk simply referred to him as "His Lordship" or "The Marquis;" to Lydia's father, John, he was simply "His Nibs," the description always accompanied with a contemptuous roll of the eyes. Lord Londonderry was back in town, this time to open the Christmas bazaar in the church hall. Discredited and ridiculed among his own class for his conduct before the war, he was deeply unpopular with many of the men he employed, and their families; some, like John Clyde, despised him, a legacy from the struggles and strikes of the 1920s and '30s. Just a few months before, in a desperate and ill-received attempt to restore his reputation, Londonderry had published *The Wings of Destiny*,[83] a book in which he once again had set out his vision for the development of the Air Force whilst in charge of the Air Ministry in the 1930s. He so desperately wanted to be proved right, and for others to accept that he had been badly done by when he had been removed

---

83   Londonderry, The *Wings of Destiny*, London, Macmillan & Co, 1943.

from the Cabinet. Whilst some of his views on the expansion of the Air Force may well have had some merit, given the benefit of hindsight, he was forever tainted by his associations with Nazi Germany and the policy of appeasement which he had promulgated so enthusiastically.

Privately, he remained extremely bitter towards his cousin Winston Churchill. Publicly, he praised him. Speaking to the parishioners and local dignitaries who had gathered in the draughty church hall on that icy Saturday afternoon, numbers somewhat depleted after an influenza epidemic had swept through the town, Londonderry paid tribute to the Prime Minister:

> *"He is imbued with the British spirit which never knows defeat and he is determined to fight the battle to the very end. He has helped us greatly by his speeches and broadcasts, and we all owe him a deep debt of gratitude for the splendid service he has rendered to the Nation."*[84]

Londonderry was clearly determined to fight his own battle to the very end too.

Beyond the wall of the churchyard, the bombed-out buildings of Sophia, Adolphus and Viceroy Streets were still clearly visible. Every time Jack came home on leave now, the ruined homes began to play upon his conscience with increasing regularity, so much so that he would avert his eyes or change his route so that he didn't have to look at them. Even when he returned to Melbourne, he found himself constantly replaying his own imagining of what had occurred in his hometown on the night of 16 May. One bomb. A single parachute mine had been responsible for the deaths of thirty-four people, people he knew. He began to try to compute the

---

84 *Durham Chronicle*, 19.12.1943.

number of bombs he and his crew had dropped over Germany.

One aircraft.

Eleven successful operations.

Maybe twelve bombs per aircraft.

Perhaps sixteen aircraft from his squadron per operation.

Seven hundred or so other aircraft.

Thousands upon thousands of Sophia, Adolphus and Viceroy Streets. Thousands upon thousands of families like the Corkhills. He was unable to remove from his mind the sight of entire cities alight, and the acrid smell of burning hung about him constantly like an aura, or so he fancied. It was always that first raid on Wuppertal, the glow of the firestorm visible from dozens of miles away, that weighed most heavily upon him. Old men, women, children, babies had perished, in the most horrific of circumstances – people just like his father, his sister, Lydia, his baby niece, Moira, and his next-door neighbours, Edie and Mrs Thornton. The nightmares troubled him infrequently at first but by now there were nights when he dreaded falling asleep, no matter how exhausted he was.

As he went about his business, running errands for Lydia down Church Street, or along Adelaide Row and Blandford Place, or calling in on friends and relations, he would often be collared by one of his father's workmates.

"Alreet, young Jackie? Are you home on leave AGAIN? There's a war on you know, son!"

21

Mephistopheles

Jack returned to Melbourne in the middle of November, with a very heavy heart. Still in shock at the loss of his friend and comrade, he struggled to come to terms with what had occurred. How could he and his crewmates continue without Roy? How would the crew be able to function without Roy's skills and knowledge and calmness under fire? Who else would have been able to get them home when the aircraft's instruments had failed or been shot up? The Pennicott crew operated as one fighting unit, a well-oiled machine. Each man knew that without Roy they would never have survived that very first mission to Wuppertal. Now they'd have to make do with whichever "spare bod" navigator was available and faced the distinct possibility that they would never fly with the same navigator twice until their tour was complete. Provided, of course, they lived that long.

The other crews on the squadron no longer sought out the Pennicott crew before a mission; there were no more pats on the back in the hope that the crew's good luck would somehow rub off. Their imagined invincibility had now disappeared, and Jack and the boys were revealed to be mere mortals, tarnished and vulnerable, the same as everyone else. No one ever dared refer to them as "the lucky crew" again. The spell had been broken. Penny, for one, was relieved.

At Headquarters, Air Marshal Arthur Harris had decided to focus the attentions of Bomber Command on sustained attacks on German cities, and in particular Berlin. Harris remained convinced that the destruction of the Nazi capital was vital to an Allied victory and could even shorten the war. The cost, in aircraft and lives, of both RAF airmen and German civilians, would prove to be monumental.

The Pennicott crew were not selected for operations until 25 November, a month after their last unsuccessful trip to Kassel. In the meantime, 10 Squadron's losses had continued to mount. Flight Sergeant Lindsey's crew had been shot down over France during a diversionary raid on Mannheim on 18 November. Two further aircraft were lost after a raid on the IG Farben chemical works in Leverkusen. Pilot Officer Lucas crash-landed his badly damaged aircraft in Sussex; miraculously all his crew survived, though several were injured. Flight Sergeant Holdsworth's crew crashed into a hangar while trying to land at Tangmere. All were killed instantly. A memorial to the Holdsworth crew has recently been unveiled there. Sixteen crews from the squadron took part in a raid on Berlin on 22 November. Those of Flying Officer Pont and Flying Officer Hall failed to return, with all crew members killed.[85]

Penny was informed on the morning of 25 November that his crew would be required for operations that evening, and that a temporary navigator, Sergeant Ryan, would be flying with

---

85   National Archives AIR/27/144 10 Sqn ORB November 1943.

them. None of the crew knew Ryan, although they'd seen his face in the canteen and in the Blacksmith's Arms on a couple of occasions. In the briefing hall, the assembled men sat awaiting news of their destination, the majority of them convinced that they'd be off to Berlin. There were no mutterings of relief when the Commanding Officer announced that their target was Frankfurt. Frankfurt, Cologne, Berlin, Hamburg… what did it matter anymore when survival was purely a question of luck? The more experienced crews understood life or death was simply a game of chance. No matter how skilled the pilot, no matter how adept the navigator or the flight engineer, each operation was a gamble against the most ridiculous odds, with the lives of the entire crew at stake.

Jack and the rest of the crew kitted up in silence that night. Upon collecting his two pigeons in their little wooden box, he decided that he would rename one of them Roy, although he kept this to himself. The other remained Walter, like all the others. As the crew trundled out to the airfield in the back of the transport truck towards their allocated aircraft, *M-Mother*, there was none of the usual chit-chat. Quite simply, nobody knew what to say. Even the groundcrew – Alec, Ronnie, Tommy and Norm and the others – usually full of witty jibes and bawdy jokes, were quiet. One by one, as each crew member scrambled up the short wooden ladder into the aircraft, hurling his kit up in front of him, before taking up his position, he cast a glance to the navigator's seat, now occupied by a stranger. Jack forced back tears as he settled into his cubbyhole beneath Penny, put on his headset and began his test transmissions.

At half past eleven, *M-Mother*, the aircraft whose instruments had failed the Pennicott crew on the trip to Kassel, accelerated along the main runway, heaving and shuddering under the weight of her bombload as her wheels lifted off the tarmac. The raid on Frankfurt was a relatively small one – only 262 aircraft took part – and was not a success, due to poor weather. Low-lying heavy cloud made target location difficult, and consequently the result of bombing was rather scattered. Twelve RAF aircraft were lost that night, eleven Halifaxes and one Lancaster. On this occasion the men of 10 Squadron were spared, and all returned safely to base. Flying conditions had been treacherous.

On return to Melbourne, Jack had recorded in his logbook:

"FRANKFURT. Target not seen, bombed on ETA. Severe icing in clouds, temperature was several degrees below minus 35. Rather a wasted effort."

In his official briefing report, Penny confirmed that *M-Mother* had bombed Frankfurt a little before three o'clock in the morning, from a height of 20,000 feet. The results of their efforts were not seen due to cloud. They'd encountered moderate flak but thankfully the searchlights had been largely ineffective.

In the cramped and isolated tail gunner's position, poor Bill had half frozen to death. The condensation created by breathing into his oxygen mask had caused icicles to form from his chin all the way down to his chest; every time he moved his head or attempted to manoeuvre his guns, the ice would dislodge his mask and he would struggle for breath. Jack kept him awake on the return leg by singing to him over the intercom and getting Bill to join in with the chorus. The whole crew would chip in from time to time and Ryan, the stand-in navigator, thought them all quite deranged, especially their singing wireless operator.

Jack and the boys were stood down for the following evening's raid on Stuttgart. All crews had returned safely, and then as winter took hold of northern England, there were no more operations for a week. As November drew to a close, Flight Sergeant Thackray and his men (one of the crews for whom Leo Groark and his groundcrew men were responsible) successfully completed their tour and were transferred out. Only five 10 Squadron crews completed their tour in the whole of 1943, although some crews had been transferred to Pathfinder and other squadrons.

On 3 December, a window in the weather meant that operations were back on. That morning, George Phillipson had been working out the crew's leave dates over the next month; he was desperate to get back home to his wife, Ethel, in the East End for Christmas, but it wasn't to be. He broke the news to the rest of the crew in the canteen at lunchtime that they'd be spending Christmas at Melbourne. Jack and Ken were crestfallen, but Freddie wasn't bothered; he was 10,000 miles away from home, so leave or no leave, he wasn't going anywhere. The squadron Medical Officer, Dr Ponder, had just signed him off flying for a month due to a severe sinus infection; whilst he relished the opportunity of being able to take full part in any festivities, he also knew that this would delay the completion of his tour, and that he'd probably have to stay on another month or so after the others were finished – if they finished. Penny was concerned that he was now going to be two regular crew members down; as well as having to rely on a stand-in navigator, he was now missing his regular mid-upper gunner.

Just to cheer up the proceedings yet further, Penny then summoned the crew and told them they'd be flying that night. Rumours abounded among the groundcrew as to the target; once again, they knew from the calculations they'd been issued for fuel and bombloads that it was likely to be a long trip. Jack had assumed they'd be going to Berlin. Surely it was their turn by now? Later that evening as the curtain was pulled back from the huge map in the briefing room, there were murmurings of surprise as Leipzig was revealed to be their target.

"Where? Thought that was in bleedin' Russia!" muttered George.

As one, the crew glanced at their "spare bod" navigator that evening, Flying Officer Duchesney, wondering if he could be relied upon to get them to the heart of Saxony in the far east of Germany, and home again. Sergeant Bywaters, their relief gunner, sat impassively; inwardly, he was both terrified at the prospect of such a long trip, and was also very apprehensive about flying with a new crew. To make matters worse for Penny, he'd been informed that Wing Commander Ayling would be flying with them that evening as Second Pilot. He'd already warned the crew to be on their best behaviour and not to use any bad language, whatever difficulties they might find themselves in.

Five hundred and twenty-seven aircraft were detailed for the Leipzig raid, including sixteen from 10 Squadron. Wing Commander Ayling wasn't the only VIP involved in the raid; the famous American journalist Ed Morrow, whose broadcasts from London at the height of the Blitz had done much to inform American opinion in the early days of the war, was on board a Lancaster belonging to 619 Squadron. Although it wasn't unheard of for journalists to go along on raids for publicity purposes, this was a brave decision by Morrow. The night before, two reporters had been killed when their Lancaster had been shot down over Berlin.

At twenty-five to midnight, *M-Mother*, her mixed bag of crew and their VIP took off from Melbourne. Their orders were to head towards Berlin, then to make a right turn and fly southeast to Leipzig. A small diversionary force of Mosquitoes flew on to the capital, enough to draw the Luftwaffe night fighters away from the main bomber stream, but losses were still heavy.

Leipzig was, and is, a beautiful city. Although the surrounds now bear testament to the brutalist architecture of over sixty years of Soviet control, the old town is a maze of baroque and medieval architecture, of alleyways and courtyards. The walls of the Thomaskirch echo with the music of one of the city's most celebrated sons, Johann Sebastian Bach, who lies there still. In a side street just around the corner from the white-gabled and red-roofed Rathaus, down a steep set of steps in a beautiful arcade now filled with designer shops, you will find the 500-year-old Auerbachs Keller. Beneath its vaulted ceilings, in a dark corner behind the stone pillars, Faust plotted to sell his soul to the devil Mephistopheles, in the German writer Goethe's dramatic retelling of the legend. Goethe was a regular visitor to the Keller while a student at Leipzig University in the 1700s, and the long evenings spent in Auerbachs provided inspiration for his writing. Three hundred years later, it's still a bustling bar and restaurant, serving typical German fare (accompanied by huge steins of beer) to hundreds of locals and tourists every week, its whitewashed walls now decked with Faustian imagery.

In the early hours of 4 December 1943, like many of the old town's cellars, it was filled to bursting point with terrified German civilians, mainly women, children and the elderly. The air raid siren had sounded around four o'clock in the morning, and across the city families gathered up their children and fled, some down into their basements, others into the busy municipal air raid shelters.

Across town from Auerbachs, five-year-old Elke Rau's parents had slept through the first siren. She later recalled that she had been the first of the family to wake up and was horrified to see that her bedroom window had been shattered and that the curtains were on fire.

"My parents quickly wrapped us in blankets and carried us down four flights of stairs to the air raid shelter. The door was already closed but after much banging and hammering the air raid warden opened the door and let us in with a flea in our collective ear for being so late. He wasn't too pleased later when my parents begged him to let them go back up to our apartment as we only had our nightclothes on and we didn't have our 'cellar bag' with us which contained all our important documents, medicines and clothes. It was a very long 20 minutes before they returned but they explained that they had helped other neighbours to put out a firebomb which had landed on the house.

We heard an awfully loud noise and thought our house had been hit but it was 'only' the house next door. A few minutes later the next door neighbours broke through the firewall and climbed over into our cellar. They were all badly shaken up, especially a young woman with a baby in her arms which was screaming very loudly… We left the cellar in the morning and set off for my grandparents' house which was a few streets away. My parents put a blindfold on both of us so we couldn't see the horrors of what had occurred, but it couldn't stop the stink which was all pervasive and still lives with me today."[86]

Elke and her family were later evacuated to the Erz mountains, where they remained until the end of the war.

The scenes described by Elke Rau were repeated across the city. In the next neighbourhood, six-year-old Regina Mathees had gone to stay with her grandparents on the morning of 3 December, while her parents were at work. Decades later, Regina recounted what had occurred that night.

---

86   University of Leipzig Archives.

"I went to bed quite early and after my Grandmother read me a goodnight story I fell fast asleep. In the middle of the night (I later found out that it was 3.50am) I was shaken out of my sleep by the sirens. I was so tired and began to cry. My grandparents comforted me but got me out of bed and insisted we go downstairs to the cellar. The bombs were falling all around and on the way down to the cellar we saw that the house behind ours had caught fire. I screamed and panicked and was shaking all over. Whilst my Grandfather and other occupants of the house attempted to extinguish the fire my grandmother took me down to the cellar. She tried her best to comfort me but I was so tired and exhausted and I couldn't comprehend what was happening. I started to cry for my best friend, Susanne.

My Grandfather came into the cellar and he had Susanne with him but her parents were not with her. I later found out that they had been killed, something which I just couldn't understand. Susanne and I comforted each other and although the bombs continued to fall we sang songs together which helped us a lot.

When the all clear sounded my Grandmother brought Susanne and me upstairs to our apartment and put us to bed. We were luckier than a lot of people who had lost everything in that terrible night.

My mother came to collect me on the 5th December, worried that something might have happened to us. She told us about the terrible scenes of devastation in the town, all the homeless people and children crying for their parents. We took Susanne home with us and as we went through the town we could see all the demolished houses and the tram wasn't operating. My mother tried to take our mind off it all by telling us funny stories but it didn't work, we just cried and cried and cried."[87]

---

87 Ibid.

(In February 1944 Susanne was evacuated to Dresden. She died in the air raid on 14 February 1945.)

The Pennicott crew had bombed Leipzig at 3.56am, six minutes after Regina Mathees and her grandparents had been awoken by the sirens. Pennicott's report in the Squadron Operations Record Book simply states:

> "Bombed Leipzig over heavy cloud at 0356 hours from 19,000 feet... Ten minutes after bombing the glow of fires was seen in marked area. Some moderate flak was encountered in target area. Searchlights were ineffective due to cloud."[88]

Jack noted:

> "LEIPZIG. 10/10th cloud cover over practically the whole trip – target pranged well – defences moderate."

From a military point of view, the raid was a success, with many factories and industrial buildings destroyed, including a Junkers aircraft factory. The exact number of civilians who perished in the raid is unknown, with figures of 614, 1182 and even 1800 being quoted by German sources. Thousands more were injured and made homeless. The older parts of the city were ravaged by a firestorm; much of what can be seen today has been rebuilt. That the death toll was not much higher was due, in part, to civilians coming out of their cellars and shelters to assist with putting out fires; had they remained there, there is every likelihood that they would have been suffocated or incinerated.

Twenty-five aircraft and their crews were lost that night. Although Leipzig was not particularly well defended, many of the Halifaxes and Lancasters had strayed into the heavy

---

88   National Archives AIR/27/144 10 Sqn ORB 3.12.1944.

defences over Frankfurt on the return leg and were brought down by a combination of Luftwaffe night fighters and flak. Of the sixteen crews who had left Melbourne the night before, only fifteen returned. Pilot Officer Walker's crew were shot down, with only Sergeant Brock and Sergeant McNeil surviving. Both were captured after baling out.

Bad weather meant that the 10 Squadron crews enjoyed a lengthy break from operational flying, until the week before Christmas. Although the winter weather meant that operational flying wasn't possible, the airmen were kept busy with daytime training sorties. On 11 and 12 December, Jack and the boys were once again aboard *M-Mother*, taking part in air/sea firing tests and practising with the H2S navigation systems.

Upon landing after a local flying exercise on 12 December, Penny had been collared by one of his superiors on his way into the Officers' Mess. He was given the news that he and his crew had been allotted a permanent replacement for Roy. During lunch, Penny mulled over how best to approach the issue with his crew, as he was unsure how they might react. He had good reason to deal with the matter sensitively.

The Pennicott crew's new navigator was Reg Cowles.

22
The Navigator

Reg Cowles was a year older than Jack. Born in Walthamstow in East London, the youngest of five children, he was a butcher's son, like Penny and Roy. The blood and bustle of Smithfield meat market was not for him, though; he was a bright lad and had done well at school. Reg had enlisted in the Royal Air Force in 1941 and was sent off to Canada and America to complete his navigator's training. He had arrived at 10 Squadron in June 1943 just a few weeks after the Pennicott crew and had already completed nineteen operations. Reg was well known at Melbourne. Small in stature, with a friendly, open face, he always wore a navy paisley silk scarf under his leather flying jacket and had acquired a reputation as something of an "ace." Awarded the Distinguished Flying Cross for his exploits with the Cameron crew just a few months earlier after the crash-landing on the return from the Hannover raid, he was now the sole survivor.

For his part, Reg was anxious about the reception he might receive from the Pennicott crew. Would they welcome him?

Would they tolerate his presence among them simply because they had to? Most of all, he feared their open hostility – would they blame him for Roy's death? All concerned knew full well that Roy would have still been alive had he not been required to replace Reg in Cameron's crew that night. Tortured by feelings of guilt and grief, he had privately voiced his concerns to Penny before the news was made public.

He need not have worried. Penny had already spoken to Jack, Ken, George, Bill and Freddie, and not one of the crew had raised any objections. Roy could never be replaced of course, but Reg was welcomed warmly. The younger members of the crew were slightly in awe of him, but each man knew that he was in safe hands with Reg. Penny reassured them that if he could have chosen any navigator within the squadron, it would have been Reg Cowles. Within days, Penny's confidence in his new navigator would be put to the test.

The newly configured crew flew together for the first time operationally less than seven weeks after Roy's death. On 20 December, Penny was notified that his crew had been detailed for that evening's operation, in company with a "Second Joe," new pilot Flying Officer Large. Penny was always very sympathetic towards the new chaps; just seven months before he had been in their position on that first nerve-wracking trip to the Ruhr Valley. Seven months now felt like seven lifetimes, and he was always happy to share the benefit of his experience and provide calm, measured advice if it was sought.

The crew were fully expecting to be sent to Berlin but sat impassively in the briefing hall that evening when their target was revealed to be Frankfurt. This was yet another "maximum effort" raid for 10 Squadron, with twenty-one crews rostered. Jack reflected upon his family at home, and the preparations for Christmas that Lydia had described in her most recent letter, which had arrived that morning, now folded up and stuffed into his breast pocket. He thought about the people of Frankfurt and wondered if they had decorated trees in their parlours, whether the women of the family would be busy baking like his sister. He tried without success to erase from his mind the thought of thousands of burning Christmas trees, the carefully wrapped gifts laid beneath them consumed by flames, showered in broken glass and falling masonry.

M-Mother was airborne early that winter afternoon. At half past four she was already rumbling along the runway with her new navigator, and her second pilot who had come along for the ride.[89] This was Reg Cowles' first operation since the rest of his crew were killed; if he was upset or afraid, he didn't show it. Reg was the master of the "stiff upper lip," the consummate professional, always with a ready smile. He fitted into the Pennicott crew perfectly, and showed no emotion, entirely focused on his job. Inside, he was quietly dying, a convoluted mess of nerves, fear and grief. Penny knew of course; they all did.

The operation did not get off to a good start for 10 Squadron; two crews were unable to take off due to their aircraft being unserviceable. German fighter control had detected the incoming bomber stream of 650 Lancasters and Halifaxes almost as soon as they had left the protection of the Suffolk coast over Southwold, and continued to track the force all the way to its intended target, with the result that Luftwaffe fighters had already been scrambled as the bomber crews passed over the Dutch shoreline into enemy territory. Many aircraft were attacked before they ever even reached Frankfurt. The clear weather forecast issued to the crews prior to departure proved to be wildly inaccurate, and there was heavy cloud, which meant that the Pathfinder ground-marking flares couldn't be seen properly. On the ground, the

---

89   National Archives AIR/27/144 10 Sqn ORB 20.12.1943.

German defenders lit a decoy site (a large area of burning material usually in a rural area, just close enough to the actual target to confuse incoming bomber crews) five miles to the southeast of the city, and also used dummy target indicators. Although some of the bombing hit the decoy zone, there was significant creepback, which meant that many residential areas and the historic centre of the city were bombed, instead of the important factories and industrial sites which had been the intended targets. "Creepback" was a regular phenomenon; bomb aimers would often release their bombs too soon when they spotted fires on the ground, with the result that the effects of bombing were seen in an area wider than the original intended target. German reports indicate that 466 houses were destroyed; there was also significant damage to the cathedral, city library, hospital and sixty-nine schools. Twenty-three thousand people were made homeless, and at least sixty-four were killed.[90]

Sergeant O'Connor and his crew in *O-Orange* had become hopelessly lost due to an error in windspeed calculation and had bombed Mannheim instead. Many crews encountered similar problems. In *M-Mother*, Penny had had to rely on a combination of Reg's calculations as to their estimated time of arrival over the target area, the HS2 navigation system and what few target indicators they could see through the dense cloud. In addition to the circling night fighters, there was also heavy anti-aircraft fire directly over the city, but the poor weather thankfully hindered the operation of searchlights. The Squadron Operations Record Book records that the Pennicott crew had observed, "... *red explosions in the target area at 19.38 hours and 19.49 hours. The glow of fires was also visible.*" *M-Mother* had also been stalked for the entire duration

---

90 Middlebrook, M. and Everritt, C., *The Bomber Command War Diaries*, Pen & Sword Aviation, Barnsley, 2014, p. 460.

of her bombing run by a Junkers 88, but no incoming fire was reported either by Freddie, who was back in his usual position in the mid-upper gunner's turret, or by Bill in the tail.[91] The trip home was much quieter, with fewer night fighters around, and the Pennicott crew landed safely back at Melbourne a little after eleven o'clock. Flying Officer Large, who had flown as "Second Joe," was ashen-faced, wondering how on earth he would ever get through his tour. As matters turned out, he would be dead within the month.

Upon landing, Jack noted in his logbook:

"*RAID ON FRANKFURT (14) Defences moderate – target illuminated by fighter flares and searchlights; one JU 88 sighted over target area – rather a scattered prang.*"

As the returning crews were debriefed and supplied with sandwiches and tea laced with rum, it became increasingly apparent that it had been a dreadful night for the men of 10 Squadron. After Sergeant Fenny and his crew landed twenty minutes before midnight in *Y-Yorker*, no further aircraft were heard to make their approach. No calls came in from other airfields to report the safe arrival of stragglers or damaged aircraft. The WAAFs and air traffic control staff were stood down at two o'clock in the morning. Three aircraft and their crews had failed to return, those of Pilot Officer Whitmarsh, Sergeant Borthwick and Sergeant Morris.

Thirty-year-old Whitmarsh and his crew were among the most experienced and popular crews on the squadron. They'd arrived at Melbourne in the same week as Reg Cowles; Frankfurt was their sixteenth operation. All were killed instantly when their aircraft, *K-King*, crashed near Dahlen. Leo Groark and his groundcrew team were devastated as

---

91   National Archives AIR/27/144 10 Sqn ORB 20.12.1943.

K-King was one of the aircraft they maintained, and they knew Whitmarsh (who had been an aeronautical engineer himself before the war) and his boys well. They now lie together at the Rheinberg War Cemetery in Germany. Sergeant Borthwick's crew had taken part in just four other raids. Borthwick was killed along with three of his crewmen; he was just twenty-two. Three others survived and were taken prisoner. Sergeant Morris and his men had only arrived at the squadron on 30 November. Morris went down with his aircraft but four of his crew had managed to bale out successfully and were captured. This had been their first, and only, operation. Their families received notification that their boys were missing, presumed dead, on Christmas Eve.

For Jack, Frankfurt had simply been one more operation to tick off the list. In the seven months that the Pennicott crew had been on the squadron, thirty-nine aircraft and their crews had been lost. The odds were poor indeed, but he took heart from the fact that Flying Officer Goodall and his lads had completed their tour earlier in December. It *was* possible. But only just.

Traditional Christmas dinner was served in the mess, followed by the usual boozing, dancing and high jinks. As the pints were downed the bravado increased; WAAFs were chatted up amid the haze of cigarette and pipe smoke, the occasional punch-up breaking out between rivals for their affections. There was noise and laughter everywhere as the gramophone belted out the popular tunes of the day. Beneath the façade of frivolity, every man knew that the chances of his seeing another Christmas were slim.

The bombing campaign against Berlin was already well underway and was about to be stepped up. A raid on 23 December had not involved the men of 10 Squadron, but on 29 December, the Commanding Officer at Melbourne was notified that his aircraft would be required for another "maximum effort" attack on the Nazi capital. Twenty crews were rostered, but again the Pennicott crew were surplus to requirements. Nineteen of the twenty crews reported successfully bombing the target, although opposition was heavy. Flight Sergeant Burcher in *P-Peter* lost an engine after his aircraft was hit by flak; at virtually the same moment, two incendiaries dropped from another aircraft at a slightly higher altitude went straight through the fuselage, causing significant damage. Astonishingly, he and his crew made it home safely. Flight Sergeant Green and his crew were not so lucky. A lurking Luftwaffe night fighter had spotted them over Holland on their way out to Berlin. They were shot down, with no survivors, on their eighth trip.[92]

As 1944 dawned the plans for the Allied invasion in June, Operation Overlord, were already well advanced, in the utmost secrecy. General Eisenhower arrived in London in mid-January to assume command of the United States forces in Europe. On the Eastern Front, the siege of Leningrad was almost at an end, at the cost of over two million lives; in the Baltic states the Red Army was making advances against the overstretched and poorly supplied German Wehrmacht, and on 4 January the 1st Ukrainian Front entered Poland. Slowly, the tide was turning for the Allies, but thousands of American, Canadian, British and Commonwealth troops were bogged down in Italy, where the advance had almost ground to a halt due to the desperate winter weather, a determined, well-trained and well-dug-in enemy, harsh terrain and an unending sea of mud. Operation Shingle, the attempt to establish a more northerly front behind the German lines at Anzio, was an abject failure. The Allies incurred huge losses and were unable to break out of the beachhead until the end of May. Jack's brother-in-law,

---

92   National Archives AIR/27/144 10 Sqn ORB 29/30.12.1943.

Jim Groark, and his unit of Royal Engineers had been ordered cross-country to take part in the campaign to break through the German Gustav Line, where X Corps had launched the first of their attacks along the Gari River, under the shadow of Monte Cassino. Both British and American attempts to cross the river had resulted in massive casualties.

At Bomber Command HQ, concerns had been mounting for some time regarding the very high numbers of Mark II Halifaxes being lost in combat operations. The new Mk III was about to be phased in to replace it, but in the meantime, a decision was made to try to limit the number of Mk II Halifaxes taking part in bombing raids over Germany. As a result, 10 Squadron's older Halifaxes were detailed for more "gardening" missions; however, when there was a "maximum effort" raid planned, such as an attack on Berlin, it was a matter of all hands to the pump, and 10 Squadron were expected to do their bit, whatever the cost. The top brass at Melbourne had been informed that they would begin receiving the new aircraft at the beginning of March, but that was still two months away. In the interim, they and the other squadrons in their group simply had to make the best of it.

For the Pennicott crew, January began with a flurry of activity. A brief weather window in the first week of that month allowed Jack and the boys to resume regular flying, and on 3 January they took part in an air/sea firing exercise. The next day they were on ferry duty, taking one aircraft to Hethel, and ferrying *M-Mother*, which had landed there on a previous trip, back to base. Just after lunch on 7 January, Penny was informed that his crew would be required for that night's operation. Once again, the boys had mentally prepared themselves for the "Big One" – Berlin – but were mightily relieved to learn that they would in fact be undertaking gardening operations, minelaying around the Frisian Islands.

The mission was unusual in that they were given a take-off time of twenty past four in the morning; normally they were almost home by that sort of time, but minelaying was of course weather and tide dependent, and subject to the whims of the Admiralty. Penny expressed some concerns that it might be growing light by the time they left the islands, and that they would be sitting ducks for any waiting flak ships. In any event he advised the rest of the crew to try to get a few hours' sleep before their very early start.

Seven crews instead of the usual five were detailed to take part in this gardening operation. At four o'clock in the morning the Halifaxes made their way towards the main runway; they took off only seconds apart, and all were airborne by twenty-five past four, heading towards the coast at Hornsea. Each was laden with two 1500-pound mines, to be carefully planted at the appointed spot. For six of the seven crews, the operation was perfectly routine, although Flying Officer Taylor's crew brought their mines back with them, unable to pinpoint their dropping zone with any accuracy, due to heavy cloud.[93]

Just as *M-Mother* was seconds away from her drop zone, all hell broke loose. The sky was suddenly lit up with the criss-cross of searchlight beams and a deadly cloud of exploding flak shells. The noise was so ear-shattering that the crew could barely hear Ken's confirmation, "Bombs gone."

"Three, repeat three flak ships to port at eight o'clock, and they're bloody close!" yelled Freddie from the mid-upper turret; he was the only man in the crew with a 360-degree view of what was going on, and had spotted the enemy vessels illuminated by their own searchlights and anti-aircraft fire just a couple of miles away. The words had barely left his mouth when there was a huge bang and *M-Mother* shuddered and jerked.

---

93   National Archives AIR/27/145 10 Sqn ORB 7.1.1944.

"Everyone alright? Crew report in," ordered Penny.

"Bomb aimer here."

"Navigator here."

"Flight engineer here."

"Wireless operator here."

"Mid-upper gunner here."

There was no reply from Bill in the rear turret.

"Tail gunner, please report in. Bill. Are you there, Bill?"

Silence.

"Clyde, go and check on Bill please."

Jack unclipped his intercom and his oxygen mask, slid off his headphones and began to clamber to the rear of the aircraft, terrified at the thought of what might await him. His heart was in his mouth as he hammered on the panel at the rear of the turret. Almost immediately the turret slid around and there was Bill, half frozen but smiling as usual, and very much alive.

"Hello, Jack, is it sandwich time already?"

Bill's intercom had become disconnected, and he simply hadn't heard Penny's request. Jack grinned, plugged Bill back in, and returned to his wireless cubbyhole.

The crew's problems were far from over. The aircraft's navigational equipment had been rendered largely useless; both Reg and George suspected that one of the aerials had been damaged by the flak barrage, although fortunately apart from a few holes in the main body of the fuselage, the damage to *M-Mother* had been relatively slight. Reg had to draw upon all his skills and experience as a navigator as it was still dark, the aircraft was over the North Sea and there were no landmarks visible along the distant enemy coast. Jack had had the presence of mind to take a radio bearing when the flak ships were first sighted; using this information, and navigating by the few stars visible, Reg was able to plot a course for home.

It was already light when Freddie spotted the coast ahead, and *M-Mother* touched down at Melbourne at nine o'clock in the morning, just in time for a late breakfast.

In his subsequent debrief report for the Squadron Operations Record Book, Penny noted:

"*Laid mines in allotted area at 0621 hours from 6000 feet, by means of HS2 fix on east end of Nordeney. Weather was 5/10ths cloud with clear patches. Aircraft was engaged by three flak ships with accurate heavy flak two miles port of track. Ships position 54.04 north by 07.13 East at 0622 hours. Enemy fire lasted about four minutes, but no damage was sustained except that the trailing aerial was shot away.*"[94]

For his part Jack wrote the following typically understated entry in his logbook after breakfast:

"*MINELAYING – Frisian Is. (15)*
    Slight flak opposition from flak ships – no damage or casualties."

In fact, the Pennicott crew had had such a narrow escape that Reg Cowles' navigational heroics that morning would subsequently be specifically mentioned in the official citation for the Bar to his Distinguished Flying Cross.

Fifteen operations down.

Halfway.

---

94 *Ibid.*

23

The Big One

In the Gesundbrunnen district of Berlin there is a large park, created in the nineteenth century, and named after the eminent natural historian Alexander von Humboldt. On the very edge of the park, far beyond the swimming pool and the children's play area, past the rose gardens, the snaking footpaths and the shrubbery, there lies a huge mound, now partially covered with trees and undergrowth. A walk around the mound reveals a vast grey concrete structure, reminiscent of two towers of a medieval castle, but now battered and worn and covered in graffiti. The occasional twist of rusted metal thrusts skywards, as if trying to escape from its concrete prison, providing some hint as to this building's dark history. A steep pedestrian ramp affords access to the very top, from which the determined visitor can gain a spectacular view of the entire city, laid out like a model village before him.

This is what remains of the Humboldthain *Flakturm*, one of eight enormous anti-aircraft towers constructed in Berlin,

Hamburg and Vienna, between 1941 and 1943. In 1940, when the RAF first began to bomb Berlin, Hitler personally sketched the designs and gave orders for the construction of these gargantuan buildings, which also doubled as barracks and air raid shelters for as many as 10,000 civilians; there was even a hospital on one of the floors. Part of his twisted vision of the future mega-city of Germania, it was anticipated that after the Nazi victory, the flak towers would be used for civilian purposes and leisure activities, pleasure castles for the master race. For that reason, the Humboldthain tower included small windows in its design, covered by steel shutters which were intended to be replaced by glass when the hostilities were over. Seventy metres square with a flat-topped turret at each corner, the flak tower was some five storeys high, with walls of concrete eleven feet thick, and was designed to be indestructible.

Built by slave labourers from the work and concentration camps in just six months (many of whom were worked, literally, to death), the tower bristled with anti-aircraft (flak) guns; two 128mm guns, which could fire shells a distance of eight miles, were positioned on each corner turret, with numerous smaller-calibre cannons on the lower-level platforms. A signal tower a short distance away picked up incoming aircraft by radar and electronically relayed the co-ordinates directly to the guns, which swung around automatically and began firing into the sky at a rate of 800 rounds per minute. There were two other such towers in the centre of Berlin, one in the Tiergarten and the other at Friedrichshain, forming an almost impenetrable triangle of air defences over the city; when fully operational, the sky was filled with so much exploding metal that it would have been suicide for any Bomber Command aircraft to go anywhere near it. Many did stray into this airspace while trying to avoid pursuing night fighters, or when off course due to the confusion of battle, and paid the ultimate price.

Jack and the rest of the Pennicott crew knew full well that it was simply a matter of time before it was their turn to run the gauntlet of Berlin's air defences. Purely by chance, the luck of the draw, they had managed to avoid it thus far. Throughout December and then into January, the Nazi capital had been attacked, night after night. After a week's leave in the middle of January 1944, the boys were back at Melbourne. By now they were the most experienced crew on the squadron. Rumours abounded amongst the other crews that Penny and his men had somehow been singled out for special treatment, that they were being rostered only for the "easy" ops as the Commanding Officer was anxious to get another crew through a full tour. On the afternoon of 28 January, those rumours were swiftly put to bed when the twenty-two crews assembled in the briefing hall were informed that their target that night was the heart of darkness itself, Berlin. The very fact that there were so many men crammed into the hall meant that the announcement came as no surprise; a "maximum effort" raid was to take place, and Berlin was the most likely target. Many of the crews present had flown to Berlin just eight days earlier; two of the squadron's crews had failed to return from that trip, those of Sergeant Arthur and Sergeant Crothers.

It was with no small amount of apprehension that Jack headed off to the locker room to get "kitted up" that evening. The mood in the crew was quiet, but determined, each man believing that if he could survive the trip to Berlin, he could survive anything. Every one of them had his own tic, his own individual foible which betrayed his nervousness. Bill would chatter more than usual, Ken would fiddle with his tie, and Jack would twist his mother's rose gold wedding band around his finger incessantly, as he always did when anxious or frightened.

Incredibly, there exists a record of one of the crew's state of mind immediately prior to the Berlin raid. Years later, Freddie Singh recalled:

> "I had done quite a few ops, but never to Berlin. I suppose I knew that it would only be a matter of time before it would come up. However, I'll never forget that briefing, when the curtain covering the map of Europe was swept aside and there, the tapes ran to a great, evil-looking, blood-red blob – Berlin, the Big City!
>
> I remember quite well how I broke into a cold sweat – and yet a feeling of relief. At last. How would I go? I was fairly confident of my ability as an air gunner by this time, but Berlin! This was different. If I could handle this one, then I could handle anything, whispered the youthful voice of self-confidence – and yet a little more fear than usual ran through me.
>
> That night, before we took off, I know my turret had an extra polish. My guns were in perfect condition – and that left only me."[95]

At two minutes to midnight, the Pennicott crew took to the air in *M-Mother*, which had now been designated their preferred aircraft. *Z-Zebra* was only used on operations as a last resort, as it had suffered extensive damage and had been patched up dozens of times. Z was now one the oldest Halifaxes on the station and was coming to the end of its operational life. 10 Squadron's aircraft were among some of the last to take off on the Berlin raid; such was the size of the raid, in terms of numbers of aircraft, that some squadrons had taken off when it was still light. Six hundred and seventeen bombers took their place in the bomber stream over the North Sea. A handful of twin-engine Mosquito bombers had carried out a preliminary raid earlier that evening, designed to confuse the German defenders

---

95 Middlebrook, Martin, *The Berlin Raids: RAF Bomber Command Winter 1943-44*, Viking/Penguin, London, 1988, pp. 33-34.

into thinking that that was it for the night's operations. The circuitous route taken by the RAF's bombers over Northern Denmark meant that attacks by night fighters on the outward route were fairly isolated, but by the time they began to approach the target area, the "Wilde Sau" Luftwaffe fighters were ready and waiting to pick them off over the city. The earlier raid had been much too small to befuddle the German controllers, who were quite expecting "the full works" later that night.

The Berlin raid got off to a bad start for 10 Squadron. Burgess and his crew in *C-Charlie* couldn't even take off due to a problem with the engine coolant. Of the remaining twenty-one aircraft, only eleven successfully bombed Berlin; on one of the worst nights of the entire campaign for the squadron, four aircraft and their crews failed to return, those of Sergeant O'Connor (his aircraft had crashed in Denmark on the outward trip), Sergeant Ling, Flying Officer Large and twenty-year-old Australian, Flight Lieutenant Neville Kilsby. Ten crewmen survived and were captured, including Pilot Officer Don Shipley, the tail gunner in Kilsby's crew. Shipley's description of his escape from the burning Halifax *D-Dog* is nothing short of terrifying:

> *"Unless you have ever been over a target area, you have not experienced the pandemonium that it is, with the searchlights coming in all directions, the bombs exploding, the flak hitting the aircraft, bombers coming in all directions at all levels, enemy fighters coming in, and having to watch the flares laid by the Pathfinders. In all, Hell let loose...*
>
> *We were attacked on the bomb run and one of our engines caught fire. Our skipper, Flight Lieutenant Kilsby, never panicked. We immediately dived and successfully put out the flames. He then did another circuit to bring us back onto the bombing route again; he was a beauty.*

Then, all of a sudden, there came the same chatter of the fighter's cannon which I will never forget till my dying day. He hit us from underneath and ignited the overload tanks carried in a portion of our bomb bays. The skipper, strict commander and split-second thinker that he was, knew of the immediate danger and gave the command to bale out…

We were going down fast. I could see one or two chutes opening, the flames coming back, the heat searing, the slipstream, being so strong, was frightening. I therefore was faced with it and I threw myself backwards to get out of this burning hulk. To my horror, I was caught up by my right leg, which was trapped, which was lectured to me many times, in the walls of the turret. This was a terrifying experience to me, as at that time the flames and the slipstream were overpowering. Even though I clawed at the sides of the turret, I was excluded from gaining entrance to free my entrapped leg. I was faced with death… The last things I can remember are the frantic attempts to get back in, the flames which were engulfing me and my despairing appeal to God… My life passed before me: people and events of years gone by were graphically depicted. It was so real. My darling mother, father, fiancée and family, all flashing before me. I knew my number was up. The next thing I can recall was seeing enormous flames and my first thoughts were that I was in Hell. But, all of a sudden, silhouetted against the flames was a Gerry helmet and Gerry soldier standing guard beside me.

Five of us got out; God only knows what happened to our poor brave skipper, Bill Kilsby, and our newly married wireless operator, Syd Daggett, whose charred bodies were found huddled together in the wireless operator's section in the remains of our burnt-out Halifax."[96]

---

96 Extract from 10 Squadron Association Newsletters, and Middlebrook, Martin, *The Berlin Raids: RAF Bomber Command Winter 1943-44*, Viking/Penguin, London, 1988, pp. 245-246.

The squadron had lost seven aircraft, and forty-nine men, in the space of just a week.

But what of the Pennicott crew? It transpired that Jack and the boys had had yet another narrow escape. Lady Luck was still on their side. Having taken off just before midnight, they were back at Melbourne well before three o'clock the next morning. Immediately upon take-off it was evident that the artificial horizon, upon which Penny was dependent to establish the angle of his aircraft in relation to the land or sea below him, was not working at all. *M-Mother* and her crew flew on for an hour or so to see if the problem would right itself, but Penny knew it was not safe to continue without it functioning correctly. After jettisoning their bombload in the North Sea, they turned for home, relieved and disappointed in equal measure. An abandoned mission would not count towards their tour total; all the nerves and fear and anticipation had been for nothing, and they still had another fifteen operations to complete. They were not alone in their frustration; five other crews from Melbourne had had to return early due to technical difficulties and icing in the harsh winter weather.

Jack's description of the abandoned trip in his logbook was brief.

*"Raid on BERLIN. DNCO (Did Not Complete Operation)
Instruments u/s"*

There is no number written next to this entry, indicating that it was not to be counted as part of his tour.

The RAF lost forty-six bombers and their crews that night, of which twenty-six were Halifaxes. Many were shot down over the target area, the *flakturme* at Friedrichshain, Humboldthain and Tiergarten operating to lethal effect in conjunction with the Luftwaffe fighters; more still plummeted into the sea on the return leg, and others crashed in England, so close to home. Despite the high losses, at Headquarters the raid was considered to be one of the most successful and concentrated attacks on Berlin so far.

Bad weather precluded any further operations in January, but in the first week of February, gardening operations picked up apace, in readiness for the forthcoming invasion. The Halifax squadrons were now requested to send out as many as fourteen crews at a time to litter the sea lanes and enemy coastline with deadly mines, and Jack and the boys found themselves rostered two nights in succession, on 3 and 4 February 1944, first in the Baltic off Kiel Bay, and then on the very lengthy and dangerous trip to the Bay of Biscay. They were slightly relieved that they weren't going to Berlin, and that they were able to tick off two further trips from their tour totals. In complete contrast to their terrifying experience with the flak ships on their previous mining sortie, the Kiel and Biscay trips passed without incident, and without encountering any form of opposition. Bill was disappointed that he did not get the opportunity to repeat his Coastal Command heroics and have another pop at the searchlights at La Rochelle on the Biscay trip, but he was still kept busy as a result of Penny's notoriously weak bladder on the seven-hour flight.

"Bill, can you come up to the cockpit again please and take over for a few minutes?"

"AGAIN?"

"Yes, again, and no bloody aerobatics, thank you very much."

The crew's relief was short-lived. After a period of heavy snowfall, followed by a few days undertaking training exercises and flight tests, on 15 February Penny was notified that his crew were required for another "maximum effort" raid. It came as no surprise to anyone present in the briefing hall that afternoon when Berlin was announced as their target. There was barely a murmur among the assembled men. Jack nudged Bill in the ribs and rolled his eyes.

"Told you so! Should've bet you ten bob."

"Ten bob?! Away with you, man, it wasn't exactly difficult to predict, was it?"

Every one of the Pennicott crew knew that he had been incredibly lucky to have seventeen operations under his belt without having to run the gauntlet of Berlin's air defences; equally, they all knew that they could not avoid it for much longer. The men dispersed and went back to their quarters for an hour's rest before their operational meal. At four o'clock there was still no sign of Penny. Bill tapped on the door of his room and walked straight in. He found Penny on his knees, elbows resting on his bed, hands joined and head bowed in prayer. Bill knew that his skipper was a deeply religious man, but on this occasion, Penny looked almost close to tears.

"What's up, Skip, praying for another safe return?"

Penny looked up, paused for a moment, and shook his head.

"No, Bill. I'm praying for the German people."

For once Bill didn't know what to say, and just nodded, closing the door softly behind him.

Just as the groundcrews were filing into the canteen for their dinner, *M-Mother* was queuing on the perimeter track with seventeen other aircraft before heading out onto the main runway. At exactly half past five the lights in the signal caravan changed from red to green, Penny pulled back on the throttles, and *M-Mother* and her crew (with Flight Sergeant Collins sitting in as "Second Joe", and Pilot Officer Devitt standing in for Freddie who was sick again) thundered along the runway, before disappearing into the darkness.

On this occasion, *M-Mother* didn't falter. There were no instrument failures, nor was there any icing. There was no reason for the crew to turn back and within two hours they were already over the Danish coast, part of a massive force of 891 aircraft intent on raining down hellfire on the Nazi capital. The time window allowed for the raid was only twenty minutes; forty bombers would drop their lethal loads over the city every sixty seconds.

The Germans had detected the incoming bomber stream not long after it left the coast of England. As the British aircraft passed over the eastern coast of Denmark into Kiel Bay, intending to make a right turn then head southeast to Berlin, the "tame boar" night fighters were despatched by the controllers in their individual "boxes" of airspace, ready to bring down the bombers long before they even approached their target. Many aircraft were shot down over the Baltic. Even if their crews were able to bale out of their stricken aircraft, there was no hope of rescue and they were dead within minutes of plunging into the icy sea. Yet more Luftwaffe fighters lay in wait over the German mainland, picking off the Halifaxes and Lancasters as they turned towards Berlin, where the "wild boar" fighters took over, hunting down the bombers as they left the target area. The anti-aircraft fire from the flak towers over the centre of the city was simply too heavy for most German pilots to risk their own aircraft; instead, they attacked the departing bombers as they headed for home.

The Pennicott crew arrived over the target area at a quarter past nine.[97] There was heavy cloud over the city, and a hellish scene as flak – and aircraft – exploded all around them. The noise was almost unbearable, as *M-Mother* shook and vibrated under the barrage. Amid the chaos, Penny lined up the aircraft for its bombing run, as Ken gave the instructions

---

97   National Archives AIR/27/145 10 Sqn ORB 15.2.1944.

from his position lying face down in the nose, peering through his bombsight.

"Hold her steady, Skip, steady... left a little, steady... bombs gone!"

As soon as Ken had taken his required photographs of the target, Penny pulled back on the throttle as hard as he could, anxious to get his aircraft and his crew out of the area as soon as was humanly possible. Over the intercom the rest of the crew could hear Jack singing. When the singing stopped, that was usually the sign that the worst of the danger was over, and that they could relax a little. That night, the singing did not cease until they reached the Dutch coast. *M-Mother* finally touched down at Melbourne a little after midnight.

All but one of 10 Squadron's crews made it back home that night. At the debrief, each skipper reported moderate or heavy ground defences. Sergeant Livesey's aircraft had lost an engine on the way out, but had still gone on to bomb the target, arriving home a full hour after everyone else; Flying Officer Le Cudenec was hit by flak and then suffered a "hang up" of his incendiaries, which his bomb aimer was later able to jettison. Twenty-one-year-old Flying Officer Clark and his crew in *S-Sugar* were all killed, shot down over Berlin.

Jack noted in his logbook, with a mixture of relief and elation:

"RAID ON BERLIN [the word BERLIN in extra-large capitals, to emphasise its importance] (18)
    Defences moderate to heavy flak, no searchlights, several fighter flares 10/10th cloud over practically whole route – wizard trip!"

How easy it is to be bullish after the event, when the fear has melted away and when one is back in safe, familiar surroundings. Jack had been terrified for the entire duration of the raid.

The Humboldthain flak tower shot down thirty-two Allied aircraft during the war, and damaged countless others. Towards the end, as Hitler's regime was fast running out of men and resources, the guns were manned by boys as young as fourteen, recruited from nearby schools and the ranks of the Hitler Youth. Not even the full weight of the Russian artillery could penetrate its concrete shell in the final days of the war; the troops holed up inside Berlin's three flak towers were the very last Germans to surrender to Soviet forces in May 1945.

The towers in the Tiergarten and at Friedrichshain were demolished, with many tons of dynamite and at great cost, not long after the war. Despite the best efforts of the Allies to erase the Humboldthain tower from the face of the earth, only two of the four turrets could be destroyed. With the help of expert guides, modern-day visitors can clamber around the partially collapsed interior, a gargantuan labyrinth of twisted steel and concrete; once the very epicentre of the Nazi defences, a place of safety for the citizens of the Third Reich, today it is home to a colony of bats.

24
Lady Luck

By 20 February 1944, 10 Squadron had lost ten aircraft and seventy men within the space of a month. Those losses were replicated at airfields up and down the country as the Battle of Berlin continued to decimate the men and machines of the RAF. Some squadrons had already received their new Mark III Halifaxes which, it was hoped, would reduce losses significantly. 10 Squadron were not expecting their replacement aircraft until early March.

The Pennicott crew were physically and mentally exhausted. The constant strain of operational flying, of witnessing death and destruction on an unimaginable scale, and of being personally responsible for a great deal of it, was beginning to tell. Tempers grew shorter and the silences longer. Penny had always encouraged the crew to talk to one another individually, and as a group, to describe their emotions and to comfort one another in times of anxiety and distress but increasingly there was simply nothing more that could be said, no words to describe how they were feeling or what they had experienced. The ever-mounting death toll of German civilians weighed heavily on Penny in particular, and he struggled to reconcile doing his duty with his religious and moral beliefs. Not a single man in the crew felt that his efforts were making any real difference to Bomber Command's expressed aim of bringing the war to a speedy end through the campaign of strategic bombing. There seemed to be no end in sight.

For Jack, the ever-present fear and anxiety was beginning to give way to something else, feelings which shocked him initially, but which gradually enveloped him: numbness, and indifference. Nothing really mattered anymore, and he simply lived, like so many aircrews at the time, from day to day. He still had twelve operations to go to complete his tour. It may as well have been a thousand. On his regular trips home, Lydia had detected the change in her brother. He no longer told her about his raids over Germany; he no longer spoke about his crewmates. If his father asked him questions while the family were gathered round the dinner table, he would immediately cast his eyes downwards and clam up; Lydia would nudge her father and quickly change the subject. She had also noticed Jack's tendency to go out of his way to avoid walking past the bombed-out houses in Sophia, Viceroy and Adolphus Streets every time he came home. He had always been a shy boy but had blossomed when he first joined the RAF; now, she could see him retreating within himself, his youthful bashfulness replaced by something altogether different.

Operations on 17 and 18 February had been cancelled due to bad weather; to their relief, Jack and the boys had not been rostered for the raid on Leipzig on 19 February. Many of the crews who took part in that operation reported close encounters with enemy aircraft. Flight Sergeant Fenny's aircraft was attacked three times, by two Junkers 88s, and then by a Messerschmitt 109, sustaining significant damage but thankfully no casualties. The tail plane of *Y-Yorker*, flown by Sergeant Pearson and his crew, was raked with machine gun fire and his tail gunner had a very narrow escape indeed. Other crews reported damage from severe flak. The words *"Missing. Nothing further heard from this aircraft after take-off"* are recorded in the Squadron Operations Record Book next to the names of Flight Sergeant Davenport and Flight Sergeant Walker and their crews.[98] Jack Walker and his men all managed to parachute to safety and were captured; Walker actually rejoined 10 Squadron many years after the war, flying VC10s in the 1960s. Alas only the navigator, Sergeant Murray, survived from Davenport's crew, and he too became a prisoner of war. The operation had proved a disaster for Bomber Command, with seventy-eight aircraft lost in total. Losses of Halifaxes on the Leipzig raid had been so high that Air Marshal Harris immediately ordered the withdrawal of all remaining Mark II Halifaxes from operations over Germany, forthwith.

The decision was to have significant consequences for the Pennicott crew.

The morning of 22 February was bitterly cold. Patches of snow lingered, and the remnants of a slight frost still sparkled on the grass outside the Officers' Mess as Penny was notified at breakfast that the Commanding Officer wished to see him. Penny assumed it must be something to do with the arrangements for the arrival of the new Mark III aircraft. Half an hour later, he emerged from the CO's office into the morning chill bearing a stunned and slightly incredulous expression, and immediately strode towards the accommodation blocks to gather up his crew.

---

98 National Archives AIR/27/145 10 Sqn ORB 19.2.1944.

"Four more, chaps. Four more and we're done," he announced as the boys encircled him, stamping their feet and blowing onto their fingers to keep warm. Only Freddie was absent. Penny had intentionally left him out of the gathering.

"Four more what?"

"What do you mean, Skip?"

"Four more bloody trips to bloody Berlin, I'll bet. We'll never get through that in one piece!"

"Four more ops. Four ops and our tour is over."

"They've made a mistake; we've still got twelve to go!"

Penny explained to Jack, Bill, Reg, Ken and George that the Commanding Officer was allowing them to include their three Coastal Command operations, as these had included flying over enemy waters, and engaging with enemy shipping and shore installations; they were also allowed to count those operations which they had had to abandon due to technical difficulties. The aborted trips to Bochum, Cologne, Kassel and the first trip to Berlin would all be taken into account.

Every one of them began counting up their ops on their fingers.

"That'll be twenty-nine for me then, Skip, I'll still be one short!" announced Jack.

"Only twenty-eight for me, I was ill that time, remember. What about me?" Bill looked crestfallen.

"That's alright, Bill, I'll have done thirty-one, you can have one of mine."

Penny sought to reassure his crew and informed them that he had already been through each of their flying records with the CO, who was fully aware that not all of them would have exactly thirty operations under their belts by the end. They would now be rostered mainly for minelaying trips or bombing raids which did not involve flying over Germany.

The boys were cock-a-hoop, almost unable to comprehend what they were hearing.

"But what about Freddie, Penny? Why isn't he here?" asked George.

"I'm going to speak to Fred separately. As you all know, Freddie missed quite a few ops when he was sick; the CO says he has to do another ten."

"Ten? Bloody hell."

The mood of the assembled crew changed in an instant. Poor Freddie.

Penny went off to find his Australian mid-upper gunner, to break the news to him. Freddie was a pragmatic young man and took the news very well. He explained to Penny that he had known all along that this would happen; as soon as he'd gone off sick in November, he had realised that he'd have to make up the time somewhere down the line. Plans were to be put in place to gradually introduce him into another crew; being the sort of man he was, he immediately sought out his crewmates, and there were handshakes and congratulations all round.

But why had the Commanding Officer made this decision? It was not uncommon for crews to be allowed to finish their tours early, particularly on those squadrons which had recently suffered very heavy losses, in order to boost morale. The Pennicott crew had completed far more operations than anyone else at Melbourne; to have lost them towards the end of their tour, say on their twenty-eighth or twenty-ninth operation, would have had a severe impact upon the morale of the entire squadron, aircrew and groundcrew alike. There was also practical reasoning; the new Mk IIIs were due at Melbourne on 7 March, and perhaps the CO felt that it would be more efficient to train the new (or at least less experienced) crews to fly them. Ultimately, he felt that Penny and his men had done their bit and served their purpose.

The "Lucky Crew" had struck gold once again.

Jack barely had time to absorb and process the information before Penny reappeared to inform him that they were flying again that night. Instead of the usual feeling of dread, the stomach-churning fear, Jack felt something new and unfamiliar: excitement. As the crews gathered in the briefing hall and awaited the standard announcement of their target, the boys could barely contain themselves. Word had already spread like wildfire among their colleagues that with any luck, they'd finish their tour in a couple of weeks. Penny had warned them to tone down their chatter and not discuss their news, out of respect to those crews who were only just beginning; he was also concerned that they might take their eyes off the ball and he wanted no lapses in standards. Mistakes or lack of attention to detail at this late stage could still prove catastrophic. Nor did he wish to tempt fate, as mining operations in mid-winter could be extremely dangerous.

By the time *M-Mother* took off late that afternoon, in company with nine other aircraft, all laden with mines for another "gardening" operation off the north-west coast of Denmark, it was already snowing at Melbourne. As the Pennicott crew began their long trek across the North Sea (with a replacement mid-upper gunner, as Freddie was still signed off sick), the weather conditions began to deteriorate still further. At times, visibility was almost nil, and the relaxed atmosphere on board the aircraft soon began to dissipate. Penny was considering abandoning the mission as it was simply too dangerous to continue, when Jack received a message from base at 17.43 hours, ordering them to turn back.[99] They had been airborne a little more than half an hour. All the crews landed back safely at Melbourne, and Jack took great pleasure in completing the following entry in his logbook:

---

99 *Ibid*, 22.2.1944.

"OPS – RECALLED – DNCO (19)"

Previously an abandoned operation would not have counted towards his tour total. The crew were in the bar by seven o'clock, accompanied by Freddie. None of them were big drinkers but they allowed themselves a couple of extra pints that evening, although Penny was keen to stamp out any premature celebrations. They weren't done just yet.

Jack did not have long to wait until his next trip. Just three days after the abandoned minelaying raid, the weather had improved sufficiently for gardening operations to be resumed. The Pennicott crew, including Freddie Singh this time, were once again pencilled in to take part in minelaying in the Baltic Sea, off Kiel Bay on 25 February. This time their role was to be slightly different. As well as planting mines in the shipping lanes, they were instructed to drop Pathfinder flares, illuminating the target areas for their colleagues who would be following closely behind in other aircraft. Unusually, 130 aircraft from squadrons throughout Yorkshire and Lincolnshire were rostered to take part in the Kiel Bay trip, including twelve other crews from Melbourne. The minelayers were to form part of a diversionary force, designed to distract attention from the main attack planned that night on the industrial city of Augsburg, which had thus far managed to avoid the attentions of Bomber Command.

The route to Kiel Bay was long and monotonous, and not without hazard, especially in the depths of winter. Due to a significant tail wind the Pennicott crew in *M-Mother* arrived over the target area early and had to spend a potentially very dangerous and extremely tense ten minutes "hanging about," circling over the dropping zone and using up precious fuel, until the time appointed for them to drop their flares and then their mines arrived. Three Halifaxes and a Stirling were lost from other squadrons, but all of 10 Squadron's men and aircraft returned home safely, without encountering any significant opposition; two had had to abandon the trip due to electrical problems. For Jack and his crewmates, the operation passed without incident. On arrival, he recorded simply:

"MINELAYING Baltic (20).
    Dropping PFF flares – no opposition."

If the crew's remaining two operations were as straightforward, Jack knew that within a matter of days he'd be enjoying a month of leave followed by a posting elsewhere. For the first time since he had arrived at Melbourne, he allowed himself to make plans, to contemplate his future, to daydream about lazy days at home; evenings spent in the Volunteer's Arms with his father and his friends (or at least those who were left), afternoons spent kicking a ball around the sooty backstreets with George, or treating Lydia to a night at the pictures, or maybe even a day out somewhere on the train. Newcastle perhaps, or maybe Whitby for fish and chips and a walk up the steep cliff path to the Abbey? Thoughts of simple, everyday pleasures which he had once taken for granted now consumed him. In one of his notebooks, he began to sketch out a rough design for a dolls' house which he intended to make for his niece, Moira, when she was old enough, eager to resume his carpentry skills. He thought about the other young joiners' apprentices, his mates at the yard near the docks, and wondered what had become of each of them. However, whenever Jack thought about home, no matter how much he tried to distract himself, his mind would run on to the bombed-out houses in nearby streets, and then to Düsseldorf. Gelsenkirchen. Hamburg. Frankfurt. Essen. Leipzig. Cologne. Always the same pattern, the same downward spiral, the same stream of consciousness which led back, inevitably, to Wuppertal and the firestorm. Despite the thoughts of warm beer, goalposts painted on backstreet walls and dolls' houses, the nightmares did not subside.

For the next few days, the eastern half of England was blanketed in snow, which prevented any further Bomber Command operations. At Melbourne, in the mess rooms and in the canteens, in the Nissen huts and in the hangars, all talk was of the new Mark III Halifaxes, which were due to arrive on 7 March. Groundcrew and aircrew alike attended lectures on the features of the new aircraft, the whole place abuzz with gossip and speculation about the capabilities of the new arrivals. Out on the pans stood *M-Mother*, *Z-Zebra* and all the other remaining Mark IIs, carefully wrapped in their tarpaulins to keep out the winter weather, but soon to be phased out and replaced, surplus to requirements – just like the Pennicott crew.

Jack and the boys grew impatient, desperate to get their remaining two sorties over and done with. By the time the weather improved on 2 March, they were champing at the bit to be rostered for the raid on the SNCA aircraft factory on the northern outskirts of Paris. Although Germany was now off limits for the older Halifaxes, the closer, less-heavily defended targets of France remained very much on the agenda. Much to their collective frustration, the Pennicott crew were not required; the twenty crews who headed off towards Paris that evening all returned safely. The very next afternoon, Penny was given the nod that he and his men would be flying that night, on yet another gardening operation, this time in the Bay of Biscay. It was a trip they had made several times before, including during their Coastal Command days; as far as some of the boys were concerned, their penultimate operation was simply a formality. Fly southwest, drop mines, fly home, file report, job done. Penny, however, was far from complacent.

He felt the weight of leadership greatly; these were *his* boys. Although only a few years older than most of his crew, and significantly younger than his flight engineer, George Phillipson, like so many Bomber Command pilots Penny felt an almost paternal responsibility for the lives of his men, both in the air and on the ground. Such responsibility was both a privilege and a burden, and the strain was beginning to tell.

As Jack and the boys kitted up in the locker room that evening, climbing into their flying suits and checking their gear, the mood was noticeably lighter. Instead of the stony silence in which they had prepared for their departure even as recently as three weeks ago, there was chatter and wisecracks, even laughter and banter among the crew. Only Ken Cox was quiet; like many airmen he was terribly superstitious, and he did not want to tempt fate by departing from his usual routine. Even Ken allowed himself a smile at one of Bill's terrible jokes as they stood around waiting in the darkness for their transport to take them out to their aircraft, puffing on cigarettes and stamping their feet on the frozen ground. The other assembled crews were much quieter and cast envious glances in their direction. Many of them hadn't even reached their fifth operation; all were keen to get in as many gardening and French ops under their belts as they could before the new aircraft arrived, and the terrifying, dreadful raids over Germany resumed.

Of the eleven aircraft detailed to take part in the operation, only nine took off. Porter and Burgess had their trips cancelled as pre-flight checks revealed technical problems.[100] *M-Mother*, with the Pennicott crew on board, took her place in the queue of waiting aircraft on the perimeter circuit, before taxiing to her take-off position on the main runway just after ten past seven. Once again, Freddie's place was taken by Sergeant

---

100 *Ibid*, 3.3.1944.

Greatrex; the boys had flown with him before, and in any event, it was not anticipated that there would be much for the gunners to do on this operation. Enemy aircraft would be concentrated on preparing for anticipated raids over Berlin, and little opposition was expected, other than from the flak batteries at La Rochelle and La Pallice on the French Atlantic coast.

M-Mother flew the length of England in darkness, heading out over the Dorset coast at Lyme Regis. The night was clear and bitterly cold, the sky peppered with stars above a gibbous moon. As they approached the French mainland, the occasional sweep of distant searchlights marked out the enemy coastline, but all was silent. No exploding flak shells, no tracer bullets, no orange glow of fires on the ground. Penny maintained a steady course towards the target area, and his crew occupied their time by running through their standard procedures to ensure that all of their equipment was functioning correctly.

After depositing their mines in the allotted patch, Ken reported that the bomb bay doors wouldn't close. This in itself was not unusual, so Penny wasn't too concerned, although it could affect the aerodynamics of the aircraft. After leaving the target area, George handed round a huge bag of toffees he'd been sent by his wife, Ethel. Jack helped himself to a handful, grateful for the sugar rush.

"Hell's bells, George, what's your missus put in them toffees? I think I've broken a tooth!"

"That's nothing, Jack son, my ruddy jaws feel like they've been glued together!"

No sooner had the words left George's lips then the whole interior of the aircraft was suddenly lit up from within, a dazzling beam penetrating the cockpit and causing the crew to raise their hands to their eyes as one. Penny was momentarily blinded, but this was no explosion. The light did not dissipate, there was no relief. Instead it remained constant, as if intent on piercing the very souls of the aircraft's occupants.

"SEARCHLIGHT, CORKSCREW PORT NOW, NOW, NOW" came the command from Greatrex in the gun turret. Immediately Penny threw the aircraft into a steep, twisting dive to his left. Toffee papers, maps, coffee cups, parachute packs, notebooks and pencils, and every other loose object aboard *M-Mother* went flying, as her crew clung onto the airframe. Almost immediately the flak barrage began, the cross hairs of every German gunsight along that stretch of coastline trained on the Halifax, which was now illuminated by multiple beams, and utterly exposed.

As the aircraft twisted and turned, Penny tried every trick in the training manual to evade the lights. Time seemed almost to stand still and Jack thought his heart would explode out of his chest. He was too frightened even to sing; the familiar words of the "Blaydon Races" became muddled in his head and stuck in his throat. For five long minutes, *M-Mother* dived and swooped, bobbed and weaved, desperate to avoid the flak shells which exploded all around her. In the rear turret, Bill desperately fired 250 rounds at the lights, though in all probability they were miles out of the range of his Brownings.

As quickly as it had begun, it was over, as the cockpit was once again plunged into darkness.

The Pennicott crew had experienced yet another miraculous escape. *M-Mother* had not suffered any major damage, and none of the crew had sustained any injuries, apart from a few bumped heads.

"What happened there? How on earth did we get out of that one?" gasped Reg Cowles from the navigator's position.

"Easy," came Bill's voice over the intercom. "I just fired a few of Ethel's toffees at the main beam and it went off."

Despite the relief on board, every member of the Pennicott crew realised just how lucky he had been. Rarely did an aircraft escape being coned in the beam of a searchlight; for an aircraft to survive for a full five minutes was virtually unheard of. On the way home, the crew was quiet, reflecting upon their incredibly close shave. None was more relieved to pass over the English coast at Selsey Bill than Penny. Once again, his quick thinking and his skills as a pilot had saved the lives of his crew, yet still he was tortured by "what-ifs" and self-doubt. Ridiculously, he blamed himself for allowing his aircraft to be caught in the searchlights in the first place. He knew full well that if they'd been coned over Berlin or the Ruhr Valley, they would not have survived to tell the tale.

M-Mother touched down at Melbourne at a quarter to two in the morning. After debrief and supper, Jack made the following entry in his logbook:

"MINELAYING *Bay of Biscay (21)*
   Coned by searchlights in target area for 5 mins, slight flak defences, bomb doors u/s unable to close – wizard trip."

Curiously Penny's account in the Squadron Operations Record Book makes no mention of what had actually occurred. It states simply:

"*Mines laid at position 46.08 north by 01.22 ½ west as ordered by H2S fix. Mines dropped at 22.20 hours from 15,000 feet. Visibility was good with no cloud. Opposition was negligible."*

Penny had had enough.

25

Permission to Land

Bomber Command scheduled no further major operations for the next two nights; instead, a small number of its aircraft were engaged in "nuisance" raids on Berlin, Duisburg and Aachen; many of the older Halifaxes which were shortly to be pensioned off took part in dropping supplies and Special Operations Agents to resistance units throughout France, in readiness for the forthcoming invasion. The next night, 6 March 1944, the RAF began a series of raids on French railway targets, designed to slow down and disrupt the German Army's ability to move men and equipment around, again in preparation for the invasion which could surely only be a matter of months away. Already vast numbers of troops, tanks, mobile artillery, aircraft, landing craft and supplies were beginning to assemble in Southern England. The Nazis knew that the invasion was coming, and soon, but they did not know when, or where. All German eyes were focused on the Pas de Calais and the shortest Channel crossing route from Dover.

Surely that was the only possible point (both from a logical and logistical point of view) from which the Allies would attempt to launch the biggest military operation in history? It was simply nonsense to even contemplate a sea crossing further west.

The first major "railway" raid on Trappes was a great success militarily, with huge damage caused to tracks, rolling stock, locomotives and infrastructure. However, of great concern to Bomber Command chiefs was the issue of what today would be termed "collateral damage" – French civilian casualties. It was absolutely essential to keep the French people "on side" as the invasion drew nearer; arguably the lives of French citizens had not been given so much weight earlier in the campaign, particularly during the raids on Montluçon and Le Creusot, in which the Pennicott crew had played their part.

On 7 March 1944, Jack and the boys learned that their final operation would take them not to Biscay or the Baltic, but to the heart of France. The Pennicott crew were rostered for a bombing raid on the railway marshalling yards at Le Mans.

Although Penny lectured his crew on the importance of maintaining concentration, and told them he wanted no premature celebrations, he was as eagerly anticipating the end of his tour as any one of his men. He knew full well that his nerves would not have been able to cope with much more.

Jack was glad; glad that their final mission would take them over enemy territory once again, one last chance to give Hitler a bloody nose, and the opportunity to go out on a high. His anticipation was also tinged with some sadness; he thought about Roy Tann and wished that he had lived to share this night. Jack knew that very soon the Pennicott crew would be broken up and dispersed, and his band of brothers would be sent their separate ways. Who knew what the future might bring? What would happen to Freddie? He wasn't flying with the rest of the boys that night, as he had been allocated to Flying Officer Pearson's crew instead. Although their adventure together was almost over, there still seemed no end to the war in sight.

As they made their way out of the briefing room, there were handshakes and pats on the back all round from some of the other crews. Many of the new crews were completely in awe of Penny and his men, and Jack smiled at a teenage wireless operator who grasped him by the hand, as the men funnelled down the corridor. Jack knew that the boy was frightened, and was simply seeking a kind word, to have his fear recognised by a kindred spirit who had lived through it and survived to tell the tale. But Jack Clyde wasn't frightened anymore. He had played his part and given his all; in doing so he had almost lost his life, and his sanity, many times over. He had nothing left to give. As he, Bill and Reg went to have a look at the new Mk III Halifax which had arrived at Melbourne that morning, each of them had a sense that this was the end of an era. It was time for others – new men and new machines – to take up the baton and continue the fight.

There was to be no grand last hurrah, no nostalgic last flight in *M-Mother* or *Z-Zebra*.[101] Instead, Penny and his crew were allotted *Q-Queen* for their last mission. It seemed like the entire groundcrew had turned out to see them off; Leo Groark for one couldn't have been more relieved that this was to be Jack's last raid. He stood at the edge of the tarmac with Tommy and Alec, and some of the other "erks" and waved the Pennicott crew off, Jack's house keys on their grubby string still jangling in the pocket of his overalls.

---

101 Both of these aircraft were eventually transferred to the Heavy Conversion Units for training purposes, and survived the war.

In dense cloud, *Q-Queen* passed over the French coast, part of the bomber stream of 304 aircraft heading for Le Mans. From the tiny window to the left of his wireless operator's cubbyhole, Jack could see nothing. No heavy opposition was expected, but as they approached their target, the familiar crud-thump of flak shells exploding around them shook the aircraft. In just a few moments *Q-Queen* passed over the flak defences, unharmed. Just before ten o'clock, Ken Cox gave the familiar signal over the intercom for the very last time.

"Bombs gone!"

"Well done, everybody, and thank you. Let's go home, shall we?"

As *Q-Queen* turned away from the target area, the red glow of fires on the ground could clearly be seen through the haze of cloud. The raid on Le Mans had been very successful; 300 bombs fell on the railway yards, causing destruction on an epic scale. Many railway lines were completely cut, over 250 wagons and six locomotives were blown up, as well as a warehouse full of wooden railway sleepers. No RAF aircraft were lost on this raid, but thirty-one French civilians on the ground paid the ultimate price. Rumours of anti-British graffiti on the walls around the town abounded; it is not known whether this was a genuine sign of French disaffection with Allied tactics, or whether it was staged German propaganda.[102]

Penny would not allow his crew any celebrations until they had passed back over the Sussex coast at Selsey Bill; only then would he allow them to relax a bit. As usual George was on coffee duty, handing the thermos round with a grin; this time he'd laced the coffee heavily with brandy. And that's when the singing began, instigated by Jack of course. The entire crew (including the stand-in upper gunner, Frost) belted out the

---

102 Middlebrook, M. and Everitt, C., *The Bomber Command War Diaries*, Pen & Sword Aviation, Barnsley, 2014, p. 479.

popular tunes of the day, everything from "Sally" by Gracie Fields to the classic "Lily Marlene," beloved by men on both sides of the conflict.

As the Pennicott crew began their approach into Melbourne for the very last time, there was only one song they wanted to sing.

"Are we ready boys?" enquired Jack. "One, two, three..."

"Ah went to Blaydon Races, 'twas on the ninth of Joon,
In eighteen hundred an' sixty-two, on a summer's efternoon"

Amid the cacophony, and after "shushing" the boys, Penny radioed the control tower to warn of their imminent arrival.

"Milk Pail, this is *Q-Queen*, permission to land, over."

A female voice, one of the WAAFs on duty in the tower that evening, responded.

"*Q-Queen* this is Milk Pail, permission to land granted. Well done, sir. Welcome home. Over."

As the Halifax touched down, the familiar refrain rang out:

"Gannin' alang the Scotswood ROOOAAADD
To see the Blaydon Races!!"

After the initial elation, the handshakes and cheers from Ronnie, Alec, Norman and the rest of the groundcrew who had anxiously waited up for *Q-Queen* to return, there was silence in the back of the truck as the boys headed back to be debriefed. None of the crew said anything. They didn't need to. They simply sat there, utterly drained, almost unable to comprehend the enormity of their achievements, but occasionally smiling at each other and shaking their heads in disbelief. After debrief and a late supper, and checking that Freddie and the Pearson crew had got back safely, Jack returned to his quarters. He had long imagined this moment, but when it had finally arrived, he was not overcome with joy, or even with relief. The anticipated feeling of euphoria had dissipated almost as soon as *Q-Queen's* wheels had touched down upon the tarmac; in its place was an aching emptiness. Illuminated only by the glow of the stove in the corner of the hut, he pulled off his boots and loosened his tie before flopping down onto his bed. He thrust his face into his pillow and sobbed, until he fell asleep.

When he awoke the next morning, he felt better. The crushing dread in his stomach which he had experienced the moment he opened his eyes every single morning since he had arrived at Melbourne was no longer there. He smiled to himself, turned over and allowed himself the luxury of an extra fifteen minutes in bed.

Later that morning the crew assembled next to one of the Halifaxes, *A-Apple*, for the traditional "Endex" photograph, which all aircrews who managed to complete a full tour received. Reg Cowles put on his flying jacket and his lucky navy scarf; the rest of the boys just turned up in their standard uniform, silver whistles still attached to their collars from the previous night's operation. Freddie Singh was sent for; despite his protests, the boys insisted he should be on the photograph. He was part of the crew at the very beginning, and as far as they were concerned, he should be part of the crew at the very end.

Amongst Jack's possessions are two large black and white photographs, taken within a couple of minutes of each other on the morning of 8 March 1944. In the bottom right-hand corner of one them, there is a faded inscription which reads, "10 Squadron Melbourne May 1943 – March 1944." A smiling Freddie stands on the left, nearest to the Halifax, in the dark blue uniform of the Royal Australian Air Force, but with his flying boots on, as if he'd got dressed in a hurry. George Phillipson stands next to him, expressionless and staring straight ahead. In the middle is Bill Bradshaw, absolutely beaming as usual, his arms around the shoulders of his comrades. Penny appears somewhat bemused and bears the expression of a man who is desperate for the photographer to get a move on. To his right stands Ken Cox, who simply looks dazed. At the front of the group Reg Cowles and Jack are sitting on the ground. Jack has his hands folded around his knees, his mother's wedding band glinting in the early morning sunlight. A half smile plays on his lips; not much more than a boy, he looks calm and happy. Next to him Reg, in his full flying gear (jacket, boots, gloves, scarf and cap), is laughing.

The second photograph shows the boys with four of their groundcrew. On the rear of this photograph, in Jack's usual neat handwriting, he has listed the names and ranks of his colleagues, including Tommy Hunter, Ronnie Rudkin, Alec Evans and "young" Norman, whose surname is not recorded. That the Pennicott crew had survived to complete their tour was due as much to the efforts of these men as Penny's skills as a pilot or Reg's abilities as a navigator. Every man – aircrew and groundcrew alike – had played an equal part. Tommy, Norman, Ronnie and Alec appear as proud as punch.

Later that day the crew handed their logbooks in to Wing Commander Radford's office to be checked and signed off. On the next clear double page of Jack's logbook, there's a large box carefully ruled out and marked in red ink. Inside the box, there are written the words:

"*Certified 1st tour completed*
No. of sorties 29
No. of ops. hours 209.20
Signed DS Radford W/C, O.C 10 SQN RAF MELBOURNE,
YORKS"

Letters were quickly written and despatched to parents, wives, sisters and sweethearts informing them of the good news. Reg Cowles wrote the following note to his older sister, Queenie, in Walthamstow:

> "*Officers' Mess, RAF Station, Melbourne, East Yorkshire.*
> *12/3/44*
> *Dear Queen,*
> *Just a line telling you to uncross your fingers at last. It's all over, I'm 'screened' – grounded. Spread the glad news but don't tell Mum yet. I shall probably be home at the end of the week and I want to see her face for myself when she hears.*
> *See you soon,*
> *Love, Reg.*"[103]

After a week or so just hanging around Melbourne, with regular trips into York to the cinemas and dancehalls and Betty's Tearoom, and making the most of their last week together, the boys were eventually sent home on extended leave. Every Bomber Command crewman who completed his tour was given a month's home leave, during which he would be notified of his next posting; thereafter he was not eligible for any operational duties for another six months, although he could always volunteer for an extended period with Bomber Command if he wished to do so. Tom Davidson, Halifax flight engineer, recalled that just as he and his crew were about to commence what they thought would be their thirtieth and final operation, their young Australian skipper announced that he'd signed them up for another six. This did not go down well, as one might imagine. Squadron Diaries usually record the onward posting of crews at the end of each month, but curiously the 10 Squadron Diary does not mention the various destinations of the Pennicott crew.

---

103 Reproduced with the permission of Maureen Cowles-Curtis.

During his six months "off ops," an airman might be sent out to one of the operational training units or heavy conversion units to train the next intake of bomber crews or be posted to Coastal Command to assist with air/sea rescues or meteorological duties. The RAF's logistical and operational needs changed from day to day as the war progressed. As Jack, Penny, George, Bill, Ken and Reg said their goodbyes to one another for the last time at York station (waved off by Freddie Singh), with handshakes and laughter and promises to keep in touch, addresses hastily scribbled on scraps of paper passing back and forth, none of them knew what lay in store.

Before 1944 had run its course, one of the Pennicott crew would be a prisoner of war. Another would be dead.

26

Absent Friends

Jack arrived home in Caroline Street for his month's leave just an hour or so after the postman had brought news from Jim in Italy. Bearing a "Napoli" postmark, Jim's letter explained that he had been stuck at Cassino for weeks in the depth of winter and hinted that things had been "a bit rough," His unit had now been withdrawn from the battle-ravaged valley, sent over to Naples, and were camped just outside Pompeii. The recently liberated city was in a desperate state, the local populace on the brink of starvation; if things weren't bad enough, just after Jim's unit had arrived, Mount Vesuvius erupted on 13 March. As well as blanketing the city and its surrounds with ash for over two weeks, the eruption had caused an earthquake and the ground still shook with alarming regularity. Years later, Jim would recall the stench and the apocalyptic scene in some of the Neapolitan cemeteries, where the graves of the recently dead were broken open, their decomposing contents thrust to the surface once more by the force of the quake.

Even the nightmarish vision in Naples paled into insignificance when compared to the hell Jim had endured at Monte Cassino. In the depths of a brutal winter, bogged down in freezing mud and under almost constant shelling, Jim and his fellow sappers worked alongside Indian Army divisions to try to keep the Allied troops moving, digging out roads and digging in trenches and artillery positions. At Cassino, Jim witnessed some of the most horrific scenes he'd encountered during the entire war, things he was barely able to speak about almost seventy years later; corpses of fallen comrades who had been driven over by tanks and armoured vehicles, and a truck full of his mates being blown to pieces as they drove over a mine. Following close behind, Jim's truck had taken the right-hand fork in the road, while the other had chosen the left. He saw the vehicle explode from about 200 yards away, after their paths had diverged. Allied forces were unable to break through the German positions until 18 May 1944, some four months after the battle had begun, when the fourth assault on the mountain top and the second by Polish divisions finally succeeded, linking up with British troops approaching from the Liri Valley. The cost had been colossal, with the Allies suffering around 55,000 casualties, and the ancient monastery at the top of the mountain destroyed. Two thousand Italian civilians lost their lives. Many of Jim's friends now lie in the Allied Cemetery at the foot of the mountain.

Throughout the Italian campaign, and indeed for the rest of the war, Jim kept with him in the breast pocket of his uniform the photograph of Lydia and his daughter, Moira, and a set of cheap olive-wood rosary beads he had purchased in one of the villages he had passed through en route to Cassino. None of the horrors he had seen were revealed in his letters to Lydia, which were full of chit-chat, and descriptions of the Italian cities he had visited, complaints about his rations, enquiries about friends and relations, and his plans for when he eventually returned home.

Jack spent the next four weeks doing all the things he had dreamed about in his Nissen hut at Melbourne: visiting friends and relations, popping into the Volunteer or the Oddfellows in Church Street for a pint, going for a walk through Seaham Hall Dene with Lydia and Moira in her pram, calling in to see his old colleagues at Tomlin's Yard, as well as regular visits to the local cinema. He took to his role as an uncle with relish. One evening his niece was particularly fractious and simply would not settle. Lydia was at the end of her tether.

"Here, Lyd, give her to me."

Jack picked up Moira, laid her in her cot, and said firmly, "Go to sleep, you little bugger!"

And she did.

For Jack himself, sleep did not come quite so easily. Although no longer weighed down by anxiety and fear, the nightmares still did not subside. Roy Tann, Wuppertal, exploding aircraft, searchlights and flak, the fires on the ground – none of it really left him. He hoped that his new posting would take his mind off things and give him a new focus; Jack had received word that he was to report at 19 Operational Training Unit (19 OTU) in Kinloss, near Findhorn Bay in the Moray Firth, to commence his new role as a wireless operator instructor, training new bomber crews before they were posted out to their operational units. Jack questioned how he'd cope, whether he possessed sufficient self-confidence to speak to groups of newly qualified wireless operators and wondered if he'd be good enough. He secretly hoped that a great deal of the training he'd be required to deliver would be "in the air" rather than in the lecture hall. On 4 April 1944, Jack once again boarded the train at Seaham station. This time he was headed north, and the following morning, in the midst of a gale, he reported for duty at 19 OTU.

Bomber Command had taken over RAF Kinloss in May 1940 and 19 OTU was formed at the same time, with the specific purpose of training bomber crews for operations over Germany. Initially equipped with Whitleys and Avro Ansons, by the time Jack arrived in the spring of 1944, the Ansons had been replaced by Wellingtons. The scattered aircraft wreckage which littered the surrounding countryside bore testament to the dangers facing the trainee crews. Poor weather, mountainous terrain and ageing, unreliable aircraft all combined to contribute to heavy losses; many of the young men who arrived at Kinloss did not survive long enough to be posted to operational squadrons. RAF funeral parties were a regular sight at the local station, as the coffins of deceased airmen were loaded onto trains to bear them home to their loved ones one last time.

*

While Jack was familiarising himself with his new surroundings, Freddie Singh was still at Melbourne, and desperate to complete his tour. The promise of a new crew had failed to materialise and instead Freddie found himself pretty much alone, a "spare bod" to be called upon if another crew was short of a gunner. He had felt the departure of the rest of the Pennicott crew keenly. There was no end in sight for him, as he was called upon rarely, and he hung around the Officers' Mess in a permanent state of limbo. He was greatly relieved when he received word on 27 April that he had been rostered as a stand-in tail gunner in Pilot Officer Den Blackford's crew, for an operation on the railway yards at Aulnoye in France.[104] By now 10 Squadron's older Mk II Halifaxes had all been replaced by Mk IIIs, and Freddie was keen to see how the

---

104 National Archives AIR/27/145 10 Sqn ORB 27.4.1945.

new aircraft handled differently on operations. The impact of the new aircraft upon the squadron's casualty rates had already been significant, even though raids over Germany had resumed apace.

Freddie had not flown operationally for seven weeks when he climbed aboard the brand-new *L-Love* a little after midnight. The mission did not get off to the best of starts when Pilot Officer Burcher's aircraft, *O-Orange*, crashed on take-off. The Halifax was seen to swerve violently, before coming off the runway and coming to a stop, its back broken. Burcher and his crew had had a very narrow escape indeed. Had *O-Orange* lifted off the tarmac, it is very likely that all would have been killed. As it was, the entire crew escaped without injury. The Squadron Operations Book records that fourteen of the eighteen aircraft detailed for this operation went on to bomb the target, the remainder cancelling due to being held up by Burcher's crash, or turning back due to technical problems. Blackford recorded:

> "Bombed primary target at 0307 hours from 14,000 feet. Visibility was good over the target, with slight ground haze and marshalling yards and railway tracks clearly identified. Bombed on green target indicators as ordered by Master Bomber. Many bomb bursts were seen in target area, and attack appeared concentrated and effective. Only weak opposition was encountered."

In his cramped rear gunner's position, Freddie had had very little to do, and his trip passed without incident. He was back in bed by half past six that morning.

If Freddie had hoped that the Aulnoye raid was to mark "the beginning of the end" of his tour, he was to be disappointed. Another month went by before he was called upon again, despite the squadron taking part in six minelaying operations and seven French "railway" raids in the interim. Instead, on 24 May, Freddie was informed that he was required for Den Blackford's crew again (two of his regular crew had gone off sick) and the squadron's first raid over Germany since Essen on 26 April. The target was announced as the Aachen railway yards. Freddie had done that trip once before with the Pennicott crew in July the previous year, when they had flown six operations in a fortnight at the height of the Battle of the Ruhr; he reflected that he hadn't even flown six operations so far this year. By now he was one of the longest-serving aircrew at Melbourne, and not by choice. Blackford and his crew were very experienced, and Freddie felt that he was in safe hands. The Aachen trip was to be their twentieth operation, and they had survived four consecutive trips to Berlin.

10 Squadron had been asked to provide only nine aircraft of the 442 allotted by Bomber Command HQ to take part in the attack on Aachen that night. Although it was another "railway" operation, a larger force was despatched than would usually be the case because Aachen was in Germany, just over the border, and the whole town was a legitimate operational target. Blackford and his crew, with Freddie resuming his role as mid-upper gunner, took off in *Q-Queen* (their regular aircraft, the new Mk III *Z-Zebra* had not yet been fitted with the H2S navigational aid) just after five to eleven, in company with the crews of Lavalley, Maw, Kennedy, Sutton, Culverhouse, Hart, Saynor and Bruce.[105] The raid was considered a big success, with extensive damage being caused to the railway lines east of the town, but also to residential areas and surrounding villages. Two hundred and seven German civilians were killed, and almost 15,000 made homeless. Bomber Command lost twenty-five aircraft and their crews.

---

105 *Ibid*, 24.5.1944.

In the 10 Squadron Operations Record Book, next to the aircraft reference LV906 "Q", and the names of Blackford and his crew, appear the words:

"Missing. Nothing heard from aircraft after take-off."

Q-Queen had successfully bombed the target and was on her way home when at around quarter past one in the morning, she was hit by a night fighter, believed to be a Junkers 88. Blackford would later recall:

> *"He fired two bursts – the first one set the fuel tanks in both wings on fire, and both the port engines were knocked out. Fires also broke out in the port wing bomb bay. Luckily the bomb bay doors which had not locked after I had closed them fell open, and this caused the plane to go into a very steep climb. I say luckily because the second burst from the night fighter went by underneath the aircraft."*[106]

As the fires burned out of control, Blackford gave the order to bale out. The navigator and the bomb aimer managed to get out through the escape hatch in the floor. The wireless operator, while handing Blackford his parachute, caught the release mechanism of his own parachute on a control knob, spilling silk everywhere inside the fuselage. He simply gathered up the open parachute and jumped. In the rear turret, gunner Jack Shenton eventually escaped the stricken aircraft but was immediately knocked out by one of the buckles on his parachute. Blackford then ordered his flight engineer Abbott

---

106 Clutton-Brock, Oliver, and Crompton, Raymond, *The Long Road-Trials and Tribulations of Airmen Prisoners from Stalag Luft VII (Bankau) to Berlin, June 1944–May 1945*, Grub Street, London, e-book version 2013, pp. 25-26.

to jump but struggled to free himself from his seat harness. Abbott turned back to help his pilot, and both were able to bale out successfully.

Freddie Singh had been hit in the leg by a cannon shell when the Junkers 88 first attacked. Bleeding heavily and amid the smoke and noise and confusion, he somehow found the strength to extricate himself from his harness in the mid-upper turret, struggle into his parachute, and jump from *Q-Queen* as she went down in flames. Freddie came to rest in a field in the dead of night; gravely wounded and barely conscious, he was unable to move, and his parachute was quickly spotted. He was captured by German troops immediately; fortunately, they had the presence of mind to take him to the nearest field hospital where he received emergency treatment which saved his leg, and ultimately his life.

The rest of Blackford's crew, scattered around the local countryside, were soon picked up and taken prisoner. Freddie never saw any of them again. They were all sent to separate POW camps, and after a long spell in hospital in Germany, Freddie spent the remainder of the war in Stalag 6J, initially at Krefeld but from October 1944 in Dorsten, after the camp was re-sited further north as a result of the Allied advances. Stalag 6J was a vast complex, and housed thousands of prisoners, many of them Italian. Freddie was incredibly lucky; he was one of the very few POWs to be repatriated before the war ended but spent the best part of the next three years in and out of hospital.

Among the film archives belonging to the Imperial War Museum of Australia, there's a short piece of silent footage, showing various unidentified dignitaries visiting Australian troops in a convalescent home on the south coast of England at the end of May 1945. About ten minutes in, the film shows some men playing snooker. Sitting on the sidelines looking on, with the occasional shy and self-conscious smile at the camera, crutches still tucked under one arm, is Freddie Singh.

Word had reached Jack at Kinloss that Freddie's aircraft had been lost. In a quiet moment, in the back of his logbook he had carefully listed the members of the Pennicott crew, and their various detachments together. Next to Freddie's name he simply recorded:

"*Missing 24.5.44.*"

To his dying day, Jack never knew that Freddie had survived.

27

"For Gallantry"

Within days of arriving at Kinloss, Jack was airborne again. As far away from the rigours and terrors of operational flying as it was possible to be, he soon settled into his new surroundings. His logbook shows that from 20 April 1944 he was back in the air, flying once a day, occasionally twice, passing on the benefit of his experience to the incoming wireless operators. The Avro Ansons and elderly Whitley aircraft seemed a far cry from the technology-packed Halifaxes that Jack had flown with 10 Squadron. Alongside him were other men who had endured and survived a full tour of operations, men who *understood*. Jack soon struck up friendships with the other instructors, particularly the pilots with whom he flew daily – Pilot Officer Hamilton, Flight Sergeant Welford and Flying Officer Weatherstone – but the camaraderie and fellowship, the bonds between the members of a crew who have faced death together, were absent.

Kinloss was a somewhat isolated spot, and there was very little to do in one's spare time other than perhaps visiting the small town for a few drinks or a parcel of fish and chips, or to attend one of the regular dances. In his days at Melbourne Jack had become used to the luxury of very regular leave; at Kinloss, even if he had a couple of days off, it was simply too far to travel back to Seaham Harbour, and several months could go by between visits home to see Lydia, George, his father and niece.

As hundreds of thousands of men waded onto the beaches of Normandy on 6 June, Jack was aboard Whitley M-5019, piloted by Sergeant Murrell, screening a new wireless operator. That evening, he and the other instructors gathered around the wireless set in the mess, listening for news of the invasion, each of them convinced that the end of the war could not be too far away. The colleagues Jack had left behind at 10 Squadron were in the thick of it, taking part in raids on the radar station at Ferme D'Urville on 1 June, and on rail installations at Trappes the following night. Three crews were lost on that raid; some were killed but others successfully baled out and evaded capture before being betrayed to the Gestapo by a Frenchman named Jacques Desoubrie. Instead of being sent to prisoner of war camps, they were transported to the Buchenwald concentration camp with other captured airmen, in direct contravention of the Geneva Convention. Days before they were due to be executed, contact was somehow made with Luftwaffe officials who intervened on their behalf, and the men were moved to Stalag Luft III, where they were finally accorded POW status. Desoubrie was tried and executed in 1949.[107] On D-Day itself, twenty-two crews from Melbourne took part in the bombing of German troop positions in St Lo,

---

107 MacMillan, Ian and King, Richard, *From Brooklands to Brize: A Centennial History of No 10 Squadron Royal Air Force*, 10 Squadron Association, 2015, pp. 146-147.

from the almost suicidally low height of 2,500 feet; all made it safely back to base.

Over the next few weeks, 10 Squadron flew almost daily, as Bomber Command mounted massive attacks on German ground positions and communications sites in support of the Allied invasion. There was a new threat too: Nazi forces had launched their new superweapon, the V1 flying bomb (nicknamed the Doodlebug), in the early hours of 13 June with devastating effect on the Greater London area. The squadron mounted daylight raids on V1 launch sites at Noyelle, Montoguel and Mont Candon. The Operations Diary for June 1944 records that seven aircraft and their crews were lost during the Normandy campaign, and another in a training accident. The tally was very nearly nine; Sergeant Bond's aircraft was involved in a mid-air collision with a Focke-Wulf 190 after a raid on the railway depot at Douai. The Luftwaffe pilot and his aircraft were seen to plummet to the ground in flames, taking with them about five feet of the Halifax's port wing. Bond and his crew had a very narrow escape indeed, managing to land their badly damaged aircraft at Woodbridge in Suffolk. All were uninjured.

There's another entry in the Squadron Diary for June. Right at the end of the records for that month appear the words:

> "The following NCOs were awarded the Distinguished Flying Medal for gallantry and devotion to duty in operations against the enemy:
> … F/S Clyde W/Op, F/S Phillipson F/E…"

Just above appear citations for the award of the Distinguished Flying Cross for Penny, and a Bar to Reg Cowles' existing

DFC.[108] Citations for Bill and Ken would follow in the subsequent months.

Every Bomber Command airman who completed a full tour was awarded the DFM (for non-commissioned officers like Jack and George) or DFC (for commissioned officers, like the rest of the crew). Today we tend to think of medals being awarded for isolated acts of bravery, perhaps for single-handedly storming an enemy machine gun position, or rescuing injured colleagues from the battlefield under heavy fire. It is difficult for us to imagine a feat so great, a task so dangerous and against the greatest of odds, that men were awarded medals for gallantry for simply still being alive at the end of it. Night after night, for months on end, the Pennicott crew had been exposed to mortal danger; that most of them had survived to tell the tale was due not to their great skill nor individual feats of courage, but largely down to old-fashioned bloody good luck. Jack received word of his citation with very mixed emotions; like many of his fellow instructors at Kinloss, men who had lived through the Battle of the Ruhr, the Battle of Hamburg, the Battle of Berlin, he carried with him a survivor's guilt, always.

Throughout the course of the war, every month the *London Gazette* listed awards of medals to servicemen and recorded their promotions. There, halfway down page 3043 of the June 1944 edition, under the heading "Distinguished Flying Medal, Flight Sergeants," was the official confirmation:

> "*1125510 John CLYDE, RAFVR, 10 Sqn*"

The defining moments of a man's life summed up in a few characters. No reason, no explanation, no details, nor any hint of what he and the many others listed had endured.

---

108 National Archives AIR/27/145, 10 Sqn Diary, June 1944.

Jack waited impatiently for his medal to arrive in the post. Weeks went by but still it did not appear. Other men on the station had already received theirs, and Jack was beginning to wonder if he had been forgotten about, or if the precious package had been lost in transit, or perhaps even stolen. He even wrote to Lydia to see if it had been sent to Caroline Street. At the beginning of August, he received an official-looking letter bearing a Royal Air Force postmark. Initially he paid it little attention and put it to the bottom of the pile of correspondence he had received from his sister and friends. When he eventually opened the brown paper envelope and read the contents of the single page, he was incredulous.

The letter contained official notification that Jack was to report to Holyrood Palace in Edinburgh on the morning of 22 September, to attend an investiture ceremony. There, he would be presented with his Distinguished Flying Medal by His Majesty King George. At the bottom of the letter was a tear-off slip for Jack to indicate how many tickets he'd like for the event. Jack could barely comprehend the words set out before him and read the letter carefully several times over to ensure that he had not been mistaken. He even asked Welford and Weatherstone to read it out aloud. Once again Lady Luck had smiled on Jack Clyde; his name had been drawn out of a lottery of hundreds of others and an invitation to the investiture duly dispatched.

On the morning of 21 September, Jack's father, John, George, Lydia (in a brand new hat) and baby Moira, then only fifteen months old, boarded the train at Seaham station with their overnight bags, bound first for Newcastle, and then for Edinburgh, where Lydia had booked the family into a boarding house. Each of them took turns to carry the baby as they walked the mile or so to their accommodation, as "infant carriages and perambulators" had not been allowed on the train. Their landlady very kindly offered to loan Lydia the use of her pram for the duration of the trip.

At nine o'clock sharp the next morning, Jack was waiting for them outside Holyrood. Passes and tickets were shown at the gate, and the Clydes trooped into the Palace to take their seats among the hundreds of assembled guests. Lydia would recall in later years that the King looked gaunt and tired, and seemed to be wearing stage makeup, perhaps to conceal the fact that he was already quite unwell. For what seemed like hours the family sat, awestruck at their surroundings and the circumstances in which they found themselves, while the names of servicemen and women were called out. Jack's thoughts turned to Roy and Freddie and the rest of the Pennicott crew. How he wished they had all been there to share this day. Eventually the announcement came.

"Flight Sergeant John Clyde, Royal Air Force Volunteer Reserve, 10 Squadron – Distinguished Flying Medal."

Jack rose from his seat and walked to the front, his cheeks aglow. He had never been more terrified, even when approaching the flak guns over the Ruhr Valley. He reminisced about the wide-eyed, innocent young lad at West Raynham who had excitedly watched the visit of the King and Queen, looking on in awe as they had chatted to the hero of the hour, Wing Commander Jenkins. This time *he* was the hero. He beamed shyly as His Majesty pinned the purple and silver ribbon to his chest, shook the King's hand firmly and gave him his best salute. It was all over in a matter of seconds. Upon returning to his seat, the applause still echoing in his ears, Lydia whispered to him loudly, wanting to know what the King had said. Much to her annoyance, Jack couldn't remember a single word.

Baby Moira, in her borrowed pram, had slept through the whole thing. After the ceremony, when the crowds had dispersed, Jack's father treated them all to lunch in one of the hotels on George Street, before the family said their goodbyes at the station.

Since arriving at Kinloss in April, Jack had spent most of his time flying, shadowing the wireless operators on trainee bomber crews or demonstrating how to obtain radio fixes of their positions. With the benefit of his experience, he was able to show them what to do if the wireless equipment malfunctioned, or what would be expected of them in the event of an emergency. He even told them about the pigeons on board the Halifaxes, and how they were to be employed if the order to abandon the aircraft was given. An enormous number of young men, many of them from the Royal Canadian Airforce, had passed through 19 OTU in the five months Jack had spent there. Fully aware of what lay ahead of them, he always endeavoured to treat his charges with empathy and fairness.

Shortly before his visit to Holyrood, Jack had received notification of his forthcoming promotion to the rank of Warrant Officer, the highest rank a non-commissioned officer could achieve, together with orders to report to RAF Enstone, near Moreton-in-the-Marsh in Oxfordshire in October, to commence his formal Instructors Training Course. If he passed the month-long course, he would then be qualified to give lectures to wireless operators, in addition to his existing airborne duties. The thought of speaking to a large group of young men filled him with trepidation, and it was with some reluctance that Jack began his long journey south, although the prospect of a few days' leave at home en route sweetened the pill a little. Back in Seaham, all talk was still of the Clyde family's trip to Holyrood; at the prompting of his sister, Jack had to repeat the whole story to every single visitor to the house, and to every single person he bumped into. This was something of an ordeal for Jack, who always shunned the limelight and hated being the centre of attention, regardless of his achievements.

Jack's notebooks from his trips to Enstone still exist. A little dog-eared now, and with the pencilled handwriting very faded in places, the pages smell faintly of tobacco. One can imagine Jack sat on his bed, resting his exercise book on his knees, a cigarette dangling from his lips as he read over his notes from the day's lessons, occasionally flicking ash from the pages. The course covered all aspects of instruction, from the preparation of lectures, to methods of delivery and even principles of leadership. It also dealt with any updated technological changes. Jack carefully noted down everything that was expected of him and appears to have taken particular notice of the presentation techniques required.

> "A strong approach is essential. Give the impression that you yourself are keenly interested in the subject and that it is one of vital importance… keep your eyes on the class, look at each man in turn, and keep the eyes moving…"
>
> "Speak to the back of your class and take great care in forming the final consonants… endeavour to cultivate a vocabulary to avoid constant repetition of the same type of expression; slang and bad language are to be avoided."

On the cover of one of the notebooks, in the bottom corners, Jack has doodled an RAF rondel and a union flag; on the inside cover, clearly proud of his new rank, he has written, in a childlike, fancy script, his name, number and new rank. Jack had only just turned twenty-two a month before; he was still not much more than a boy. He eventually passed the course with the very respectable mark of 75.9%, a vast improvement on his initial wireless operator's course when he had barely scraped through.

Just a few days after Jack left Kinloss for Enstone, a Whitley bomber, AD685, took off from the Scottish base on a training flight. All but one of the six crew on board were Canadian, recently arrived at Kinloss to commence their training for Bomber Command, like thousands of young Canadian men had done before them. The pilot, Flying Officer Kenneth Reed, was from Alberta; the navigator, Flying Officer Walter Wall, the mid-upper gunner, Alexander Sunstrum, and the young air gunner, John Dowding, were all Ontarians. The eldest member of the crew at the grand old age of twenty-nine, Sergeant Leslie Olmstead, hailed from Sasketchewan. The only British member of the crew was nineteen-year-old Sergeant Ernest Leivers from Derbyshire, a wireless operator and one of Jack's students at the OTU.

John Dowding was only seventeen, having lied about his age to enlist. He hoped to follow in the illustrious footsteps of his elder brother, Harry, a Squadron Leader and Spitfire ace, who had been awarded the Distinguished Flying Cross for his heroics in 1943. His parents, complicit in the deceit and perhaps influenced by their elder son's successes, had signed John's enlistment papers and provided a letter in support, giving their permission for him to join the Air Force. John was just sixteen when he joined the RCAF on 3 August 1943.[109]

There was nothing unusual about the Whitley's flight that night. It was a routine training operation, a cross-country exercise down the eastern coast of Scotland and northern England, following a regular route taken by the trainee crews designed to introduce them to night flying before they moved onto Halifaxes or Lancasters, at a Heavy Conversion Unit.

At 21.45 hours, AD685 was recorded as missing.

109 Boileau, John and Black, Dan, *Too Young to Die: Canada's Boy Soldiers, Sailors and Airmen in the Second World War*, James Lorimer & Co Ltd, Toronto, 2016, pp.392-403.

Half an hour or so later, in the midst of a severe thunder storm, several Seaham farmers – Bill Bulmer at Stotfold, Roy Snowdon at Seaton and Mr Ford at Slingley, between Seaton Village and Murton – were disturbed by the arrival of police officers who informed them that an aircraft was missing and was believed to have come down on their land. The three farmers and their farmhands were asked to assist in locating the crash site – no mean feat in the dark – and to search for survivors.

The search was in vain.

A subsequent investigation revealed that the aircraft had developed problems over the coast, possibly due to a combination of turbulence and icing. As the pilot had turned to come inland, perhaps in the hope of making a crash-landing, the aircraft had begun to break up in mid-air. The exact reason for the disintegration was never firmly established. "Control lost in cloud" was listed on accident documents. "Fairly frequent flashes of lightning" were reported by another Whitley bomber in the area at the time, and a local observatory in Durham reported "a violent localised electrical storm moving through the area from the west" at half past nine that evening. Perhaps extreme turbulence from the storm had caused the aircraft to break up.

One cannot even begin to comprehend the horror experienced by those on board as the Whitley began to disintegrate, as it flew over Seaham Harbour and over the new Deneside Estate, roughly on a course directly above The Avenue. One wing fell to the ground by the George Inn on that very street, a few hundred yards from Greta Meek's home, the other a quarter of a mile or so further on, landing in a backyard in Mount Pleasant. It is a miracle that no one on the ground was killed or injured. The two engines fell in farmland beyond, while the fuselage containing those poor boys hurtled into the ground in a field just behind Slingley Hill Farm, not too far from the now-disused railway line. There had been no fire, no explosion, and the bodies of the crew were found intact, but with horrific impact injuries, in and around the upturned fuselage.

The incident is well remembered by the older residents of Seaton and Murton. Alan Lowes, who has lived in Murton his entire life, still has very striking memories of going to view the wreckage with his elder brothers the next morning. The bodies of the dead men were laid out beneath a tarpaulin; Alan, who was a small boy of six at the time, vividly recalls seeing their feet, still in their flying boots, protruding from beneath their temporary canvas shroud.

The bodies of the crew were removed immediately. The Canadians were all buried together in the Harrogate Regional Cemetery, alongside so many of their compatriots, whilst Sergeant Leivers' body was returned to his family in Derbyshire. If you walk along the old railway line (now a trackway popular with cyclists and dog walkers) from Seaton Village towards Murton, you will pass Slingley Hill Farm on the right, silhouetted against the wind turbines beyond. There is no hint as to the tragic events of 17 October 1944, nor is there any memorial to the young men who perished; their story has been largely forgotten.

Young John Dowding's parents were informed of his death by telegram, three days after the crash, on 20 October. A second telegram followed two days later, informing them that their son's funeral service was to take place at Harrogate the very next day. By the time that message reached them in Sarnia, Ontario, their boy had already been buried. John's commanding officer at Kinloss, Group Captain Cole, wrote to them on 27 October, relaying details of the funeral service and the circumstances of John's death:[110]

---

110 www.sarniahistoricalsociety.com/warmemorialproject, accessed
    27.9.2018.

"As air gunner of his aircraft, he took off in the evening of Tuesday 17th October to carry out a cross-country detail. Contact was maintained with the aircraft until 21.22 hours, which was the last contact made. Information was received later that the aircraft had crashed at approximately 21.30 hours, a few miles inland west of Seaham Harbour, near Durham. It may be of some consolation to you to know that death must have been instantaneous. The cause of the accident has not yet been established."[111]

The same letter, with the names, circumstances and dates changed, that Group Captain Cole had written countless times before. Some 8240 Canadians were killed on operations with Bomber Command, and another 1740 died from non-operational causes, the vast majority in training accidents.

Jack had been unaware of the fate of John Dowding, wireless operator Ernie Leivers and the rest of the Whitley crew until he returned to Kinloss at the end of October. AD685 had crashed little more than three miles from his home.

---

111 *Ibid.*

28

Return to Happy Valley

As the final winter of the war began, the net was slowly beginning to close around the Third Reich, or what was left of it. With the benefit of hindsight, it is very easy for modern day observers to say, "Oh but the war was almost over then," but such a bald statement could not be further from the truth. After the initial early successes of the invasion after D-Day, Allied commanders had expected hostilities to be all but over by October 1944, but the pace of the advance slowed almost to a crawl as the ground troops became caught up in vicious fighting against an entrenched and determined enemy in Normandy and the Pas de Calais. A failed German counter-offensive by the German 7th Army led to 50,000 Wehrmacht soldiers being trapped in the Falaise Pocket, where thousands of men and horses perished under the weight of the Allied bombardment. Operation Dragoon, the invasion of France from its Mediterranean coast on 15 August 1944, swept northwards at a pace, but pockets of German resistance remained, especially on the Atlantic coast. Paris had finally been liberated after the surrender of the German garrison on 25 August 1944, and Allied troops were in Brussels by 2 September.

Nazi ground forces had been pushed back into Holland, where bitter fighting continued at the expense of the Dutch civilian population, who would endure months of starvation over the coming winter. Following the ill-fated attempt by British and American paratroopers to seize the bridge over the Rhine at Arnhem during Operation Market Garden in October 1944, Allied troops finally began to make substantial territorial gains, but were taken completely by surprise when German forces mounted a sudden and massive counter attack in the Ardennes just before Christmas. In Italy, the Allies had finally liberated Rome in June 1944 and were now making swift progress northwards. In response to the threat to the Reich's domestic borders, Hitler had issued a mobilisation order in October, and all men between the ages of sixteen and sixty were conscripted to defend the Fatherland.

By the end of the year, the Germans still occupied the western half of Poland; the Eastern Front was still 200 miles beyond where the border had been in 1939. The Germans had repelled the Russians' summer offensive and had established a firm line along the Narew and Vistula rivers southward to the Carpathians in Romania. In October they had held back the Soviets' attempted push into East Prussia, but Russian forces in the Balkans had been gradually moving across Hungary, and Yugoslavia, assisted by the Partisans. The Germans struggled to maintain the supply of men, fuel and equipment on all fronts as the Allied bombing campaign gradually brought the Reich to a state of paralysis.

In the Far East, the Japanese were in retreat in the Philippines, pursued by American Naval and ground forces, while British and Commonwealth troops were finally making ground against Japanese Imperial Forces in Burma, after victories at Imphal and Kohima earlier in the year.

Throughout, the men and aircraft of 10 Squadron had been at the forefront of the war in the European theatre, supporting the invasion, attacking German troop positions and bombing transport networks in France, Holland and Germany, as well as continuing to lay mines in enemy harbours and sea lanes. By late summer 1944, the Allies were able to build their own technology and radar sites on European soil, which greatly enhanced the efficiency of the bombers' navigation systems, thereby allowing for greater accuracy. The aerial onslaught against German towns, cities and industrial targets continued, paving the way for the eventual arrival of Allied ground forces.

Jack and his former crewmates were no longer at the sharp end of the fighting, although the risks of flying with trainee crews remained substantial. In the twelve months Jack spent at 19 OTU, eleven aircraft and their young crews were lost; many more men were injured, and aircraft written off or extensively damaged in training accidents. Penny, Bill and George had all received instructor postings too, and they were all sent together to 1652 Heavy Conversion Unit at RAF Marston Moor to teach the next intake of crews how to fly, defend and maintain a Halifax. Their duties meant that they never flew together as part of a crew again, although they were occasionally able to socialise in the mess and in the NAAFI on an evening. Penny and Bill in particular remained very close friends. There is no record of Ken Cox after his departure from 10 Squadron, nor of his subsequent posting.

Unlike the others, Reg Cowles had very quickly realised that instructing was not for him. He found that he missed the adrenaline and the intellectual challenge of operational flying, and despite the assurances he had previously given to his mother and elder sister, Queenie, in October 1944 Reg volunteered for a second tour with Bomber Command. His considerable skill and experience as a navigator meant that he was very quickly assigned to a new squadron. After a short refresher course, he was duly ordered to report to RAF Waterbeach in Cambridgeshire, the home of 3 Group's 514 Squadron. For the first time in the war, Reg was to fly on Avro Lancasters.

Waterbeach was a very different kettle of fish from Melbourne. It was a much bigger station and had a larger fleet of aircraft at its disposal. It was not unheard of for the squadron to despatch as many as thirty Lancasters on a single raid. Reg was attached to a very young and inexperienced crew, that of Pilot Officer Ellis Hill. Reg was the oldest member of the crew; his two gunners, Sergeants Balman and Bowen, were both only nineteen. Hill welcomed Reg's expertise and his experience of operational flying, though the entire crew were in awe of him, his thirty operations and his Distinguished Flying Cross (with Bar).

The Hill crew's first operation took place on 29 November 1944, on the German city of Neuss, part of the Düsseldorf conurbation. Squadron records show that Reg and his new crew in Lancaster NG350, *C-Charlie*, successfully bombed the target at 05.35 hours from 20,000 feet, landing safely back at base at 07.10.[112] They certainly fared better than another Waterbeach crew who undertook their first operation to Osterfeld the following day. Pilot Officer Gallicano and his Canadian crew had managed to get themselves lost on the way home, and erroneously landed at Mildenhall, an American air base in Norfolk, twenty-five miles away. The Squadron Operations Record Book somewhat generously notes, "*landed at Mildenhall by mistake owing to lack of local geographical*

112 National Archives AIR27/1978/10 514 Sqn ORB.

knowledge." One can only imagine the dressing down the Canadians received when they eventually made it home to Waterbeach.

The operational demands placed on bomber crews in the second half of 1944 were nothing short of horrendous. On 14 and 15 October 1944, 2000 sorties were flown to Duisburg in less than twenty-four hours. In addition to the area bombing of German towns and cities, Bomber Command now began to focus upon the destruction of enemy fuel oil plants and railways. German tanks, vehicles and aircraft were useless if their supply of fuel was cut off; troops and equipment could not be moved around the country without a functioning rail network. The targeting of the oil refineries had a secondary effect: millions of German civilians faced a bitter winter with rapidly dwindling supplies of fuel for domestic heating. Reg had not witnessed anything like it since the height of the Battle of the Ruhr in the summer of the preceding year. Operations continued daily, interrupted only by occasional bad weather, and the Hill crew were rostered for five operations in a week and a half. Although Bomber Command continued to attack targets at night, many of the raids now took place in daylight, to increase the accuracy of bombing.

During the whole of Reg's time at 10 Squadron, first with the Cameron and then the Pennicott crews, he had not taken part in a single daylight raid. Daytime raids over German targets would have been utterly suicidal earlier in the war, but as the German radar sites on the northern fringes of Europe were overrun by the Allies, the RAF began to gain air supremacy. However, the perils posed by flak and marauding Luftwaffe fighters over the target areas in German territory persisted. In order to try to reduce aircraft losses, the RAF had adopted American-style tight formation flying for the daylight raids, frequently escorted by USAAF P-51 Mustangs, but this tactic was fraught with danger, not least the increased risk of mid-air collision.

The Hill crew took part in the daylight raid on the Hansa Benzol factory in Dortmund on only their second operation, on 2 December 1944.[113] Flying over the Ruhr Valley in darkness had been frightening enough; doing it in daylight was utterly terrifying. Of the fifteen aircraft which left Waterbeach, five were hit by flak, although all managed to make it home. After a four-day pause in operations due to inclement weather, Reg and his colleagues were rostered for a massive evening raid on the oil refinery at Merseburg, near Leipzig, on 6 December. Four hundred and seventy-five Lancasters attacked the refinery, causing significant damage. "Intense, heavy flak" was reported over the target area, and five Lancasters and their crews were lost.[114] Less than thirty-six hours later, the Hill crew's baptism of fire continued, with another daylight operation, this time on the railway yards at Duisburg in the dreaded Ruhr Valley. Reg must surely have begun to question his own judgement, and perhaps bitterly regretted his decision to volunteer for a second tour.

A little after half past eight on the morning of 11 December, Reg (on his thirty-fifth operation) and his crew took off from Waterbeach in *C-Charlie*, Lancaster NG350, in company with sixteen other aircraft bound once again for "Happy Valley."[115] *C-Charlie* was carrying a single 4000-pound bomb and five 500-pound bombs fitted with long-delay fuses, designed to inflict maximum carnage in the aftermath of the raid. Flying in tight formation, several crews from 514 Squadron reported seeing two aircraft blow up at close range. These appear to have been German fighters, as only one of the 150 Lancasters which took part in the raid was lost.

---

113 *Ibid*, 2.12.1944.
114 *Ibid*, 6.12.1944.
115 *Ibid*, 11.12.1944.

In the 514 Squadron Operations Record Book, next to "C-Charlie" and the list of her crew, appear the stark words "Aircraft missing."

After making her bombing run, C-Charlie had been hit by flak as she attempted to make for home. There was simply no time for her crew to bale out, and the aircraft came down in the Sterkrade district of Oberhausen, in the industrial heartlands of the Ruhr, crashing into a row of houses. The fate of the occupants of those properties is unknown. Reg Cowles, pilot Ellis Hill, wireless operator Cyril Atter, air bomber Frank Guest, flight engineer Norman Readman and the two teenage gunners, John Balman and Alan Bowen, were killed instantly.

Flying Officer Reginald Andrew Clifford Cowles (DFC and Bar) lies in the Reichswald Forest War Cemetery in Germany, near the Dutch border, alongside his crew and 7587 other Commonwealth servicemen. He was twenty-three.[116]

Jack and the rest of the Pennicott crew remained unaware of their navigator's fate.

*

Bad weather on the Moray Firth coast throughout December meant that flying opportunities were somewhat limited. By then, 19 OTU's ancient Whitleys had all been replaced by Wellingtons – the Whitley which had crashed near to Jack's home the previous October was the last to be lost in the war – but the Wellingtons weren't much safer. In the whole of December, Jack flew fewer than eight hours, as "screen" wireless operator, shadowing the progress of his trainees. For a great deal of the time he was incredibly bored, and would occupy the empty hours reading, playing cards and drinking at the NAAFI bar. He tried to keep himself busy, as inevitably it

---

116 International Bomber Command Losses Database.

was in the quieter moments that his thoughts would return to Melbourne and to Roy, the noise of battle, the claustrophobia of his wireless operator's cubbyhole, and the empty chairs and tables at breakfast. Gradually, with the passage of time and the absence of further trauma, the frequency of his nightmares and flashbacks began to diminish, but they never disappeared.

Because he had enjoyed a week off in early December, yet another Christmas was to be spent away from his family in Seaham Harbour. Despite Jack's absence and the paucity of rations, Christmas at the little house in Caroline Street was a much jollier affair than in previous years. A few days after Jack had set off to return to Kinloss, late at night on 16 December Lydia answered a knock at the front door. To her considerable surprise there, on the front step, grinning from ear to ear, kit bag at his feet and "tommy" gun still slung over his shoulder, was Jim. It was the first time he had seen Lydia since they had said goodbye to one another in Scotland in 1942, and the first time baby Moira met her "paper daddy."

Jim's unit had reached Forli at the end of November. There, the men were informed that a new home leave scheme was being introduced for those soldiers who had served abroad for more than two years. Two percent of these men were to be selected by lottery and sent home for Christmas; Jim's name was one of the very few drawn out of the hat. It all happened so suddenly that he had not even had time to write to Lydia to tell her of his imminent arrival.

Jim was immediately struck by the fact that at home, life already seemed to be returning to normal, the war ever more distant. The blackout restrictions had been lifted in July and partial street lighting had been reintroduced (Greta Meek still recalls her childish amazement when the street lights were turned back on), the Home Guard had been stood down, and in Seaham Harbour folks went about their daily business just as they had done six years previously, before the madness had begun. Much to the delight of Ron Toft and the other local children, many of whom had never swum in the sea or played on the sand before, part of the coal-stained beach had been reopened. The sight of the bombed-out houses around the corner did not shock Jim, indeed they barely registered, such was the scale of the devastation he had witnessed throughout Italy. However, despite the outward appearance of peace and normality, a steady stream of "REGRET TO INFORM YOU" telegrams continued to be delivered to families throughout the town, destroying dreams of shared futures in an instant.

On Monday 22 January 1945, the day after Lydia's twenty-fourth birthday, Jim said goodbye to his little family, and walked the few yards towards Church Street, where the town's shopkeepers were just beginning to open up. As he turned the corner and lost sight of Lydia and Moira waving at the front door, he paused, and almost turned back, overcome with emotion. Throughout the hell of the desert campaign, and even in the face of the unremitting horrors of Cassino, in his twilight years Jim confessed that he had never come so close to deserting as in that brief moment. He wiped away his tears, gathered his composure, threw his kit bag over his shoulder, and strode off towards the station. Within a week, he had met up with his unit in Faenza, near Bologna. He would not see his family again until March 1946.

As usual, 10 Squadron had been in the thick of the action. After a break of three months between April and late July 1944, when they had concentrated purely on French targets and the V1 rocket sites in support of the invasion, operations over Germany had resumed with alarming regularity. As Reg Cowles had done, the Melbourne crews were now taking part in daylight raids, with an increasing number returning to base with significant flak damage. Although the rate of losses was not as high as in the early days of the Battle of the Ruhr, the squadron records are still littered with the familiar phrase, "Failed to return." One of those aircraft was flown by Flying Officer Saynor and his crew, believed to have been shot down in error by another Halifax en route to Brunswick on 12 August, on what should have been the last operation of their tour. All baled out successfully but spent the rest of the war as prisoners.[117] In addition to the usual raids on industrial targets, 10 Squadron also carried out successful attacks on Luftwaffe night fighter bases in Holland.

By late January 1945, the Luftwaffe had been all but grounded, having largely run out of pilots, aircraft and fuel. Many German cities were left more or less undefended, reliant solely on the remnants of their anti-aircraft flak batteries, manned by boys and old men; much of the artillery had been moved to the Eastern Front in a desperate attempt to halt the Soviet advance. Bomber Command continued to flatten German cities regardless, but questions began to be raised about the morality of a campaign in which the majority of the victims were German civilians who now lacked the resources to defend themselves.

On the night of 13 February, 10 Squadron were called to take part in a "maximum effort" raid on yet another oil plant, this time at Böhlen. Twenty-three of the squadron's aircraft took part, but their attempts were somewhat hampered by low cloud. Just seventy miles from the refinery, two waves of Lancasters were heading towards the city of Dresden, in South East Germany. Dresden, a marvel of Baroque and Medieval architecture on the banks of the River Elbe, had

---

117 MacMillan, Ian and King, Richard, *From Brooklands to Brize: A Centennial History of No 10 Squadron Royal Air Force*, 10 Squadron Association, 2015, p. 151.

largely been spared from the Allied bombardment thus far. The German authorities had considered it to be of too great historical significance to be a target; it had very few air defences, nor any municipal air raid shelters. Plans had been drawn up by Allied commanders earlier in the year for attacks on Chemnitz, Dresden and Leipzig, with the intention of aiding the Soviet advance in the east; with the Russians now close to the German border, the time had arrived for the plan to be implemented. As the Halifaxes of 10 Squadron began to head home from their raid on Böhlen, the fires of hell were about to be visited upon on Dresden, in the first of four raids by RAF and USAAF aircraft over the course of two days.

At around quarter past ten, the bombardment began. The attackers were completely unopposed, and within minutes of the first bombs being dropped, the ancient city, crammed with wooden medieval structures, was on fire. Fanned by a strong wind, individual conflagrations soon spread to envelope the city in one huge firestorm. The blackened and anonymous corpses of those who had attempted to flee towards the safety of the river were scattered upon every street. Thousands huddled together in the medieval cellars of their homes, only to be suffocated as the firestorm engulfed house after house, sucking up all the oxygen from the air. Others still tried to take refuge in the large water tanks situated in the city's squares, where they drowned or were boiled alive as the flames overtook them.

Arguments have raged for decades as to the actual death toll (the city population was swelled by a large number of refugees from the Eastern Front on the night of the raid); over the years estimates have been put at figures ranging from 18,000 to 135,000 (Nazi leaders announced a grossly inflated of 200,000 dead in the immediate aftermath for propaganda purposes). The true figure is believed to be between 25,000 and

41,000, and probably at the lower end of that range. Dresden was destroyed, devastated on a scale perhaps comparable only to that witnessed in the aftermath of the atom bomb attacks on Hiroshima and Nagasaki. Even now, seventy-five years later, there are still tell-tale signs of the firestorm all over the city. The Altstadt has been diligently and beautifully rebuilt in recent years, but if you look carefully, particularly around the bases of buildings at pavement level, the fire-blackened stones remain. The debate as to the morality, and indeed the legality, of the raid on Dresden continues to this day.

Barely visible on a stone plinth in the centre of the Alt Markt, next to the pedestrian entrance to an underground car park, there is a memorial to the Dresden victims. It is deliberately very understated, and not immediately apparent. The inscription is striking and thought provoking:

> "The horror of the War that went out from Germany into the world came back to our city."

In the gaps between the cobbles just below, there is a small splash of what appears at first sight to be molten silver. Engraved upon it is a dedication to the memory of the 6865 people whose bodies were stacked and cremated upon that very spot in the days after the raid.

The remaining months of the war passed very quietly indeed for Jack at Kinloss. He began to grow in confidence as an instructor, and soon found that lecturing held no more fears for him. As the dank and dreary Scottish winter lingered, he barely flew in January or February, but by mid-March and the first tentative signs of spring, the weather had begun to improve. He was relieved to escape the stuffy classrooms and get back in the air. Jack's last flight of the war took place two days before VE Day, on 6 May 1945, a late evening cross-country exercise incorporating some practice bombing and air sea firing in Wellington A-883, with Flight Lieutenant Pickler at the controls.

On the following day, the 10 Squadron Operations Book at Melbourne states simply:

"7th May 1945 – 10 Squadron Operations Book is now closed."

From that point onwards, 10 Squadron was repurposed as a transport squadron, a function it still performs today. Curiously, Jack's logbook makes no mention whatsoever of the end of hostilities. After VE Day, he and his colleagues were sent home on leave for several weeks. Some bomber squadrons were on standby for transfer to the Far East, but were stood down after the Japanese surrender. As the result of a somewhat baffling logistical decision by the RAF hierarchy, Jack was then posted from Kinloss to 11 Ferry Unit at RAF Dunkeswell in Devon, at the opposite end of the country. Ironically, he spent his entire summer there flying Lancasters from base to base, with Pickler, his pal from Kinloss. Jack had never set foot in a Lancaster for the entire course of the war; like many of the men who had flown the Halifax operationally, he thought it far superior to its more glamorous and better-known counterpart.

On the same day that Jack received notification of his transfer to 11 Ferry Unit, his former crewmates were also on the move. Penny, Bill and George were all transferred to 158 Squadron at Stradishall in Suffolk, by then a transport unit. Originally a 4 Group Squadron flying Halifaxes out of RAF Lisset in Yorkshire, after VE Day it was converted to fly Short Stirling bombers adapted as troop carriers, to bring hundreds of thousands of British servicemen back home from India, and to return Commonwealth servicemen to their "home" countries.

This huge undertaking, codenamed "Operation Sketch," involved flying the fairly ancient Stirlings, with their insides ripped out in order to accommodate a five-man crew and twenty-four passengers (with kit), from Suffolk to Melsbroek in Belgium (a former Luftwaffe base), then across the Mediterranean to Castel Benito in Libya. There, the crews would change over before flying on to Shallufa in Egypt, Lydda in Palestine, Mauripur on the outskirts of Karachi and finally to Arakkonam in Tamil Nadu, in the far south of India. Thousands of trips were made back and forth along this tortuous route, by 158 and other transport squadrons. Penny and George flew more hours after the war with 158 Squadron to India and back than they had throughout the whole of their time at Melbourne; Bill had been sent off to assist in the decommissioning of various RAF bases, and it was during this time that he received his promotion to Flight Lieutenant.

A little after midnight on 12 December 1945, seven months after the war had ended, a Short Stirling PJ950 took off from RAF Castel Benito, with a full complement of crew and passengers. The flight had originated in Mauripur, where it had picked up twenty-four British soldiers bound, at last, for home. There was no cloud, and visibility was good as the aircraft, piloted by 158 Squadron's Flight Lieutenant Wilson, sped down the electrically lit runway. The Stirling appeared to be in trouble almost immediately and struggled to gain height. Just a minute after take-off, and from an altitude of only 200 feet, it was seen to hit the ground a short distance from the end of the runway and burst into flames. Except for one passenger, all were killed or died shortly afterwards.[118] The cause of the crash was never established, but all Short Stirlings were

---

118 National Archive AIR 27/1050/15.

removed from troop transports with effect from the end of December 1945.

George Phillipson never did get back home to Upton Park and his beloved wife Ethel. He is buried in the Commonwealth War Cemetery in Tripoli, Libya.

29

At Ease

A few miles southeast of the city of York, a narrow country lane snakes through flat, fertile farmland, criss-crossed with drainage ditches and hedges of hawthorn and bramble. The skyline is interrupted by stands of poplar, lime and oak, and occasionally the spire of a long-empty church. Where the lane straightens for a short distance, a small sign marks the entrance to Melrose Farm, one of the many scattered across the landscape in this part of Yorkshire. The track towards the farmhouse leads past a small single-storey whitewashed building, then through a maze of functional sheds and barns, and bears slightly right through the muddy farmyard, past tractors and feed silos. Just around the corner, and invisible from the main road, stands something quite remarkable, a window into the past. There, restored to its original state, is the control tower of RAF Melbourne, looking out across what remains of the concrete runway.

The handful of rooms of the ground floor have been converted into a tiny museum, containing treasures from the very earliest days of 10 Squadron, during the First World War, right up to the 1970s and '80s, and its reinvention as a transport and tanker squadron. The walls are filled from floor to ceiling with framed photographs of dozens of bomber crews and their aircraft, but also of many of the men who served as groundcrew. Always at the centre of the action, and never one to shy away from the camera, Leo "Titch" Groark appears on many of them. Tucked away in a corner, perhaps a foot or so above the skirting boards and so easily overlooked, is the photograph of the Pennicott crew taken after their last operation. It's the same one that can be found amongst Jack's personal effects and bears the caption "Pennicott Crew with Halifax *A-Apple*" – an aircraft they never actually flew. Many of the names printed beneath the hundreds of photographs seem familiar to me now; many I recognise as belonging to those young men who "failed to return."

A narrow staircase leads up into the control room, which has been painstakingly restored to represent how it would have looked on VE Day. On two large blackboards just near the door appear the names of the crews who flew on the penultimate day of the war, among them the wonderfully named Flight Lieutenant Bastard. The windows look out to the old runways beyond, where a solitary orange windsock hangs limply from a pole, occasionally flapping listlessly in the breeze. The windmill at Seaton Ross, a familiar and welcoming sight for the returning crews, is long since gone. It is a silent place now, but it is not difficult to imagine the clatter of feet running up and down the concrete stairs of the control tower, the eagerly awaited crackling of the radio in the early hours of the morning, and the roar of engines as the returning Halifaxes began to arrive home.

Once a year, on Remembrance Sunday, the tower comes back to life, as members of 10 Squadron Association crowd inside for tea and biscuits after the service at the memorial which stands at the entrance to the farm. Each year, the number of those present who served here dwindles yet further. Thousands of men passed through RAF Melbourne; there are but a handful of these brave and revered gentlemen left.

During the course of the war, "Shiny Ten" flew more operations than any other 4 Group Bomber Command squadron, at enormous cost. In the nine months Jack spent at Melbourne, fifty-four Halifaxes were lost and 285 of his colleagues killed. Dozens more were taken prisoner of war. By the time the conflict was over, 835 10 Squadron men had perished, many of whom have no known grave.

The statistics make extremely sobering reading. Over 125,000 aircrew flew with Bomber Command, each man a volunteer; 55,571 of those men were killed, representing losses of 44%, the highest attrition rate of any Allied unit in the Second World War. Like Roy Tann and Reg Cowles, the average age at death was just twenty-three. A staggering 72% of aircrew were either killed, severely injured or taken prisoner.

Seventy-five years on, these figures can be recited with cold academic detachment, perhaps without pausing to contemplate the enormity of their meaning. Behind each of those statistics is a man with his own story, stories like those of Jack, Penny, Roy, Bill, George, Ken, Reg and Freddie. For the survivors, the statistics were meaningless; instead, they lived (and indeed continue to live) daily with the blurred boundaries between duty and conscience, between summoned recollections and uninvited memories.

The majority of those who survived attempted to return to the familiarity of their old lives and occupations, and to recapture their own particular "normality," whilst trying to process the terror they had lived through. Life simply went on.

Penny returned to Berkshire after being demobbed from 158 Squadron and resumed his career as an estate agent. In January 1946, he became a father for the first time, and a second son followed shortly afterwards. He eventually set up his own successful surveyor's practice and estate agency, and lived very comfortably in the affluent town of Sunningdale with his wife, Joan, until his death in 1982. Pennicott & Co continues in business to this day. Penny remained a deeply religious man his entire life, and his eldest son, Anthony, became a Catholic priest. Now retired himself, Anthony recalls taking his father back to Melbourne to visit his old haunts not long before he passed away; they stood together in the old control tower, long before its restoration, looking out over the abandoned and overgrown runways, in a moment of silent reflection.

After spending several years in and out of hospital in England receiving treatment on his shattered leg, Freddie Singh eventually returned to Australia. In 1947, Freddie changed his surname to Stuart. Perhaps he felt his Indian heritage and surname hampered his career prospects. He rejoined the Royal Australian Air Force and rose eventually to the rank of Squadron Leader. After his retirement, he joined 10 Squadron Association when it was in its infancy in the early 1980s; Freddie was a frequent correspondent to the Association newsletter, and despite living half a world away, was a regular visitor to the annual Remembrance Day Service at Melbourne and Association reunions. Freddie Stuart (formerly Singh) died in 1990, at the age of seventy-two. He is buried in Toowoomba, Queensland.

Of Ken Cox and Bill Bradshaw, I could find no trace. Ken simply disappears after his departure from 10 Squadron; the last mention I could find of him anywhere was the entry in the

London Gazette for the citation for his Distinguished Flying Cross, in the summer of 1944. Bill also remained elusive, and I wondered if perhaps he had returned to Northern Ireland after the war. His name was listed on the Roll of Honour on the wall of his local church in Newcastle, but thereafter the trail went cold. I trawled through newspaper archives and genealogy websites, and even made requests on social media, to no avail. I thought perhaps I had found him when I stumbled upon newspaper articles relating to a Group Captain W.H.A. Bradshaw. However, this gentleman was not "my Bill", but rather an RAF Battle of Britain pilot who had enjoyed an illustrious career after the war. It appeared that Ken Cox and Bill Bradshaw had become just two of the many thousands of names remembered only in fading squadron photographs and once treasured logbooks, hidden away in boxes in attics or stuffed into plastic bags in the backs of wardrobes, or on inscriptions on weather-beaten gravestones in quiet country churchyards.

I had been deeply moved by the neglected state of Roy Tann's grave when I visited him in September 2018 and I took the matter up with the Commonwealth War Graves Commission upon my return home. Roy now has a gleaming new headstone of Portland stone, the inscription clearly visible. I hoped that Jack and the boys would have been glad that Roy is still cared for.

Jack returned to Seaham Harbour and was finally officially demobbed in June 1946, the only member of the Pennicott crew never to be commissioned. The role of wireless operator was traditionally considered to be a "trade" rather than a profession, and very few wireless operators ever progressed beyond NCO ranks. His RAF Certificate of Service and Release states, *"His records show a very satisfactory war service both as regards character and work done."*

Upon returning home, he simply picked up where he had left off in the winter of 1940 and returned to the joinery yard to complete his apprenticeship. His father had remarried; Jack moved out of 7 Caroline Street (by then occupied by Lydia, Jim and Moira) and went to live with him, his stepmother and younger brother, George, just round the corner in Henry Street, but continued to visit his sister daily on his way home from work.

After the initial VE Day festivities and street parties had run their course, Seaham Harbour continued its slow return to normality. Construction work continued apace throughout the town, as hundreds of new homes were built to replace not only the bombed-out houses but also the slums where so many of its residents had been born. Gradually, Seaham's servicemen began to return to a town they hardly recognised and in many cases, children they barely knew or perhaps had never even met.

It would be easy to pretend that everything was suddenly better the day after the war ended, but that simply wasn't the case. Rationing continued right up until 1954, and returning servicemen throughout the country (particularly in urban areas where there had been heavy bomb damage) were faced with a severe housing shortage as need outstripped supply; some Seaham families were forced to squat in the huts abandoned by the Army on the cliff tops opposite Seaham Hall, as the new housing estates couldn't be built quickly enough. As well as homes, jobs were also in short supply as the economy struggled under an enormous mountain of debt.

Seaham men were lucky in some respects as bodies were always needed at the local collieries; despite his intelligence and capabilities, that's precisely where Jim ended up when he returned home in March 1946, working for Lord Londonderry after ten months assisting with post-war reconstruction work in Austria. Jim would spend the remainder of his working life at the Vane Tempest colliery. Londonderry himself saw his greatest fears realised when a socialist government was elected in 1945; his coal mines, the source of his family's wealth for almost 130 years, were taken out of private ownership and nationalised two years later. He died at Mount Stewart on 10 February 1949, still vilified by his peers for his pre-war connections with Nazi Germany and his support for the policy of appeasement, his reputation never restored. The last of Seaham's pits finally closed in 1992, the end of 150 years of mining in the town.

Jack's father, John Clyde, passed away in 1951, and he continued to live with his stepmother, first in Henry Street but later in a tiny terraced cottage in Bethune Avenue on the Deneside estate. No trace remains of the Clyde family home in Caroline Street, which was demolished in the 1950s. The Volunteer Arms is still there, recently reopened after years of neglect, and the only building left in Frances Street. Viceroy Street, so badly damaged in the May 1943 air raid, was completely rebuilt, and Sophia Street was eventually replaced with 1960s housing.

After Mrs Clyde died (or Nana Clyde as she was known in the family), Jack lived alone. He never married, and never had any children. His days were spent in the joiners' yard or working out on site; his evenings were passed in the RAFA club, which he helped build, in the company of men who had shared similar experiences. He eventually became secretary of the Seaham Royal Air Force Association, and he continued to fly on RAFA trips whenever he got the opportunity. At the back of his logbook, Jack carefully recorded every flight, the type of aircraft, and the name of the pilot. Old habits die hard.

There's a black and white photograph of him on one of these trips in 1961, sitting back to back with his mates on the grass, laughing. All are wearing the navy RAFA blazer and tie; Jack is a little more rotund than in his squadron days, but he looks happy and relaxed. He was always terribly proud of his RAF service, and in another photograph, he is seen marching with the RAFA standard in the Remembrance Sunday Parade on Seaham seafront, his DFM proudly pinned to his chest.

The Jack I knew was a quiet old man, with pale, watery blue eyes, a shy smile and a faint aroma of mothballs and tobacco, who built me a dolls' house and who always had sweeties for me which he kept in a glass ashtray in the middle of his dining table. I saw him at Jim and Lydia's house most Sunday mornings after church. I would sit on the gatepost watching out for him while my grandmother, Lydia, made the Sunday lunch; as soon as I spotted him walking down the road I would jump down and run into the house to announce his arrival. After Lydia passed away at the age of just sixty in 1981, Jack and Jim would come to our house on a Sunday. Jim was always full of funny stories about his wartime experiences; we heard the same tales a thousand times over but every now and again he would surprise us and come up with a new one. Jack would sit there listening, taking it all in, occasionally with a wry smile, but always saying nothing.

In real life, happy endings are few and far between. It would be comforting to think that Jack and the Pennicott crew had remained lifelong friends, like Tom Davidson and his Australian crew, or like Leo Groark, Tom Thackray and Doug Evans. In reality, after the war they simply drifted apart, returning to their families and professions, and the friends and associates of their own class. Most working folk did not have a telephone in those days; as people moved house and moved on with their lives, addresses were misplaced, the sending of Christmas cards eventually fizzled out, and contact was lost. Perhaps that was how he had wanted it; maybe Jack had wanted to try to forget. He never did join 10 Squadron Association, unlike Leo who was a regular at squadron reunions at Brize Norton with his wife, Patsy, until his death in 2014. Leo remained the life and soul of every party he ever attended, right until the very end.

Jack never really talked about his Bomber Command days with his family in later years. It wasn't that he refused to discuss it, he simply just never mentioned it. Lydia knew a great deal of course, especially from his early days at Melbourne, and much of what Jack told her has passed into the family mythology. I remember sitting on the floor in her kitchen as a child, listening open-mouthed as she relayed to me what had happened to Jack and his crew on the Wuppertal raid, about Roy Tann, and how Jack had received his medal from the King. One of my earliest memories is watching *The Dambusters* film with Jim and Lydia, Lydia carefully pointing out the wireless operators on board the Lancasters and explaining Jack's role. It never once occurred to me to ask him directly about it.

With Jim of course, it was different. We all thought we knew everything there was to know, that we'd heard each tale until we could repeat it verbatim, until I realised (when Jim was in his early nineties) that in fact he had told us nothing very much at all, just the same handful of amusing anecdotes. One afternoon in March 2008, I sat down with him and persuaded him to tell me everything, from the fears he had experienced while walking through the minefields of the North African desert, to the horrors of Monte Cassino and the pain of being separated from his wife and child. Perhaps he thought it was time we knew the truth; Jim passed away peacefully in his sleep six months later at the grand old age of ninety-two. Like the old soldier that he was, he simply faded away.

Jack's silence was nothing unusual. So many men who served with Bomber Command never spoke about their experiences at all, and their families knew absolutely nothing about their war service. The reasons for their reticence are many and complex. Even before the war ended, questions were being asked about the wisdom of continuing the area bombing campaign when Germany was all but defeated; after Dresden and the extent of the devastation wrought upon German cities became widely known, politicians (including Churchill) very quickly began to distance themselves from the actions of Sir Arthur Harris and Bomber Command. Throughout the 1960s and '70s, there were many who argued that Bomber Command had been guilty of committing war crimes. Many still do. Those who had served as aircrew, a fair proportion of whom were already secretly tortured by multifaceted feelings of guilt and shame, were publicly humiliated by the debate. For some, their service, their huge personal contribution to the war effort, and in many cases their near-death experiences, had become a burden of dishonour. The bomber crews received no campaign medal; there was no permanent memorial built in their honour until 2012.

Among the population at large there was a feeling of wanting to lay the past to rest, and to look forwards to the future. The average citizen – veterans and ordinary civilians alike – simply wanted to put the war behind them and move on with their lives. Some former servicemen felt that they had nothing new to say, in circumstances where most of their workmates and friends had all, to some extent, experienced something similar, whether it was being evacuated from Dunkirk, serving on the Arctic convoys or fighting the Japanese in the jungles of Burma. Why should one man's experiences be given any more weight or consideration than those of another? Why would anyone be interested?

Some men didn't talk about their time with Bomber Command because they simply couldn't. A large number suffered, to varying degrees, from what we would now call post-traumatic stress disorder; there was no counselling in those days, no support groups, no therapy. How many poor souls must have suffered in silence for years, in the depths of despair, powerless or unwilling to vocalise their pain and their grief for their fallen comrades, their guilt at the devastation and enormous loss of life in which they had played a part, or perhaps unable to make the link between the trauma they had experienced and their current state of mind. The shameful legacy of the RAF treatment of those considered to "lack moral fibre" still lingers. A few of the last remaining veterans are only just beginning to come to terms with their feelings in their nineties; it has taken over seven decades for them to be able to open up about their experiences. Jack maintained his silence right to the very end.

Jack Clyde passed away suddenly, quietly, at home on 25 February 1988, at the age of sixty-six. There was no fuss, no RAFA guard of honour, nor any standard bearer at his funeral. As in life, in death. His Bomber Command logbook, his notebooks from Wireless School, his RAF clothing card, paybook, medals and even his identification dog tags were all found bundled together in a plastic bag, along with a small pile of photographs of the Pennicott crew.

Jack's Distinguished Flying Medal was missing from his personal effects. It has never been found.

His mother's rose gold wedding band, which he had worn for the duration of his service with Bomber Command and which had accompanied him to hell and back, passed into the possession of his younger brother, George, upon his death. It was stolen in a burglary at George's home some years later.

*

In the last ten to twenty years or so, attitudes towards the Bomber Command campaign and the men who took part have begun to change noticeably. Their contributions are now valued, their service revered by many. People *want* to hear veterans' stories; their testimonies are now rightly considered to be of great historical significance and are carefully and diligently recorded. The very few gentlemen who are (thankfully) still with us are treated with respect and dignity. As a result, some find that they are now able to talk about their experiences for the first time in their lives. The beautiful bronze Bomber Command memorial which now stands in Hyde Park in London depicts an exhausted crew looking skywards, waiting for their comrades to return; the fact that it took until 2012 for an official memorial to be created is to our eternal shame as a nation. It remains controversial, and sadly has been vandalised several times. The Mayor of Dresden lobbied the British Government to abandon the plans for the memorial when they were announced in 2010. Upon learning that the planned inscription honoured the war dead of all nations in the 1939–45 conflict, in a gesture of reconciliation, the Mayor withdrew her objections.

Public interest in the men of Bomber Command continues to grow. Every year, a wonderful team of volunteers organises Project Propeller, a reunion for Second World War aircrew, who are flown into a working airfield on light aircraft from airports all around the country to meet up with their former squadron colleagues, for a spot of lunch and a chinwag, and the inevitable flypast by the Battle of Britain Memorial Flight. It is a beautifully moving and happy occasion, but sadly the number of attendees grows fewer each year.

In January 2018, the International Bomber Command Centre on Canwick Hill, Lincoln, opened its doors to the public for the first time. Its stated purpose is "to provide a world-class facility to serve as a point for recognition, remembrance and reconciliation for Bomber Command." It is not an aircraft or a war museum; instead, set among pretty gardens, you will find a visually arresting state-of-the-art building containing a vast archive – both physical and digital – of historic documents and objects, as well as a thought-provoking and very moving interactive experience which attempts to further our understanding of the Bomber Command campaign. The centre isn't devoted solely to aircrew, as it recognises the contribution of the million service personnel from sixty-two nations who supported them: from the groundcrews to the cooks, the drivers to the intelligence officers, the WAAFs who packed the parachutes to the training instructors, the recovery crews who retrieved human remains from crashed aircraft and the chaplains who provided moral support – all are remembered here. The experiences of German civilians are thoughtfully and respectfully considered too.

Set away from the building on the hilltop directly opposite the city of Lincoln stands the Memorial Spire. Constructed from rusted steel, it is 102 feet tall, the same height as the wingspan of an Avro Lancaster. At its base, there is a series of panels, etched with the names of all 57,861 members of Bomber Command (including those killed on the ground) who made the ultimate sacrifice. Among them are Roy Tann and Reg Cowles, and the young Canadian crew who crashed near Seaham in October 1944.

Leading up to the Spire and the vast panels of names there is a long, straight footpath. Down each side are laid a number of memorial stones, forming a "Ribbon of Remembrance", each inscribed with a dedication, where family members can pay tribute to anyone who served with Bomber Command, groundcrew and aircrew alike. The contribution of *all* who served, including those who survived, is given equal weight.

On a glorious Saturday afternoon in July 2019, I brought my parents to visit the IBCC for the first time. We made our way slowly towards the Spire, which shimmered in the heat, carefully reading the dedications on the stones. Halfway up on the left-hand side we paused.

There, on a single stone, are listed all eight members of the Pennicott crew. In the distance just opposite is Lincoln Cathedral, so frequently the boys' first indication that they were very nearly home, having survived yet another raid over Germany.

"Penny's Prangers", together again at last, looking up towards familiar skies.

Above them, only the stars.

Postscript

Four days after returning from my emotional trip to the IBCC in Lincoln in July 2019, I was busy reading through archived newsletters from the early 1980s on the 10 Squadron Association website. I was looking for correspondence from Freddie Singh (Stuart) and any crumbs of information about everyday life at RAF Melbourne, when a list of new members from around 1986 caught my eye. There, at the top of the page, was a W.H.A. Bradshaw, with an address in West Yorkshire. I felt certain that this must be *the* Bill Bradshaw, due to the unusual combination of initials, and the fact that despite it being a common surname, there weren't actually that many Bradshaws who had served as aircrew with 10 Squadron during the war.

After much online searching and raking through old telephone directories, I alighted upon a telephone number for the address given, which was relatively recent. I decided to call, on the off chance that the current occupants of the property may have some inkling as to what had happened to the previous residents. The number rang out for a while but then a gentleman answered. I explained that I was trying to trace the family of a William (Bill) Bradshaw who had lived at that address many years ago.

"William Bradshaw, you say?" enquired the gentleman with a chortle. "You're speaking to him, my dear!"

I was so overcome, I could barely explain who I was or what I wanted, or my connection to Jack. Here he was, after all those years of searching, all those hours spent looking at his photograph, researching every aspect of his experiences with the Pennicott crew. Once I had collected myself, I explained to Dr Bradshaw, to give him his correct title, that I was Jack Clyde's great-niece. I think Bill was as shocked to hear from me as I was from him.

"Ah yes. Clyde! Fantastic chap, excellent wireless operator. He was from a little place called Seaham Harbour, you know. A Geordie. His people were coal miners. We gave him the nickname Andy, after Andy Clyde, the American film star. He was always singing, especially when he was frightened. He used to sing the 'Blaydon Races' all the time, I remember. They were the best crew, the absolute best."

We chatted for about twenty minutes or so, and arrangements were subsequently made with his lovely daughter Angela for me to visit.

Three weeks later, Angela kindly picked me up at the station and we drove to Bill's home. Upon entering, there he was, sat on the sofa, with a shock of white hair, looking at least two decades younger than his ninety-seven years (he had celebrated his birthday just a few days before), and still with the same dazzling smile as in Jack's photographs from a lifetime ago. I was smitten immediately. We chatted for hours, and much of what he told me appears in this book – the details about the crew, their personalities, crewing up, Dr Ponder, Wuppertal, Pennicott and his Catholic faith and his prayers for the German people, the searchlights at La Rochelle and being allowed to include their Coastal Command trips as part of their tour. He hadn't known of the fate of Reg Cowles or George Phillipson and looked downcast as I related what had happened to them.

Bill explained that he had been raised on a farm in Northern Ireland, near Strangford Lough, in a staunch Protestant area. His mother had once been "sent to Coventry" by the other women in the village for attending the funeral of a Catholic woman; his aunts were appalled when they discovered the pilot of his bomber crew was a Catholic.

"I joined the RAF at seventeen, as soon as I could," he told me. "When I was eighteen, I volunteered for Bomber Command and was recommended for pilot training. I was sent across the Atlantic by ship to train in Canada in 1941, but I failed the training. I could have retrained as a navigator or bomb aimer, but that would have taken ages. I was so fed up and I wanted to get into the action as soon as possible, so I chose to be a gunner, as the course was only a month long. I was one of the few pilot officers who became rear gunners! I was sent back to England for my gunnery training. Crossing the Atlantic at that time was incredibly dangerous because of all the German U-boats. We sailed on the SS *Volendam* in a convoy to Reykjavik. We spent some time in Iceland, and it took us three weeks and four days altogether to get back home."

Bill recalled well the process of "crewing up" at RAF Honeybourne. "We were all put in this one big room and given cups of tea and told to mingle. I started talking to a few people and then spotted Penny. It was all pretty much done on instinct, on the basis of 'well, he looks like a nice lad'."

Throughout our meeting, Bill would pause occasionally, then smile, shaking his head in disbelief.

"You're Clyde's niece. His niece! And you've come to see me! Well I never..."

I sensed that he still found talking about the crew's bombing operations difficult, so I skirted around the issue. "Wuppertal was rough," he said, "very rough indeed. We got hit and lost a lot of fuel, but Penny got us back. He was a very good pilot and got us out of trouble on many occasions."

Bill spoke with enthusiasm about his crewmates.

"Ah yes, Freddie was a super bloke. It really was one of the best crews, you know – people always say that, but we were. We used to go out and socialise together, but we didn't drink a huge amount. Penny was a few years older than the rest of us, except George, and he was very sensible. He had a terribly weak bladder though, and if he needed a wee I had to come all the way up from the rear turret and fly the aircraft till he was done, because I'd done a bit of pilot training and knew roughly what to do. 'No aerobatics! Keep it in a straight line!' That's what he always used to tell me.

"Ken Cox was a Londoner, very shy and quiet. He kept in the background, but he used to get incredibly upset about his family back in London during the air raids. I'm not sure but I think he may have emigrated after the war. I got on very well with George, he was much older than the rest of us. He was a quiet chap as well. Roy was from a farming background. He was an excellent navigator, very meticulous in his record keeping. Poor bloke went on a 'spare bod' trip and never came back."

I asked him about the crew's response to Roy's death.

"We'd just gone into breakfast, and he was missing, he just wasn't there anymore. The padre was very good, he came around to see us all individually, and I remember talking to him about Roy, with him sitting on the end of my bed."

I told him of my visit to Roy's grave, and that I had laid flowers with a photograph of the crew, and he seemed glad.

Bill explained that they were all very lucky, as the Pennicott crew was a very supportive environment.

"We were very good as a crew – we used to meet regularly to talk about things, about how we were feeling. We used to have little meetings in my room quite often. People used to confide in Penny, as he was the skipper, but Penny needed someone to talk to as well, and he often used to confide in me. The other blokes used to talk to me too – maybe because I was one of the youngest in the crew and was non-judgmental. That's why I became a doctor after the war, because I felt able to listen to people's problems."

I asked Bill about how the crew felt about Reg Cowles joining them after Roy was killed.

"Oh, he was welcomed into the crew straightaway. We had a tradition of looking after each other, you see. We didn't need any psychiatrists. When things got really bad, which they often did, we talked to each other all the time."

Bill recounted one incident which was most definitely not recorded in any of their logbooks or in official squadron records, and which would have got the crew into huge trouble if anyone had found out about it.

"We had an intelligence officer at Melbourne, he was getting on a bit (he was in his fifties) as he'd fought in the First World War. His nickname was 'Young'un'. He was a super fellow and we used to take him out with us when we went out socially. He was desperate to fly on ops so one night we took him with us!"

(Bill could no longer recall which operation this was, and that is the reason why this incident does not appear in this book.)

After leaving 10 Squadron, Bill had gone off to be an instructor, like most of the others. One of his superior officers had ascertained that he could speak a little French, and much to his alarm he was asked to deliver a lecture to a group of "Free French" trainee gunners. Bill spent hours upon hours preparing his talk, which he duly delivered in his best schoolboy French. At the end of the lecture, the seated Frenchmen applauded loudly, before one of them stood up and thanked Bill for his efforts, in perfect English.

After the war, Bill had returned to Northern Ireland, and won a place at Queen's University in Belfast to study medicine. The RAF paid his fees, and he eventually qualified as a GP in the 1950s, settling in Huddersfield. In those days the local GP would also be responsible for delivering babies.

"Ah yes, I delivered thousands of babies!" he recalled with great pride, beaming.

Bill had lost contact with the rest of the crew towards the end of the war. He'd been with Penny right up until the time they were demobbed, and they remained great friends. He showed me photographs of his wedding in 1951, of himself and Penny, who of course was his best man, standing outside the church awaiting the arrival of his bride. They looked so different out of their RAF blues.

I told Bill what had happened to Jack after the war, and of his passing in 1988. He spoke of Jack with great warmth and fondness.

"Jack, or Andy as we often called him, was a typical Geordie. He had pals all over the place – the wireless operators used to chat to each other over the airwaves, you see. If we ever landed away from base, he'd be on the radio straightaway. By the time we got inside he would know all about what was on at the local picture house, and where the best places were to eat. We had two pigeons on board the aircraft on operations, and he would look after them, he always gave them names."

I asked if he could remember Jack's mother's wedding ring.

"Oh yes, of course I remember it! He always wore his mother's wedding ring, he never took it off, not even in the shower – that was his good luck charm."

After several hours chatting, and lunch at a local café, I could see that Bill was tiring a little. Before we said our goodbyes, I gave him a framed colour photograph of the crew, the one taken after their last operation, on 8 March 1944. Bill had never seen this photograph before, not even in the original black and white, and he was quite overcome. "You've brought this for me? I can keep it?" he repeated.

As I began to take my leave of this wonderful old gentleman, he looked down at the photograph, still smiling and shaking his head.

"Well I never. Jack Clyde. My Jack. The singing wireless operator."

Bibliography

Original Source Material

Flt Sgt John Clyde, DFM – RAF logbook and other personal papers.

National Archive (accessed via 10 Squadron Association website) – Operations Books, Squadron Diary, 10 Squadron RAF.

George Edwin Walter Clyde – Personal papers and recollections.

Lydia Groark (nee Clyde) – Personal papers and recollections.

James Martin Groark – Personal papers, recollections and interviews.

Edith Threadkell – Personal papers.

Interviewees

Bomber Command:

Tom Davidson DFM
Dr William H.A. Bradshaw, DFC
Harry Irons DFC
Tom Sayer DFC
Ken Thomas DFC

Arthur Atkinson DFM
Doug Newham DFC
Andy Andrews DFM
Rusty Waughman DFC
Reg Payne DFM

SEAHAM HARBOUR:

Cornelius Vickers
George Meek
Greta Meek
Cecily Guy
Ron Toft
Harry Sayers
Alan Lowes

BOOKS

Alexander, Leslie – *Seaham, A Town at War, 1939-1945*, Cleveland, Lighthouse Publishing, 2002.

Ballantyne, Kenneth – *First Wave*, Wellington, Laundry Cottage Books, 2013.

Boileau, John and Black, Dan – *Too Young to Die: Canada's Boy Soldiers, Sailors and Airmen in the Second World War*, Toronto, James Lorimer & Co. Ltd, 2016.

Bowman, Martin W. – *Voices in Flight: The Heavy Bomber Offensive of WWII*, Barnsley, Pen & Sword Books, 2014.

Boyd, Julia – *Travellers in the Third Reich*, London, Elliott and Thompson, 2018.

Chorlton, Martyn – *The RAF Pathfinders: Bomber Command's Elite Squadrons*, Newbury, Countryside Books, 2012.

Clutton-Brock, Oliver – *The Long Road: Trials and Tribulations of Airmen Prisoners from Stalag Luft VII (Bankau) to Berlin*,

June 1944-1945, London, Grub Street, 2013.

Cooper, Alan – *Air Battle of the Ruhr*, Shrewsbury, Airlife Publishing Ltd, 1992.

English, Allan D. – *The Cream of the Crop: Canadian Aircrew 1939-1945*, Montreal, McGill-Queen's University Press, 1996.

Falconer, Jonathan – *Handley Page Halifax Owner's Workshop Manual (Haynes)*, Yeovil, Haynes Publishing, 2016.

Falconer, Jonathan – *RAF Airfields of World War 2*, Midland Publishing, 2012.

Falconer, Jonathan – *RAF Bomber Command 1939-45 Operations Manual (Haynes)*, Yeovil, Haynes Publishing, 2018.

Falconer, Jonathan – *RAF Bomber Crewman*, Oxford, Shire Publications Ltd, 2010.

Gordon Shirt, J. – *Gordon's Tour with Shiny Ten: A Wartime Record of a Tour with RAF No 10 Squadron*, Warrington, Compaid Graphics, 1994.

Harris, Sir Arthur – *Bomber Offensive*, London, Collins, 1947.

Hastings, Max – *Bomber Command*, London, Michael Joseph Ltd, 1979.

Hawes, James – *The Shortest History of Germany*, Devon, Old Street Publishing, 2017.

Holland, James – *Big Week: The Biggest Air Battle of World War Two*, London, Bantam Press, 2018.

Huber, Florian – *Promise Me You'll Shoot Yourself*, London, Allen Lane (UK Edition), 2019.

Kaplan, Philip – *Bombers: The Aircrew Experience*, London, Aurum Press Ltd, 2000.

Kershaw, Ian – *Making Friends with Hitler: Lord Londonderry and Britain's Road to War*, London, Penguin, 2005.

Leivers, Roger – *Stirling to Essen*, Fighting High Ltd, 2017.

Levine, Joshua – *The Secret History of the Blitz*, London, Simon & Schuster, 2016.

Londonderry, The Marquis of – *Wings of Destiny*, London, Macmillan & Co, 1943.

MacMillan, Ian and King, Richard – *From Brooklands to Brize: A Centennial History of No 10 Squadron Royal Air Force*, 10 Squadron Association, 2015.

Middlebrook, Martin – *The Battle of Hamburg: The Firestorm Raid*, London, Allan Lane, 1980.

Middlebrook, Martin – *The Berlin Raids: RAF Bomber Command Winter 1943-44*, London, Penguin Group, 1988.

Middlebrook, Martin – *The Nuremberg Raid 30-31 March 1944*, London Allen Lane, The Penguin Press, 1973.

Middlebrook, Martin and Everitt, Chris – *The Bomber Command War Diaries: An Operational Reference Book, 1939-1945*, Barnsley, Pen & Sword Aviation, 1985 & 2014.

Moorhouse, Roger – *First to Fight: The Polish War 1939*, London, Bodley Head, 2019.

Neillands, Robin – *The Bomber War: Arthur Harris and the Allied Bomber Offensive 1939-1945*, London, John Murray Ltd, 2001.

Nichol, John – *The Red Line: The Gripping Story of the RAF's Bloodiest Raid on Hitler's Germany*, London, Harper Collins, 2013.

Ohler, Norman – *Blitzed: Drugs in Nazi Germany*, Allen Lane/Penguin Random House/Kiepenheuer & Witsch, 2015 & 2016.

Partridge, Eric – *A Dictionary of RAF Slang*, London, Michael Joseph Ltd, 1945.

Pogt, Herbert – *Vor Funfzig Jahren: Bomben Auf Wuppertal*, Wuppertal, Born-Verlag, 1993.

Rolfe, Mel – *Flying into Hell: The Bomber Command Offensive as Seen Through the Experiences of Twenty Crews*, London, Grub Street, 2001.

Skelly, Paul – *At the Foot of Our Stairs: The History and Crews of*

Handley Page Halifax JD314, USA, XLibris Publishing, 2011.

Taylor, Frederick – *Dresden Tuesday February 13, 1945*, London, Bloomsbury Publishing, 2004.

Wadsworth, Michael, *Heroes of Bomber Command Yorkshire*, Newbury, Countryside Books, 2007.

Ward, Chris – *4 Group Bomber Command, An Operational Record*, Barnsley, Pen & Sword Aviation, 2012.

Weale, Adrian – *The SS: A New History*, London, Abacus, 2012.

Wilson, Kevin – *Bomber Boys: The Ruhr, the Dambusters and Bloody Berlin*, London, Weidenfield and Dickinson, 2005.

Publications

Sunderland Echo Archives 1940-45.
Durham Chronicle (Durham County Archives)

Websites

www.bpears.org.uk/Misc/War_NE
www.losses.internationalbcc.co.uk
www.nationalarchives.gov.uk
www.10sqnass.co.uk
www.iwm.org.uk/collections
www.griffon.clara.net/19/
www.wallyswar.wordpress.com
www.ne-diary-genuki.uk
www.ancestry.co.uk
www.australianindianhistory.com
www.rafcommands.com/forum
www.yorkshire-aircraft.co.uk
www.thegazette.co.uk
www.tailendcharlietedchurch.wordpress.com
www.lancaster-ed559.co.uk
www.sarniahistoricalsociety.com/warmemorialproject

For exclusive discounts on Matador titles,
sign up to our occasional newsletter at
troubador.co.uk/bookshop